THE JOHNNIE WALKER

ENCYCLOPEDIA OF
GOLF

THE JOHNNIE WALKER

ENCYCLOPEDIA OF
GOLF

edited by
Bob Ferrier and
Graham Hart

GUINNESS PUBLISHING \\\\

Payne Stewart, out of a bunker and onto the green, during the 1989 Ryder Cup. (The photograph facing the title page is of Seve Ballesteros).

First published in 1994 by
Guinness Publishing Ltd,
33 London Road, Enfield,
Middlesex EN2 6DJ

Designed by Peter Simmonett

Printed and bound in Italy
by New Interlitho SpA, Milan

Text copyright © 1994 by
Guinness Publishing Ltd

Colour originated in Singapore
by Master Image Pte Ltd

Illustrations copyright © 1994
as credited

Front cover design
by AdVantage Studios

A catalogue record for this book is
available from the British Library

'Guinness' is a registered trademark
of Guinness Publishing Ltd

ISBN 0-85112-747-9

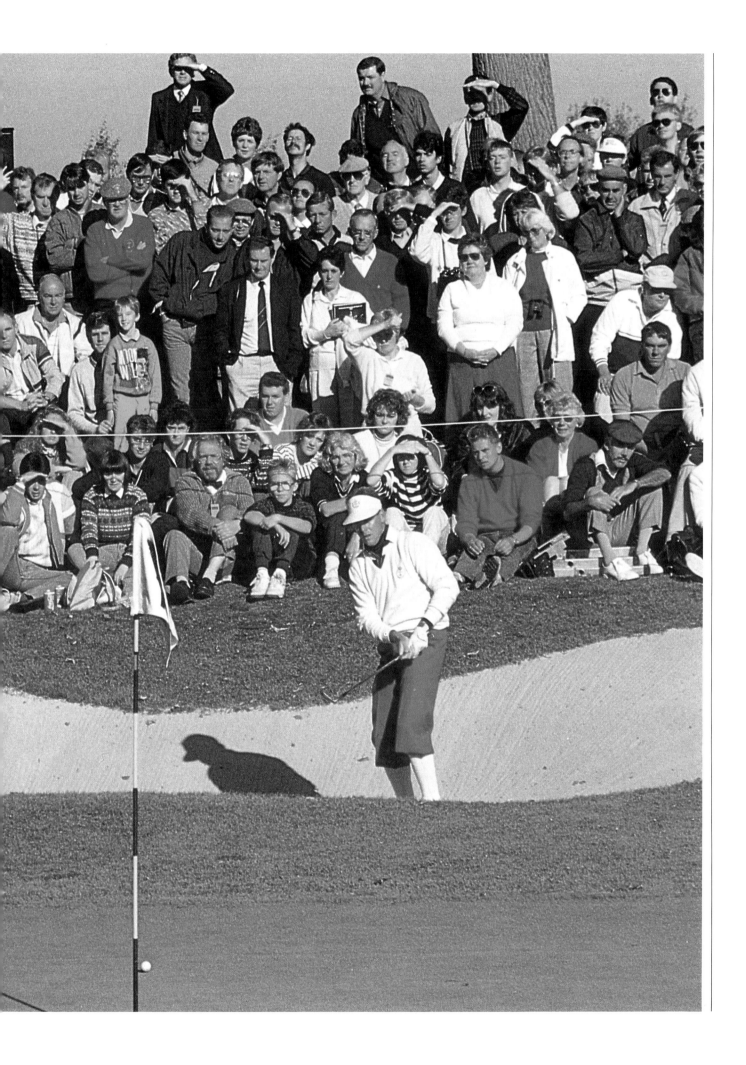

Introduction

A perceptive man once wrote that a complete history of an Open Championship - one single championship - would require a 'Decline and Fall' running to fifteen volumes or something of the kind. He was predicting of course that the entire event and all the experiences of its 1600 entrants and thousands of acolytes would be recorded. It would demand a survey of all local and regional qualifying competitions as well as the championship proper; it would describe every shot of every player, many thousands of them; it would have to recount the history and preparation and condition of the host club and its course, the setting up and staffing of all the support systems and services, the administration of the event, and so on and so on almost ad infinitum.

Applying this proposition to an 'encyclopedia of golf', which of its nature must embrace a game with its origins in the Middle Ages, means that our present work inevitably must be subjective. However, we have tried to touch all the elements of this beautiful and intriguing game - players amateur and professional, men and women; courses, their designs and designers; governing bodies and administrators, champions and championships and the evolution of golf's equipment and laws.

Our subjectivity is particularly plain in our choice of the photographs you will find here. Many are old friends, widely recognised and none the worse for that. Many have been seldom seen before. We trust that among them will be your favourites. Above all else, they confirm the loveliness of the golfing environment.

The game has lent itself to fine, discursive writing over the years, some of this reflected here. We are indebted to the leading golf writers of the day for their erudite essays. Patricia Davies of The Times has written on Ian Woosnam and Sandy Lyle; Michael McDonnell of the Daily Mail on Jack Nicklaus; Mitchell

The 1993 Ryder Cup: the Britain and Europe team line up prior to the match... and the victorious Americans at the conclusion.

Platts, formerly of The Times and now Media Director of the PGA European Tour, on Nick Faldo; Renton Laidlaw of the London Evening Standard has written about Henry Cotton;, and finally, Douglas Lowe of The Herald (Glasgow), has deciphered the convolutions of the handicapping systems.

In addition to the writers there are several others who have contributed significantly to the production of the book. In particular we would like to thank Simon Duncan, Charles Richards and David Roberts at Guinness Publishing, Peter Simmonett who designed and laid out the pages, Gill Attwood our typist, Sarah Wright, Gill McLeod and Susannah Wills who helped on the editorial side, Lee Martin of Allsport UK Ltd and Paul Hudson of United Distillers.

Bob Ferrier
Graham Hart

The editors and publishers are grateful to the following for permission to reproduce the photographs used in this book:

The photographers of Allsport UK Ltd: Howard Bolan: page 38; Simon Bruty: pages 122, 158, 183; David Cannon: pages 8, 18, 24, 37, 57, 63, 80, 85, 91, 103, 105, 113, 117, 120, 129, 133, 136, 144, 162, 167, 170, 174, 179, 180, 182, 189, 199, 202, 208, 211; Russell Cheyne: page 164; Stanley Chou: page 48; Chris Cole: page 196; Michael Hobbs: pages 11, 21, 31, 34, 41, 89, 100, 134, 148, 156, 187, 220; Stephen Munday: pages 28, 36, 69, 147, 193, 221; Gray Mortimore: page 174; Gary Newkirk: pages 26, 210; Richard Saker: pages 33; and also from Allsport UK Ltd: pages 29, 47, 78, 108, 142, 153, 178.
The Charles Walls Group: page 53 (x3).

Michael Hobbs (The Hobbs Golf Collection): pages 14, 32, 44, 65, 102, 106, 107, 110, 115, 146, 177, 184, 196, 205, 212, 215.

The Hulton-Deutsch Collection: pages 25, 39, 50, 61, 70, 73, 97, 98, 102, 112(x2), 131, 149, 176, 213, 214.

Topham Picture Source: pages 48, 64, 118, 125, 188, 194, 219,

United Distillers Photo Library: pages ii, iii, vi, vii, 12, 13, 14, 16, 17(x2), 20, 22, 23, 52, 54, 55, 56, 58, 60, 66, 67, 75, 76, 77, 82, 86, 87(x2), 93, 94, 96, 114, 124, 126, 127, 150, 160, 169, 171, 172(x2), 173, 186, 200, 205, 218.

ALISON, Charles

Charles Alison was born in Preston, and educated at Malvern and Oxford University, where he was an outstanding cricketer and golfer. Indeed he was the youngest member of the Oxford and Cambridge Golfing Society team which toured America in 1903, winning every match he played.

After a spell in journalism, Alison became secretary of the newly formed (1903) Stoke Poges club, where Harry Colt of Sunningdale fame was laying out the course. Alison worked with him on finishing Stoke Poges, then with the construction work on St George's Hill and several other courses in the London area. He survived the First World War, emerging as a major, and when Colt returned from America in 1920 they formed a partnership which lasted for a good 20 years. Alison worked mainly abroad. Colt handled the design work for the UK and Europe and Alison worked extensively in North America and the Far East. The partnership included at different times other prominent architects in JSF Morrison and Dr Alister Mackenzie.

Between the wars, Alison laid claim to a good body of work, with some courses that became prominent, some that became famous, and quite a few of these paradoxically in Britain and Europe. They included Trevose in Cornwall, the Wentworth courses, East and West, Rosses Point in Ireland, Puerto de Hierro in Madrid, Falkenstein in Hamburg and the Frankfurter club in Germany, Kennemer at Zandvoort in Holland. In the US he made revisions and additions at Sea Island in Georgia, Burning Tree and Chevy Chase in Maryland, North Shore at Glenview, Illinois and the Milwaukee Country Club.

Charles Alison worked in Australia and South Africa, but found rich fairways in Japan. His record there includes Fuji GC, Kanawa GC, and the Tokyo club which moved to a new site in 1936. He also remodelled 36 holes at perhaps the single most famous Japanese club, Kasumigaseki, in 1931. It was to become the venue of the Canada Cup, now World Cup, in 1957 when the victory of Japan started the first great golf expansion in that country. Alison introduced deep bunkers to Japanese golf courses – to this day they are called 'Arisons'.

ALLISS, Peter

Born	1931
Nationality	British
Turned Pro	1946

Peter Alliss was born on 28 February 1931 in Berlin, where his father Percy was professional at the affluent Wannsee club during much of the twenties and into the thirties until the coming of Hitler. Peter grew up in the Ferndown area of Dorset with its many fine courses, and he and his brother Alex almost automatically became golf professionals. Peter played for England Boys International team in 1946, and turned professional at the age of 15. He held club

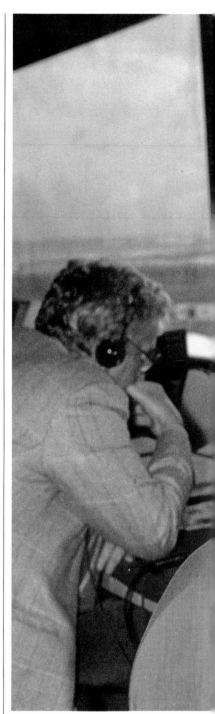

Peter Alliss, Ryder Cup and World Cup player, winner of a score of tournaments, has become the BBC's 'Voice of Golf' as their top television commentator at all major championships.

positions at Parkstone and Moor Allerton, but much of his early career embraced tournament play. He won a score or more of events, his first championship being the Spanish Open in 1956. In 1958 he won the Italian Open, Spanish Open and Portuguese Open in successive weeks with a spell of sustained and brilliant scoring. He led the Order of Merit in 1964 and 1966.

He played in eight Ryder Cup teams, and ten World Cup teams for England. Many of his friends thought he retired prematurely, before he was 40, but he went on to become an outstanding broadcaster and BBC Television's lead announcer. His technique was conversational, talking as if it were to two people in their own living room, and he was occasionally taken to task for prattling. But it was highly successful, so much so that Alliss was contracted as a broadcaster to other networks in the United States and Australia from time to time.

He has written several books on golf, and has had a busy life as a raconteur and in particular with golf course designs. With David Thomas, he designed and built the courses at The Belfry; the bigger course there has been the setting for some marvellously exciting Ryder Cup matches. Peter has subsequently joined with Clive Clark in course design, and so has touched on almost every aspect of modern professional golf.

AMATEUR GOLF

Amateur golf is the game that is played by millions all over the world. Professional golf is the other game, the one played by the club professional with his members, whom he may teach and to whom he will sell golf merchandise from a retail outlet at the club; or by the tournament professional, who plays competitive golf for prize money. They are the golfers, the great

teaching or playing assistant to a professional golfer. Being an assistant or a salesman in a golf shop does not necessarily infringe the rules – they are basically concerned with the giving of golf instruction, playing for money, and being paid or getting any kind of compensation because of golfing skill or golfing reputation.

Golf instruction is permitted by a teacher in an educational institution provided that this takes less than 50% of his or her total tuition time. In amateur competitions, prize vouchers may be given to players. For an event of more than two rounds, limits in Europe are £300, elsewhere $500 or their equivalents, and for two rounds or less £200 and $350 respectively. These vouchers are for the purchase of goods from a professional's shop or other outlet which may be specified by the committee of the competition. They may not be used for travel or hotel bills or the like. In certain circumstances, amateur players may receive expenses not exceeding the actual expenses incurred; –

• from a member of the family or legal guardian;
• when playing in a competition limited to players who have not reached their 18th birthday;
• when representing a team, club, country, national or similar body.

There are other detailed circumstances in which controlled expenses may be paid.

Also seldom considered by the average amateur golfer is the fact that he or she can be deemed a professional for accepting membership of a golf club without full payment of fees, because of his or her golfing skill. And even more important, the R & A would act on 'any conduct, including activities

champions, who now get massive publicity and exposure on television and in the Press, and become household names.

The distinction between amateur and professional golfer is clearly set out in the 'Rules of Amateur Status', which are governed in Great Britain by the Royal and Ancient Golf Club of St Andrews (R & A) and in all other countries by the national golf association. They are copyrighted by the R & A, and by the United States Golf Association (USGA). These two bodies consider the Rules of Amateur Status every four years, when their joint committee also reviews the Rules of Golf.

The millions of golfers throughout the world who play the game for pleasure seldom consider their amateur status, but in fact this status is defined and protected by extensive and quite sophisticated legislation. The specific definition is:- 'An amateur golfer is one who plays the game as a non-remunerative or non-profitmaking sport.'

This status of 'amateur' is one which should be valued. It can be forfeited at any age by any one of a fairly lengthy list of transgressions set out in the Rules of Amateur Status. Many of them are fairly obvious, such as receiving payment or compensation for serving as a professional golfer, or as a

THE AMATEUR CHAMPIONSHIP

Winners British, except where stated

Year	Venue	Winner	Margin
1885	Royal Liverpool (Hoylake)	Allan MacFie	7 & 6
1886	St Andrews	Horace Hutchinson	7 & 6
1887	Royal Liverpool (Hoylake)	Horace Hutchinson	1 hole
1888	Prestwick	John Ball	5 & 4
1889	St Andrews	Johnny Laidlay	2 & 1
1890	Royal Liverpool (Hoylake)	John Ball	4 & 3
1891	St Andrews	Johnny Laidlay	at 20th
1892	St George's (Sandwich)	John Ball	3 & 1
1893	Prestwick	Peter Anderson	1 hole
1894	Royal Liverpool (Hoylake)	John Ball	1 hole
1895	St Andrews	Leslie Balfour Melville	at 19th
1896	St George's (Sandwich)	Freddie Tait	8 & 7
1897	Muirfield	Jack Allan	4 & 2
1898	Royal Liverpool (Hoylake)	Freddie Tait	7 & 5
1899	Prestwick	John Ball	at 37th
1900	St George's (Sandwich)	Harold Hilton	8 & 7
1901	St Andrews	Harold Hilton	1 hole
1902	Royal Liverpool (Hoylake)	Charles Hutchings	1 hole
1903	Muirfield	Robert Maxwell	7 & 5
1904	Royal St George's (Sandwich)	Walter Travis (US)	4 & 3
1905	Prestwick	Gordon Barry	3 & 2
1906	Royal Liverpool (Hoylake)	James Robb	4 & 3
1907	St Andrews	John Ball	6 & 4
1908	Royal St George's (Sandwich)	EA Lassen	7 & 6
1909	Muirfield	Robert Maxwell	1 hole
1910	Royal Liverpool (Hoylake)	John Ball	10 & 9
1911	Prestwick	Harold Hilton	4 & 3
1912	Royal North Devon (Westward Ho!)	John Ball	at 38th
1913	St Andrews	Harold Hilton	6 & 5
1914	Royal St George's (Sandwich)	JLC Jenkins	3 & 2
1920	Muirfield	Cyril Tolley	ay 37th
1921	Royal Liverpool (Hoylake)	Willie Hunter	12 & 11
1922	Prestwick	Ernest Holderness	1 hole
1923	Cinque Ports (Deal)	Roger Wethered	7 & 6
1924	St Andrews	Ernest Holderness	3 & 2
1925	Royal North Devon (Westward Ho!)	Robert Harris	13 & 12
1926	Muirfield	Jess Sweetser (US)	6 & 5
1927	Royal Liverpool (Hoylake)	William Tweddell	7 & 6
1928	Prestwick	Philip Perkins	6 & 4
1929	Royal St George's (Sandwich)	Cyril Tolley	4 & 3
1930	St Andrews	Bobby Jones (US)	7 & 6
1931	Royal North Devon (Westward Ho!)	Eric Martin Smith	1 hole
1932	Muirfield	John de Forest	3 & 1
1933	Royal Liverpool (Hoylake)	Hon. Michael Scott	4 & 3
1934	Prestwick	Lawson Little (US)	14 & 13
1935	Royal Lytham & St Annes	Lawson Little (US)	1 hole
1936	St Andrews	Hector Thomson	2 holes
1937	Royal St George's (Sandwich)	Robert Sweeny (US)	3 & 2
1938	Troon	Charlie Yates (US)	3 & 2
1939	Royal Liverpool (Hoylake)	Alex Kyle	2 & 1
1946	Birkdale	James Bruen (Ire)	4 & 3
1947	Carnoustie	William Turnesa (US)	3 & 2
1948	Royal St George's (Sandwich)	Frank Stranahan (US)	5 & 4
1949	Portmarnock	Max McCready (Ire)	2 & 1
1950	St Andrews	Frank Stranahan (US)	8 & 6
1951	Royal Porthcawl	Richard Chapman (US)	5 & 4
1952	Prestwick	Harvie Ward (US)	6 & 5
1953	Royal Liverpool	Joe Carr (Ire)	2 holes
1954	Muirfield	Douglas Bachli (Aus)	2 & 1
1955	Royal Lytham & St Annes	Joseph Conrad (US)	3 & 2
1956	Troon	John Beharrell	5 & 4
1957	Formby	Reid Jack	2 & 1
1958	St Andrews	Joe Carr (Ire)	3 & 2
1959	Royal St George's (Sandwich)	Deane Beman (US)	3 & 2
1960	Royal Portrush	Joe Carr (Ire)	8 & 7
1961	Turnberry	Michael Bonallack	6 & 4
1962	Royal Liverpool (Hoylake)	Richard Davies (US)	1 hole
1963	St Andrews	Michael Lunt	2 & 1
1964	Ganton	Gordon Clark	at 39th
1965	Royal Porthcawl	Michael Bonallack	2 & 1
1966	Carnoustie	Bobby Cole (SA)	3 & 2
1967	Formby	Robert Dickson (US)	2 & 1
1968	Troon	Michael Bonallack	7 & 6
1969	Royal Liverpool (Hoylake)	Michael Bonallack	3 & 2
1970	Royal County Down (Newcastle)	Michael Bonallack	8 & 7
1971	Carnoustie	Steve Melnyk (US)	3 & 2
1972	Royal St George's (Sandwich)	Trevor Homer	4 & 3
1973	Royal Porthcawl	Dick Siderowf (US)	5 & 3
1974	Muirfield	Trevor Homer	2 holes
1975	Royal Liverpool (Hoylake)	Vinny Giles (US)	8 & 7
1976	St Andrews	Dick Siderowf (US)	at 37th
1977	Ganton	Peter McEvoy	5 & 4
1978	Troon	Peter McEvoy	4 & 3
1979	Hillside	Jay Sigel (US)	3 & 2
1980	Royal Porthcawl	Duncan Evans	4 & 3
1981	St Andrews	Philippe Ploujoux (Fr)	4 & 2
1982	Royal Cinque Ports (Deal)	Martyn Thompson	4 & 3
1983	Turnberry	Philip Parkin	5 & 4
1984	Formby	Jose-Maria Olazabal (Sp)	5 & 4
1985	Royal Dornoch	Garth McGimpsey	8 & 7
1986	Royal Lytham & St Annes	David Curry	11 & 9
1987	Prestwick	Paul Mayo	3 & 1
1988	Royal Porthcawl	Christian Hardin (Swe)	1 hole
1989	Royal Birkdale	Stephen Dodd	5 & 3
1990	Muirfield	Rolf Muntz (Neth)	7 & 6
1991	Ganton	Gary Wolstenholme	8 & 6
1992	Carnoustie	Stephen Dundas	7 & 6
1993	Royal Portrush	Ian Tyman	at 37th

connected with golf gambling, which is considered detrimental to the best interests of the game.'

The R & A committee concerned with all of this has wide powers. Its decision is final. A golfer losing his amateur status would certainly be asked to resign from his club. He would not be able to play in competition at any level. On the other hand, there is a detailed procedure set out for reinstatement. In general, two years would have to elapse before that became possible. This period would depend on how long the applicant for reinstatement had been in breach of the definition of an 'Amateur Golfer.' And a golfer would certainly not be reinstated more than once in his career.

With the huge rewards now on offer to the tournament golfer, the temptation for talented amateurs to take up professional careers is becoming irresistible and many turn professional at an early age, as soon as they have proved themselves by winning an important national amateur championship or being selected for a national or Walker Cup team.

Among the outstanding amateur players since 1945 have been Michael Bonallack, who won five Amateur Championships; Joe Carr of Ireland who won three; RDBM (Ronnie) Shade, who won five successive Scottish Amateur Championships in the 1960s, before turning professional; and Charlie Green, who won three and was five times a finalist. In the United States, Harvie Ward, Deane Beman, Jack Nicklaus and Jay Sigel each won the US National Amateur Championship twice, Beman and Nicklaus, of course, later turning professional and having successful careers.

THE US AMATEUR CHAMPIONSHIP

Winners US, except where stated

Year	Venue	Winner	Margin
1895	Newport	Charles Macdonald	12 & 11
1896	Shinnecock Hills	HJ Whigham	8 & 7
1897	Chicago	HJ Whigham	8 & 6
1898	Morris County	Findlay Douglas	5 & 3
1899	Onwentsia	Herbert Harriman	3 & 2
1900	Garden City	Walter Travis	2 up
1901	Atlantic City	Walter Travis	5 & 4
1902	Glen View	Louis James	4 & 2
1903	Nassau	Walter Travis	5 & 4
1904	Baltusrol	Chandler Egan	8 & 6
1905	Chicago	Chandler Egan	6 & 5
1906	Englewood	Eben Byers	2 up
1907	Euclid	Jerome Travers	6 & 5
1908	Garden City	Jerome Travers	8 & 7
1909	Chicago	Robert A Gardner	4 & 3
1910	Brookline	William Fownes	4 & 3
1911	Apawamis	Harold Hilton (GB)	at 37th
1912	Chicago	Jerome Travers	7 & 6
1913	Garden City	Jerome Travers	5 & 4
1914	Ekwanok	Francis Ouimet	6 & 5
1915	Detroit	Robert A Gardner	5 & 4
1916	Merion	Chick Evans	4 & 3
1919	Oakmont	Davidson Herron	5 & 4

1920	Engineers	Chick Evans	7 & 6
1921	St Louis	Jesse Guilford	7 & 6
1922	Brookline	Jess Sweetser	3 & 2
1923	Flossmoor	Max Marston	at 38th
1924	Merion	Bobby Jones	9 & 8
1925	Oakmont	Bobby Jones	8 & 7
1926	Baltusrol	George Von Elm	2 & 1
1927	Minikahda	Bobby Jones	8 & 7
1928	Brae Burn	Bobby Jones	10 & 9
1929	Del Monte	Harrison Johnston	4 & 3
1930	Merion	Bobby Jones	8 & 7
1931	Beverly	Francis Ouimet	6 & 5
1932	Baltimore	Ross Somerville (Can)	2 & 1
1933	Kenwood	George Dunlap	6 & 5
1934	Brookline	Lawson Little	8 & 7
1935	Cleveland	Lawson Little	4 & 2
1936	Garden City	Johnny Fischer	at 37th
1937	Alderwood	Johnny Goodman	2 up
1938	Oakmont	William Turnesa	8 & 7
1939	North Shore	Marvin Ward	7 & 5
1940	Winged Foot	Richard Chapman	11 & 9
1941	Omaha Field	Marvin Ward	4 & 3
1946	Baltusrol	Stanley Bishop	at 37th
1947	Pebble Beach	Robert Riegel	2 & 1
1948	Memphis	William Turnesa	2 & 1
1949	Oak Hill	Charles Coe	11 & 10
1950	Minneapolis	Sam Urzetta	at 39th
1951	Saucon Valley	Billy Maxwell	4 & 3
1952	Seattle	Jack Westland	3 & 2
1953	Oklahoma City	Gene Littler	1 up
1954	Detroit	Arnold Palmer	1 up
1955	Virginia	Harvie Ward	9 & 8
1956	Knollwood	Harvie Ward	5 & 4
1957	Brookline	Hillman Robbins	5 & 4
1958	Olympic	Charles Coe	5 & 4
1959	Broadmoor	Jack Nicklaus	1 up
1960	St Louis	Deane Beman	6 & 4
1961	Pebble Beach	Jack Nicklaus	8 & 6
1962	Pinehurst	Labron Harris	1 up
1963	Wakonda	Deane Beman	2 & 1
1964	Canterbury	William C Campbell	1 up Score
1965	Southern Hills	Robert Murphy	291
1966	Merion	Gary Cowan (Can)	285*
1967	Broadmoor	Robert Dickson	285
1968	Scioto	Bruce Fleisher	284
1969	Oakmont	Steve Melnyk	286
1970	Waverley	Lanny Wadkins	279
1971	Wilmington	Gary Cowan (Can)	280
1972	Charlotte	Vinny Giles	285
1973	Inverness	Craig Stadler	6 & 5
1974	Ridgewood	Jerry Pate	2 & 1
1975	Virginia (Richmond)	Fred Ridley	2 up
1976	Bel-Air	Bill Sander	8 & 6
1977	Aronimink	John Fought	9 & 8
1978	Plainfield	John Cook	5 & 4
1979	Canterbury	Mark O'Meara	8 & 7
1980	Pinehurst	Hal Sutton	9 & 8
1981	Olympic	Nathaniel Crosby	at 37th
1982	Brookline	Jay Sigel	8 & 7
1983	North Shore	Jay Sigel	8 & 7
1984	Oak Tree	Scott Verplank	4 & 3
1985	Montclair	Sam Randolph	1 up
1986	Shoal Creek	Buddy Alexander	5 & 3
1987	Jupiter Hill	Billy Mayfair	4 & 3
1988	Hot Springs	Eddie Meeks	7 & 6
1989	Merion	Chris Patton	3 & 1
1990	Englewood	Phil Mickelson	5 & 4
1991	Honours Course	Mitch Voges	7 & 6
1992	Muirfield	Justin Leonard	8 & 7
1993	The Champions Club	John Harris	5 & 3

* play-off

Bobby Jones, the non-pareil, with the British Amateur Championship trophy at St Andrews in 1930, the year of his magnificent Grand Slam.

AMERICA, Golf in

When Francis Ouimet, a 20-year-old salesman in the Boston office of a sporting goods company, won the US Open Golf Championship in 1913 at The Country Club at nearby Brookline against the famous English champions Harry Vardon and Ted Ray, he set American golf on the road to an international dominance which it has maintained to this day.

Ouimet had been a caddie at The Country Club and knew the course backwards. But before 1913 amateur golf in America had been elitist and professional golf had been bossed by immigrant Anglo-Saxons, Scots in the main. The Age of Ouimet changed all that. The Americans had already matched the British in such sports as tennis, athletics, swimming and polo. Golf was next on the list. Ted Ray, on another tour of America in 1920 did win their Open then, but that apart, after Ouimet it was not until Gary Player in 1965 and Tony Jacklin in 1970, a South African and an Englishman, that any other 'foreign' players would win that championship.

The power of young Ouimet's achievement in beating Vardon and Ray (in a play-off) can be seen in the context of Vardon's tours in America. He made three: in 1900 when he won the US Open with JH Taylor, his countryman, second; in 1913 when he and Ted Ray finished second; and finally in 1920 when Ray, over the last half dozen holes in a storm, beat Vardon into another second place.

Just 25 years before Ouimet's seminal victory, an equally significant round of golf had been played on a cow pasture in Yonkers, New York. On an unseasonably mild day, on George Washington's birthday, February 22, in fact, John Reid and a few friends played golf over a few holes they had set out in the pasture.

A year earlier Reid, a Dunfermline emigrant, had asked his friend Robert Lockhart, also from Dunfermline, to bring back some clubs and balls from the business trip he was planning to make back to Scotland. Lockhart stocked up at Old Tom Morris's shop in St Andrews. In the spring of 1888, Reid and his friends moved to a larger pasture, where they laid out six 'more proper golf holes'. So golf was born in the United States. By the end of the year, Reid and his friends were able to sit down and form the St Andrews Golf Club, and from that November it has had a continuous existence to this day.

Earlier indications, albeit sketchy, of golf in America have been established. Positive evidence places golf in the southern ports of Charleston and Savannah in the 18th century. Notices relating to the South Carolina Golf Club appeared in the *Charleston City Gazette* from 1788. It is not entirely clear that proper courses were laid out, and such clubs as had been established did not survive into the next century. What with the Revolutionary War, it is not suprising that it was not until a century had passed that American golf became formalised.

Soon after John Reid's St Andrews Club was formed, others sprang up in fashionable localities in the East – Newport, The Country Club near Boston as we have seen, Shinnecock Hills out on Long Island. In Chicago, Charles Blair Macdonald, a powerful figure in the early days of American golf, had created the first 18 holes course in the United States – the Chicago Golf Club at Wheaton, 25 miles west of the city. In December of 1884, delegates from these five clubs met in the Calumet Club in New York City, had a good dinner, and formed what became the United States Golf Association. These early delegates were men of substance, with such names as Havemeyer, Vanderbilt, Biddle, Tallmage. But they were to see the first great explosion of American golf – by the turn of the century, no fewer than 1000 golf clubs were established in the US including courses as far afield as Texas and even this early some public, municipal courses. Golf was on its way to becoming a sport of the common man.

Critical in this expansion was the 'Haskell' ball, the creation of one Coburn Haskell, a Cleveland golfer. The existing golf ball had been made of nothing but gutta percha, moulded and painted. Haskell, visiting a friend at the Goodrich Rubber Company Factory, noticed a pile of rubber strips lying around, and thought that if he wound them tightly around a rubber core and encased the whole

John Daly, a big name in every sense of the word, brought life to a slightly sagging American golf scene around 1990 with his massive driving and his much publicised, and troubled, personal life.

thing in a gutta percha cover, he would have a much improved golf ball. He was right. By the time the new century dawned, almost the entire world of golf was using the 'Haskell' ball. It flew further, and nothing could be more encouraging to the ambitious golfer than an extra 20 yards on his drive.

The early years of the great American championships, the National Amateur and the National Open, were dominated in the former by British students and businessmen temporarily in the United States and in the latter by foreign-born immigrant professionals. By contrast any Americans who ventured over to play in the old country made few headlines. Walter Travis, born in Australia but resident in America from the age of four, won the US Amateur Championship in 1903. The next year he stunned the world by winning the 'British Amateur' at Royal St Georges – but was made less than welcome by the golfing establishment in England. Johnny McDermott in 1911

and repeating in 1912 became the first native born US Open Champion. Ouimet came in 1913, and Walter Hagen appeared in 1914. The power of America was clearly established, and increased after the First World War in the championship and Ryder Cup, Walker Cup and Curtis Cup play on both sides of the ocean.

Hagen was the US Champion again in 1919, and was golf's gift to the Jazz Age. He became the first professional to be essentially a freelance tournament player, spurning club jobs to travel endlessly to tournaments and exhibitions throughout the world, dressing snappily, driving the most elegant of automobiles, living in the grandest hotels – and winning championships galore. His counterpart was Bobby Jones, a very different personality. Jones was the amateur who beat the professionals in their own championships and a man who has been considered the finest golfer the game has known. Jones retired full of

honours, in 1930. He was 28 years old.

The effect of Hagen and Jones on the health of the game was immeasurable. The twenties saw a boom in real-estate in Florida and every hotel resort and property development seemed to need a golf course, and an exhibition or tournament to publicise it. Walter Hagen and Bobby Jones were the stars who kept golf in the news and in the national consciousness. The game slowed a little in the depression years of the thirties, but golf in America, like all its other sports, has always had its heroes. After the Second World War came Byron Nelson, Ben Hogan and Sam Snead, Arnold Palmer who took golf into the television age, and Jack Nicklaus and Tom Watson. In the 1980s, the sun states of Arizona, New Mexico and California saw staggering expansion of courses and golf-related developments, as Florida had done more than half a century earlier.

Although at the end of the eighties and into the nineties, European teams of

professionals and amateurs, men and women alike, were at last able to win international matches on both sides of the Atlantic against US teams, American golf remained immensely powerful. It was also inclined to be expensive, certainly in comparison with golf in Scotland for example, particularly since various national governments have withdrawn some of the tax advantages of golf club memberships. The sheer size of the US, the scale of everything there, sustained comfortably the philosophy that a golf club should be a country club, offering its members more than just a golf course, expensive though that might be. Thus even as early as 1892, the Shinnecock Hills clubhouse designed by Stanford White, a leading architect of the day, might have satisfied the needs of a minor Indian rajah. Almost all private clubs since then have rejoiced in swimming pools, tennis courts, restaurants, grill rooms, bars, and in many cases living quarters. All of this has required large investments, high entry fees and subscriptions, 'dues' as the Americans call them. In golf as in so much else, Americans expect service. They are prepared to pay for it, and they get it. The affluence of this enormous country makes it all quite commonplace.

ANDERSON, Jamie

Born 1842

Nationality British

Turned Pro 1857

Majors Open Championship 1877, 1878, 1879

Jamie Anderson, Open Champion in 1877, 1878 and 1879, shares with Young Tom Morris in the1860s and Peter Thomson in the 1950s, the distinction of having won three successive championships. Anderson was very much a St Andrews man, the son of David Anderson ('Old Daw') who was a caddie and very much a town character. Jamie took to golf at the age of ten, and became probably the best

Jamie Anderson of St Andrews, winner of three successive Opens.

iron player of his time and a fine bad weather player. He was very accurate and machine-like in his play and in his attitude to the game. Jamie was not over modest – he once claimed that he had played 90 holes at St Andrews without playing a bad shot! He also declared that, 'As soon as the hole is within reach, I play to hole the shot.' A century on, the Arnold Palmer version of this was, 'If you can hit it, you can hole it.'

Jamie Anderson lived in a distant age of great matches, and great match players – Young Tom Morris, Davie Strath, and the Parks of Musselburgh, for example. He and Young Tom Morris once challenged 'any two', laying £100 to £80. There were no takers. Jamie spent some time at the Ardeer Club, and in Perth, but St Andrews always called him back.

AOKI, Isao

Born 1942

Nationality Japanese

Turned Pro 1964

As the Japanese professional best known around the world, Isao Aoki came within a few short putts of becoming the first Oriental golfer to win one of the Grand Slam tournaments. In the US Open Championship of 1980, played at the Baltusrol Club in New Jersey, Aoki finished second to Jack Nicklaus by two strokes, and over four days play all but matched the great man

Isao Aoki, the most famous Japanese player, in action during the Johnnie Walker Asian Championship.

stroke for stroke. His total of 274 set a new championship record, but it was not quite enough against the Nicklaus total of 272, which included a record-shattering opening round of 63. Oddly, both men were paired together throughout the four rounds, in which Aoki scored 68, 68, 68, 70.

Born on 31 August 1942 at Abiko in Chiba, across the

bay from the city of Tokyo, Isao caddied at his local club there as a boy and having turned professional, took seven years to win his first tournament. Since then, he has won on all four major professional tours – in the US, Europe, Australia and Japan. He won the World Match Play Championship at Wentworth in 1978, the European Open and the Hawaiian Open in 1983, the Open of Japan twice and the Japanese PGA Championship five times. He has been leading money winner in Japan five times.

At six feet tall and weighing 12 stone, Aoki is rather tall for a Japanese, and is polite, deferential, and inscrutable on the course. Technically he is a quite exceptional golfer. He crouches at address, his hands held low, down around knee level it seems, then picks the clubhead up sharply with an excessive wrist cock, comes down and goes through the ball powerfully with his right hand. With this swing he is liable to finish in any one of half a dozen positions, but he makes it all work. His putting technique, too, is highly personalised. Again he crouches very low, with hands held low and the toe of the putter pointing upwards. From that position he gives the ball a crisp rap and proves to all and sundry that he is one of golf's finest putters.

ARMOUR, Tommy

Nationality British

Turned Pro 1924

Majors Open Championship 1931; US Open 1927; US PGA 1930

The Braid Hills, that age-old Edinburgh playground, was the golfing classroom of Thomas Dickson Armour

before the First World War, and the starting point which took him to the pinnacles of the game. Armour served in the Tank Corps in that war, losing the sight of an eye, but when it was over he was soon making a name in international golf. He won the French Amateur Championship in 1920, beating Cyril Tolley in the final. With Tolley and Roger Wethered he made a first trip to the United States that year, playing in the US Amateur and all but winning the Canadian Open as an amateur. He lost in a play-off to an English born professional, J Douglas Edgar. Armour did win it as a professional in 1927.

He played for the Great Britain team which met a visiting American team informally at Hoylake in 1921, a precursor to the Walker Cup series, and then for Scotland against England in 1922.

But Tommy had tasted the American way, and enjoyed it. He took himself across the

ocean to become secretary of the Westchester-Biltmore club in New York. After turning professional, he found himself part of a US team which played the British at Wentworth in 1926. This was to be an overture to the Ryder Cup series, which started the following year. This 1926 appearance gave Armour the unique distinction of having played for GB against the US as an amateur, then for the US against GB as a professional.

Armour had huge powerful hands, giving his iron play in particular, from a slightly closed stance, a relentless quality. He was brilliant, inconsistent, moody,' never a man to miss the chance of a bet, a desperately slow player but a fast, vinegarish talker who was one of the few golfers of the time who could match the pranks, ploys and gamesmanship of Walter Hagen, and often best him.

Tom won both the US and Canadian Opens in 1927 and the Open Championship at

Two 'emigrants' to the US who became champions. Tommy Armour of Edinburgh (left) and Jim Barnes from Cornwall.

Carnoustie in 1931 with a solid closing round of 71. That year, the Argentine golfer Jose Jurado had the championship all but won, but lost it over the last few holes.

When his competitive career was over, Armour proved to be an outstanding teacher of the game. His instructional books became bestsellers, and as the professional at the elite Congressional Club in Washington DC in summer and at Sarasota or Boca Raton, Florida in winter, Tommy Armour became wealthy, through teaching an endless line of well-endowed golfing students, and from his 'Silver Scot' personalised line of golf clubs manufactured by the Macgregor company.

ASIA, Golf in

The development of golf in Asia followed the flag of empire. The British in general, the Scots in particular – soldiers, administrators, traders – unpacked clubs and balls almost as soon as they were settled in foreign parts, often starting with half a dozen holes. And no doubt setting up a bar.

If we take Asia to be India and the countries to the east, plus the whole Pacific rim, then the Royal Calcutta, the first club established outside

Vijay Singh from Fiji, one of Asia's top golfers.

the UK, was also the first Asian course. It was started in 1829, probably by the Scottish troops, as the Dum Dum Golf Club, Dum Dum being a district and now the site of Calcutta's airport. Critical to the development of golf in all the monsoon countries of the east has been the fact that Royal Calcutta established that grass, in their case a type of Bermuda known as 'dhoob' grass, could be maintained in such a climate.

Royal Hong Kong dated from 1889 when the Argyll and Sutherland Highlanders were involved and with Captain RE Dumbleton of the Royal Engineers laying out a rough and ready nine holes in Happy Valley on Hong Kong island. Within a few years, growth in

membership was such that another move was made to Deep Water Bay on the other side of the island. In the early years of this century another move was needed, this time to Fanling, dubbed the 'new' course. After the Japanese occupation during the war, it was 1953 before these neglected courses had fully recovered, and ten years later in response to demand, yet a third 18-hole course was opened, giving Royal Hong Kong Old, New and Eden courses, just like distant St Andrews.

Golf in another British island city, Singapore, followed the Hong Kong pattern. Emerging from the Singapore Sporting Club (1842), a group of members met in 1891 to form the Singapore Golf Club with

nine holes near the old racecourse. By 1920, it was clear that a proper course away from the growing city was needed. A 258-acre site was leased and after massive jungle clearance was opened for play in 1924.

It was designed by James Braid, who never set foot in Singapore. He disliked travel and designed the course by correspondence, working from topographical maps.

Some members chose not to go to the new course, and formed the Island Club in 1932. Both courses suffered under the Japanese occupation in the Second World War. The Singapore club, appointed Royal in 1938, reopened in 1947. The Island Club was functioning again by 1952, when it too had become Royal, and in

1963 the clubs merged, becoming simply the Singapore Island Golf Club. Now it is one of the wonders of world golf, with four full-size courses and 7000 members, at least 2000 of whom are active players, and all of this in one of the world's smallest nation states.

With an almost parallel history is the Royal Selangor, up the coast of Malaysia in Kuala Lumpur. Thirty 'expats' started it in 1893 and the club has been compelled to move only once, in 1918 when the State of Selangor government took over its land for a building project but provided in return a nine hole course and a new clubhouse. By 1931, 18 holes which became known as the Old Course were ready for the inspection of Harry Colt, the famous English architect. He made only minor changes.

In Indonesia, a dozen or so courses existed before the Second World War, almost all of them owned or managed by tea or rubber plantations, most of which in turn were British owned or managed. The Jakarta Golf Club was probably the most widely known, but after the Second World War it lost much of its land to a state building project. When General Suharto, a golf fan, became President of Indonesia in 1967, golf was given a substantial impetus. Suharto saw the value of golf as a tourist attraction and encouraged golf developments in Bali and throughout the islands.

Sir James Fergusson, an Edinburgh Scot, is said to have taken golf with him to Adelaide when he become Governor of South Australia in 1869, and certainly by the last decade of the century the game was well established in Australia and New Zealand.

And things were stirring further north. The first golf course in Japan was the Kobe Golf Club, started in 1903 by Arthur Groom, an English tea merchant, and his friends. The earliest Japanese clubs were essentially by and for foreigners – not until 1914 was the first club formed by Japanese for the Japanese. That was the Tokyo Golf Club. And when the Japanese Golf Association, the governing body, was formed in 1924, the founders were five Japanese and six foreigners, and the constitution was written in English!

The American military occupation of Japan following the Second World War had a major effect on the development of the game there, but the start of an explosion unparalleled in the history of the sport came in 1957. That year the international Canada Cup competition, now the World Cup, was played at Kasumigaseki and Japan won. The fact that the Japanese professionals Torakichi (Pete) Nakamura and Koichi Ono beat such outstanding players as Sam Snead and Jimmy Demaret, the United States team, and Gary Player and Harold Henning of South Africa, brought a staggering boom to the game in Japan which has persisted ever since. It also made Kasumigaseki the most famous club in Japan.

Visits from such champions as Arnold Palmer, Jack Nicklaus, Gary Player in the sixties, Tom Watson and Severiano Ballesteros later, and now all the current champions, have helped the game further. Leading architects like Peter Thomson, Robert Trent Jones, Peter Dye and David Thomas have worked extensively in Japan and it now sustains a professional tour of 83 tournaments and a total prize fund of some £15 million. Sponsors include some of the greatest corporations in the automobile and computer industries and the game is given massive coverage on television, radio and print. The leading money winner in Japan is likely consistently to earn more than his US or European counterpart. The game is highly fashionable, and such is the demand for hugely expensive club memberships that there has been a 'stock market' in them, traded openly. All of this has simply been a reflection of the extraordinary affluence of the Japanese economy over several decades.

Sang Ho Choi playing in the 1992 Johnnie Walker Asian Classic. To date only a few Asian golfers have achieved much on the world stage, but many are waiting in the wings.

AUGUSTA NATIONAL

The Augusta National Club's course vies with the Old Course at St Andrews as the most photographed, best known golf course in the world. And in the same way, the Augusta Masters tournament rivals the Open Championship as the most famous golf tournament in the world, despite the fact that it is 74 years younger. All of this is the product of the work of three remarkable men, and of course the development and spread of television which has allowed millions of viewers throughout the world, not all of them golfers, to see the Masters tournament as it is happening, and to enjoy the beauty of a magnificent course.

The club was founded by Bobby Jones who, having won the Open and Amateur Championships of Great Britain and the United States in 1930, promptly retired from championship competition. In ten years of competitive play at the highest level on both sides of the Atlantic, Jones had formed very clear ideas as to what constituted a challenging golf hole, and had often considered, and discussed with his friends, the creation of a course which would allow him to express these ideas and make them fact.

Jones was in the habit of travelling the 100 miles from his home in Atlanta to the small Georgian town of Augusta, for winter golf. It is not generally known that Atlanta, at an altitude of 1000 feet, can be rather tart in the winter, whereas Augusta, more or less at sea level, has a

The beautiful par-3 course at the Augusta National club, used annually in an overture to the US Masters tournament

AUGUSTA			
HOLE	**NAME**	**YARDS**	**PAR**
1	Tea Olive	400	4
2	Pink Dogwood	555	5
3	Flowering Peach	360	4
4	Flowering Crab Apple	205	3
5	Magnolia	435	4
6	Juniper	180	3
7	Pampas	360	4
8	Yellow Jasmine	535	5
9	Carolina Cherry	435	4
OUT		**3,465**	**36**
10	Camellia	485	4
11	White Dogwood	455	4
12	Golden Bell	155	3
13	Azalea	465	5
14	Chinese Fir	405	4
15	Firethorn	500	5
16	Redbud	170	3
17	Nandina	400	4
18	Holly	405	4
IN		**3,440**	**36**
TOTAL		**6,905**	**72**

much milder winter climate. Another winter golf friend, Clifford Roberts, a New York investment banker, had discussed the golf course idea with Jones and was to be a critical personality in the formation of the club, and in the subsequent organisation of the Masters tournament. In 1931, 'Fruitlands', a nursery property of 365 acres on the edge of town, became available for sale. Jones expressed an interest, as usual 'subject to viewing'. One look was enough. A splendid tree-lined avenue ran to an old colonial mansion, which has become the core of the present clubhouse. Beyond it the property fell away, more than 100 feet down to Rae's Creek and the boundary, a ridge of tall pines which make a backdrop to the entire scene. Jones was enchanted. With the help of Roberts, the financing was arranged, the property bought.

The third of our three remarkable men now enters the scene. Dr Alister Mackenzie, a Yorkshire-born Scot who had given up medicine in favour of golf course design, was responsible in the twenties for Royal Melbourne West and Cypress Point, quickly recognised as two of the world's finest courses. Jones invited him to work at Augusta. The Jones concept of the course was that it should be a test for the very best players and at the same time a pleasure for all golfers to play – a tall order. The fact was that the club was to draw its membership from friends of Jones, from 'like minded people' from all over America, which meant in effect successful and prosperous not to mention influential people (the club was later to be dubbed 'The Republican Party at Play'). Not all of these men would be first-class golfers!

Thus they settled on very wide fairways, allowing for some waywardness from the tees. There would be no rough, few fairway bunkers. But against the best of golfers, such a course would be defenceless. During his playing career, Bobby Jones had been much taken with the greens he had encountered on the great championship links of Scotland and England – the huge double greens at St Andrews, the plateaued greens with firm, fast surfaces, sand-based, contoured and quick. So they resolved that the defences of Augusta would be concentrated in the greens. They are huge, plateaued and severely contoured. The challenge to the player is to hit the ball into positions on these greens from which he may escape three-putting.

All of the holes are challenging, many of them spectacular, in particular the 'water' holes on the inward half. The run of the 11th, 12th and 13th has been dubbed 'Amen Corner', on the grounds that only prayer will get the golfer through them without disaster. Changes have been made to the course over the years; the inward half was originally the outward nine. At the 11th hole, a lake guards the left side of the green, with a spur reaching into the water for a quite diabolical pin position. The par-3 12th is played over Rae's Creek, a wide stream fronting the green. The 13th is a sharp dog-leg to the left, with a stream running along the left side and across in front of the green. The 15th green is crowned, with a pond covering the entire front, and the 16th is a par-3 with a carry entirely across water to a sloping, two-level green.

The Augusta National course fits the American concept of golf at its most grand – spacious, imaginatively designed, rigorously maintained, everything in its proper place and quite, quite lovely. This is as it should be. The course is open for winter play only, November to April. The club is not a country club – there are no swimming pools, tennis courts, whatever. One does not ask to join the Augusta club, one is invited to join. The Augusta National is exclusive – armed guards man the lodge at the entrance to the club.

B

BAKER-FINCH, Ian.

Born 1960

Nationality Australian

Turned Pro 1979

Majors Open
Championship 1991

Ian Baker-Finch, apart from anything else, may just be at 6' 4" the tallest of the Open Champions. His win at Royal Birkdale in 1991 featured brilliant closing rounds of 64 and 66, and a first nine holes of 29 in that final round shattered a class international field. That sequence of 'perfect golf' was an example of the near-monastic state of trance which the modern championship player seeks in major competition. Baker-Finch played those holes as though enchanted, shutting out everything save the course and the stroke, and producing a stream of stunning golf shots. He claimed this was a result of 'mind control', which he had been studying and practising.

Ian Baker-Finch, one of a few bespectacled players in the modern game... and one of a select group of Australians to be currently challenging for the major prizes. His outward half of 29 in the last round at Royal Birkdale scattered the field and made him Open Champion of 1991.

Ian was born in Nambour, just north of Queensland – Greg Norman country – and turned professional when he was 19. He won the New Zealand Open in 1983, and while playing the European Tour for several seasons in the mid-eighties, the Scandinavian Open of 1985. He has competed in the United States since 1988, and by the end of 1991 his earnings had reached £1.5 million. He has won 15 events, and finished second in 'more than twice that number', in his own words.

Ian Baker-Finch is dark, with film-star looks, and is widely considered to be one of the nicest men in golf. Technically, his putting is probably the one outstanding part of his game.

BALL, John

Born 1862

Nationality British

Majors Open Championship 1890; Amateur Championship 1888, 1890, 1892, 1894, 1899, 1907, 1910, 1912

One of the greatest of all the amateur champions, John Ball from Hoylake won eight Amateur and one Open Championships, against the best of the professionals, around the turn of the century.

The name of John Ball is linked eternally with those of Hoylake, the Royal Liverpool Golf Club and the Amateur Championship. John's father owned the Royal Hotel at Hoylake, adjoining the Warren racecourse, the property of the Royal Liverpool Hunt Club. When the golf club was formed in 1869, the land became the Hoylake course. John Ball was seven years old, with a golf course literally on his doorstep. He played in the Open Championship when only 15, finishing fourth. The Hoylake Club was instrumental in starting the Amateur Championship in 1886 and John Ball was to win it an astonishing eight times in the 24 years from 1888 to 1912.

When he won the Open Championship at Prestwick in 1890, he became the first amateur to win, the first non-resident and the first non-Scot. And victory that year in the Amateur Championship on his own ground at Hoylake meant he was the first man to win Open and Amateur in the same year. He played his last Amateur Championship at Hoylake in 1921, the year of the first American 'invasion', and reached the sixth round – aged 61.

He served in the Cheshire Yeomanry in the Boer War from 1899 to 1902, as did his friend and golfing rival Freddie Tait, in the Black Watch. He and Tait had fought out a classic final at Prestwick before going to South Africa, Ball winning only at the 37th hole.

With a palm grip and a very full swing in the fashion of the times, he was very long, hitting long shots right up to the pin, but also had a great mastery of the half shots. The swing was smooth and repeating and John Ball was clearly the greatest amateur player of his time.

BALLESTEROS, Severiano

Born 1957

Nationality Spanish

Turned pro 1974

Majors Open Championship 1979, 1984, 1988; US Masters 1980, 1983

Severiano Ballesteros is the seminal figure in world golf in the final quarter of the 20th century. He has won the Open Championship three times, the US Masters twice. He has won more than 50 events on the PGA European Tour and almost a score of others across the world, including the national championships of Holland, France, Germany, Switzerland, Spain, Ireland and Japan. He has been an inspirational figure in the European team which won the Ryder Cup, then retained it, in thrilling matches against the United States in the 1980s. And he has inspired a whole new generation of golfers in Spain, a land once considered only for bullfights, football and cycling.

'Sebbie', as the Spaniards say, was born in Pedrena, a small town of some 5000 farmers and fishermen on the northern coast of Spain near Santander, west of Bilbao.

His father was a landowner and working farmer. His grandfather had sold some land in the twenties to help make the 1st, 4th and 6th holes of the neighbouring Royal Club de Golf de Pedrena. There was a golfing background. His uncle Ramon Sota, his mother's brother, had been the best golfer in Spain and prominent internationally in the fifties and sixties. In addition, three of Seve's brothers are golf professionals, so the boy had a club in his hand as soon as

Three times Open Champion, twice US Masters champion, Severiano Ballesteros of Spain has been the dominant personality of his time, and above all an inspiring Ryder Cup player.

he could walk. He was to hit practice shots on the beach at Pedrena, and illicitly on the Royal Pedrena course, and had turned professional before he was 17.

One single shot, televised around the world, made him famous internationally. It was a chip shot to the last green, the 72nd, at Royal Birkdale in the Open Championship of 1976. He was 19. He had led after 36 holes, but needed to make a four on that last hole to tie Jack Nicklaus for second place behind Johnny Miller. Ballesteros had pulled his second shot wide of the green to a piece of bare ground. His ball was 30 yards from the flagstick, which was about 20 feet past a pair of bunkers with only a very narrow pathway between them. The obvious safe shot, a pitch, would surely run far past the hole. Seve chipped his ball, ran it audaciously up

the narrow path, saw it finish close to the hole and sank the putt.

His first Open was not long delayed. He won at Lytham in 1979, becoming the youngest champion since Young Tom Morris in 1872. Here too came one of his spectacular recoveries at a critical time – at the 70th hole, when he hit a pitch shot from a car park, and holed for a birdie!

By the end of 1991, he had won close to £3 million on the European tour alone, and other victories probably brought this career total to more than £5 million. Ballesteros had demonstrated that at last, Europeans were the equals of the Americans in golf and had little to fear from them.

This then was Ballesteros – young, handsome, with a flashing smile and a hugely uninhibited golf swing, a

Even the greats can use a little help; Seve receiving guidance from the most celebrated teacher of recent years, David Leadbetter.

cavalier who laced out enormous drives, marched after them with the brio of an Arnold Palmer, peppered the flagsticks with iron shots, holed preposterous putts. His short game was deft and dynamic, but above all it was his recovery play that astonished the world of golf. That chip shot at Birkdale personified his game, and wherever Ballesteros was on the golf course, there would be the crowds, expecting the impossible from him. Ballesteros was a reincarnation of Walter Hagen and Arnold Palmer combined.

BALLYBUNION, OLD

Herbert Warren Wind, the highly respected American golf writer and essayist, wrote, 'Ballybunion revealed itself to be nothing less than the finest seaside course I have ever seen.'

Peter Dobereiner, the highly respected British golf writer and essayist, wrote, 'If sheer pleasure is the yardstick, Ballybunion gets my vote as the best course in the world.'

Tom Watson, champion golfer, wrote, 'A man would think that the game of golf originated here.'

The village of Ballybunion, a modest place, lies on the south shore of the Shannon estuary, at the top end of County Kerry in the Republic of Ireland some 50 miles west of Killarney, 25 miles north of Tralee. Its face is turned to the wide Atlantic Ocean which has pounded the western shores of Ireland since time began, creating golden beaches, towering cliffs, tumbling sand dunes. And it is along and through and across these dunes that

OLD BALLYBUNION		
HOLE	YARDS	PAR
1	392	4
2	445	4
3	220	3
4	498	5
5	508	5
6	364	4
7	423	4
8	153	3
9	454	4
OUT	3,457	36
10	359	4
11	449	4
12	192	3
13	484	5
14	131	3
15	216	3
16	490	5
17	385	4
18	379	4
IN	3,085	35
TOTAL	6,542	71

Ballybunion Old has its being.

It had an uncertain start. The original minute book, preserved to this day, shows 4 March 1896 as the inauguration, with George Hewson from nearby Listowel as president and Mark Montserrat as honorary secretary. Alas, they got their finances wrong and on 13 August 1898 the minute book closed. But one Colonel Bartholomew, retired from the Indian Army, formed the present club in 1906 with, sensibly, BJ Johnstone of the Bank of Ireland on his committee, plus Patrick Murphy from the original group and John Macauley of Listowel, who had played Rugby football for Ireland.

They asked a prominent figure in Irish golf, Lionel Hewson, editor of *Irish Golf* for many years, to lay out nine holes. In 1926 a further nine were laid out by a Mr Smyth, a designer for Carter and Company, the London sports ground company. By 1937, Ballybunion had been chosen to stage the Irish Mens Close Championship and the club invited Tom Simpson, a prominent English architect, to review the course. He made but a few changes, for in a sense Ballybunion designed itself. The dunes heave and tumble in all directions, giving valleys for fairways, high tops for teeing grounds, and green sites set out dramatically by the edge of the cliffs. Indeed in the late 1970s, serious cliff erosion saw the 'Friends of Ballybunion' from all over the world produce £100,000 needed to stabilise the cliffs.

As always in links golf, wind, seldom absent here, is a factor in playing the course. An even greater distraction for the newcomer may simply be the dramatic loveliness of the entire setting.

BALTUSROL, LOWER

Seven times the US Open has been played at the Baltusrol course in New Jersey, over the lower of the club's two courses, clear evidence of the regard that the US Golf Association has for one of its vintage venues. It is a classic American parkland course, yet not so severe as, for example, the Olympic in San Francisco or Oak Hill at Rochester, New York, where the fairways are pinched and overwhelmed by the fringing forests. Indeed for the 1993 'National Open', as the Americans call their championship, won that year with startling control and composure by Lee Janzen, the USGA and the Baltusrol club presented a course which was much less of a monster than some previous US Open courses which had attracted much criticism. The landing areas for the drives were made wider and the rough, prepared previously to be quite penal, allowing the golfer nothing more than an escape shot, this time was benevolent enough for the player to get a full shot.

Baltusrol is very demanding, but fair. In the 1920s, when the club had enough land, AW Tillinghast, an outstanding architect of the day, was asked to design two new courses, taking in the existing 18. His Lower course, brought up to date subsequently by Robert Trent Jones, another outstanding designer, typified his work. Tillinghast's greens were often on the small side, but subtle and with exceptionally deep bunkering. Often he would splash a ripple of sand traps across the fairway, perhaps 30 yards short of the green, but he always provided an open entrance to his greens, so that they could take a running approach shot. He used water only if it was already there naturally.

The club is one of America's oldest, dating from 1895. Its name comes from the oft-told story of one Baltus Roll, of Dutch extraction, who was farming the land when in 1831 he was dragged from his home and murdered by two thieves. Later in the century, Louis Keller, much taken with this 'new' game, bought what was still farmland, and set about forming a golf club and course. Keller was the founder and publisher of *The New York Social Register*, and surely had enough friends and influence to have the whole thing moving along smartly. By 1903, Baltusrol had its first Open, won not surprisingly by Willie Anderson, originally from North Berwick, the club's first professional and the only man to win three successive US Opens (he won four in all).

An even more often-told story of Baltusrol is that of its fourth hole, the club's signature hole, a magnificent par 3. It was made by Trent Jones when he was invited to ready the course for the US Open of 1954, won by Ed Furgol. Jones made it a challenging shot of 196 yards over water. He expanded an existing brook into a lake, rather as he did with the 16th hole at Augusta. He made the green two-tiered, very wide, but quite shallow. When the club committee were shown the hole and suggested it might be too severe, Jones, a

The famous short 4th on the lower course at Baltusrol, New Jersey, the venue of the 1993 US Open. The entire carry is over water.

LOWER BALTUSROL		
HOLE	YARDS	PAR
1	469	4
2	390	4
3	438	4
4	194	3
5	388	4
6	470	4
7	470	4
8	365	4
9	206	3
OUT	3,390	34
10	449	4
11	410	4
12	193	3
13	383	4
14	399	4
15	419	4
16	214	3
17	623	5
18	524	5
IN	3,632	36
TOTAL	7022	70

capable player in his time, teed a ball, hit a shot over the water, and made a hole in one. There was no further discussion.

Baltusrol is an altogether splendid course, demanding in particular fine long-iron play and very, very careful putting. It finishes with a soaring climax of two huge par-5 holes of 623 and 524 yards. The 17th is the longest hole in American championship golf.

BEMAN, Deane

Born 1938

Nationality United States

Turned Pro 1967

When Deane Beman succeeded Joe Dey as 'commissioner' (ie chief executive) of the US PGA Tour, he began a second career which made him the most successful and longest reigning commissioner in American sport, controlling a business which now has revenues of almost $200 million and tournament prize

background in insurance had given Beman a lively insight to tax law, and he was disturbed to learn that the PGA Tour was paying tax on its profits, as were the governing bodies of other professional sports. He reckoned the tour could qualify as a non-profit association. Hauling in his tax attorney, wife and secretary, he simply formed a new organisation, registered it and the tax authorities approved it, simply by correspondence. Beman then transferred the tour's board of directors to the board of the new organisation, and for a few hundred dollars in lawyers' fees, he had a non-profit PGA Tour.

During Beman's time in control of the organisation, off-course activities have grown to such an extent that the weekly tournaments often seem almost incidental. 'Tournament Players Clubs' is a concept that sees private developers join with the PGA Tour to build golf courses and property developments, with courses of a quality which meets tournament demands. There are now at least 15 in the United States and one in Japan, with others scheduled. The 'Family Golf Centre' is a variation on the theme, with the PGA Tour managing municipal courses for local authorities.

The tour had its own film company, making

money of close to $100 million.

Born in 1938 in Washington DC, Deane had an outstanding amateur career, winning the Amateur Championship at Sandwich in 1959, the US Amateur in 1960 and 1963 and playing on four US Walker Cup teams. In 1967 he left a healthy insurance broking firm in Bethesda, Maryland, a suburb of Washington, to turn professional and play on the PGA Tour full-time. In the following six years, he won four tournaments before becoming PGA Commissioner in 1974. As a golfer, Beman was never quite long enough to keep up with his more powerful contemporaries, Jack Nicklaus among them, but he was a deadly finisher and a ruthless competitor. These qualities stood him in good stead when he became the tour 'boss'.

His first executive decision in the new job was probably the best he will ever make. A

networked television programmes. PGA Tour Partners is a membership scheme for serious golf fans which drew 37,000 applicants in its first year. The PGA Senior Tour for the 'over-fifties' started in 1980 with two events. Now it has 43, and features such great names as Gary Player, Arnold Palmer, Lee Trevino, Jack Nicklaus, Raymond Floyd. The Ben Hogan Tour, now the Nike Tour, was started to give young professionals a stepping stone to the big tour, and now Beman's organisation administers a total of 120 events each year. All of this is a reflection of the affluence of the American economy, but it also owes a great deal to the energy and vision and management skills of the commissioner, Deane Beman.

BONALLACK, Michael

For any amateur golfer, winning the Amateur Championship, playing in the Walker Cup match, or representing his country in the Home Internationals might be honour enough. But what is to be said of the golfer who won the Amateur Championship five times, including three years in succession, with a win in each of the four countries of the UK? Or who was on nine Walker Cup teams, including two as captain and once as the victorious captain? Or

Michael Bonallack, secretary of the Royal and Ancient club, in his golden years. They brought him five Amateur Championship wins, five English Championships, and the captaincy of a winning Walker Cup team, at St Andrews in 1971.

who played for England every year without a break from 1957 to 1972, and again in 1974, 17 times in all?

All that is left to say is that Michael Francis Bonallack, who dominated British amateur golf in the decades of the 1950s and 1960s, has the greatest record of any amateur golfer in his country's history, and certainly ranks with the John Balls and Harold Hiltons of the game. His achievement is staggering.

Born in Chigwell, Essex on 31 December 1934, he was British Boys Champion in 1952 and two years later county champion for the first of 11 times. He was five times English champion, and four times English Stroke Play champion. He played on Great Britain's Commonwealth Trophy and Eisenhower Trophy teams, and captained both. He played for Great Britain amateur teams against the professionals, against European Amateurs and in the European Team Championship. He won amateur events galore and was leading amateur in the Open Championship of 1968 at Carnoustie and 1971 at Royal Birkdale.

Off the course, Bonallack was full of good works. He was chairman of the R & A Selection Committee 1975-79 and of the Amateur Status Committee 1976-79. He was chairman of the PGA in 1976 and of the Golf Foundation in 1977. He was a member of the R & A Rules of Golf Committee 1979-80.

In 1983, Michael Bonallack became Secretary of the Royal and Ancient Golf Club of St Andrews, which concerns itself with the Rules of Golf and of Amateur Status, not to mention the organisation of the Open and many other championships, and the requirements of an international membership of more than 1000!

In his playing days, Bonallack was a powerful figure who hit a long ball, not always precisely, with an easily identifiable swing – from a full follow-through, the club was whipped back down almost to the impact position.

But his greatest single talent was an outstanding short game. He was a deadly chipper and putter, talents which brought him bursts of phenomenal scoring to demolish match play opponents. He putted with an uncommon stance, legs wide apart, head down almost to the putter handle. He scored the first 18 holes of the English Amateur final at Ganton in 1968 in 61 strokes, with but one putt of less than two feet conceded. He was out in 32, back in 29. The par was 71. The match, against PD Kelley, was won 12 and 11. Bonallack's Amateur Championship wins were at Turnberry and Troon in Scotland, Hoylake in England, Royal Porthcawl in Wales, and Newcastle, Co. Down in Northern Ireland.

BRAID, James

Born 1870

Nationality British

Turned Pro 1896

Majors Open Championship 1901, 1905, 1906, 1908, 1910

James Braid was tall and taciturn, reserved but resolute, a powerful, placid man and by any reckoning one of the finest professionals in the history of the game. He was the first man to win five Open Championships (all in the first decade of this century), later passed by Harry Vardon with six and equalled by his contemporary JH Taylor, much later equalled also by Peter Thomson and Tom Watson. With Vardon and Taylor, Braid formed the romantically named 'Great Triumvirate' which dominated British golf for almost thirty years before the First World War.

Braid also won the first PGA Match Play Championship, in 1903 at Sunningdale, and repeated three more times. In 1910 he added the French Open. He played for Scotland against England eight times from 1903 to 1912, and for Great Britain against America in 1921 at the age of 51. His first Open Championship win, at Muirfield in 1901, was the last championship won with the gutty ball. Braid named his son Harry 'Muirfield' Braid by way of celebrating when he won there again in 1906. Indeed all his championships were won in Scotland, as befitted a Fifer – 1905 St Andrews, 1908 Prestwick, 1910 St Andrews again.

A very strong left-hand grip occasionally saw him suffer a spell of hooking, but he was an immensely long driver and a masterly iron player. From time to time, he suffered on the greens. 'Jimmy' Braid was born into golf, at Earlsferry by Elie on that coast of Fife where there is no shortage of fine links courses. He was handling a club at the age of four, was scratch at 16 and making his presence felt on the courses of the area. His parents put him to learning carpentry and a family friend, CR Smith, offered him a job in London's Army and Navy Stores as a clubmaker. Soon his presence was felt around the London courses. In a' challenge match against the great John Henry Taylor, Braid halved the match by winning the final two holes with birdies. No doubt it helped him to land the professional's job at the new Romford club in Essex in 1896.

In the early years of the century, JH Taylor was instrumental in forming an organisation which evolved into the PGA, its objective being to safeguard the welfare of golf professionals, and Braid was an enthusiastic lieutenant and one of the founder members. When his competitive career was over, he was constantly in demand for golf course designs. His most famous course is no doubt the King's course at the Gleneagles Hotel, little changed in fact since he laid it out in the early 1920s, but he worked all over the British Isles and Ireland, one way or the other on a hundred or more courses. Never much of a foreign traveller, he never did make a trip to America such as Vardon, Taylor and Ted Ray had done. In fact he remodelled the St Andrews Club's course at Hastings-on-Hudson, and designed the Bukit Timah course of the Singapore Island club, by correspondence and from topographical maps! But typically, he was highly regarded for the accuracy and detail of his drawings.

In 1904, he moved to the newly opened Walton Heath Club, and remained there for 46 years, as a latter day Old Tom Morris, until his death. It was said that no one could possibly be as wise as Braid looked. For the final 25 years, he was an honorary member of the club, and shortly before his death, was made an honorary member of the Royal and Ancient. But it was said that he never once entered the Walton Heath clubhouse by the front door.

James Braid, standing, watches Harry Vardon drive. The third member of the 'Great Triumvirate' is JH Taylor, seated.

JOHN HENRY TAYLOR

JAMES BRAID

HARRY VARDON

CALLOWAY SYSTEM

The Calloway System of Handicapping is designed to help competition organisers with a large number of players in the field who do not have authorised handicaps. It is essentially a system for deciding the player's handicap on the day. Devised by Lionel Calloway, a professional at Pinehurst, the system in simple terms deducts a given number of worst holes from the card, with the addition of a maximum of two strokes per worst hole in their place. The gross score decides how many "worst holes" may be deducted (the higher the gross score the more of these deductions may be made). This is set out on a comprehensive table which covers gross scores from 70 to 130. In practice, the net scores come out surprisingly close to each other – since a few bad holes cannot hurt the card, the system encourages bold, even aggressive play, in competitions using the Calloway system.

CAMPBELL Bt, Sir Guy Colin

Guy Campbell was the great grandson of Robert Chambers, who had a hand in the design of the original nine-holes course at Hoylake, and was an early golf historian. Guy, at Eton and the University of St Andrews, was an outstanding sportsman, excelling at rowing and cricket as well as golf. He was a semi-finalist in the Amateur Championship of 1907, and played for Scotland against England in 1909, 1910 and 1911. He was wounded in the First World War, in which he served as an infantryman, and actually served again in the Second World War although advanced in his fifties.

In 1920, he joined the staff of *The Times* and wrote several books and magazine articles on golf.

In the late twenties, he began designing courses, working variously with CK Hutchison, SV Hotchkin and Henry Cotton. Among his design credits are Princes at Sandwich, Mahony's Point at Killarney and the Hague course in Holland. He remodelled Rye GC in Sussex, Royal Cinque Ports, Royal Dublin, and North Berwick's West Links. He assumed the rank of baronet on the death of his father Sir Guy T Campbell in 1931. Guy Colin Campbell died in Irvington, Virginia in 1960, aged 75, but was interred at St Andrews.

Dorothy Campbell of North Berwick, champion on both sides of the Atlantic.

CAMPBELL HURD, Dorothy

Born in Edinburgh in 1883, Dorothy Campbell was a North Berwick golfer who won the British Ladies Amateur Championship in 1909 and 1911. Three times Scottish champion, she played for Scotland in international matches and in the early British v American Ladies matches, but her outstanding achievement was to win the three major championships of her time, the British, American and Canadian events. The American she won in 1909, 1911 and 1912. In the year of 1911, she came close to doing the treble in one year. Defending her US title, she fell only in the semi-final to Margaret Curtis, one of the sisters who later donated the Curtis Cup for ladies competition between the United States and Great Britain and Ireland. The only other lady to win all three titles has been Mrs Marlene Stewart Streit.

CARNER, Joanne

Born	1939
Nationality	United States
Turned Pro	1970

One of the finest records in women's amateur golf was compiled by 'Gundy', Joanne Carner (her maiden name was Gunderson). She won the US Women's Amateur Championship five times, in

Joanne Carner jigs for joy as another putt drops. Born to golf, Joanne was US Girls Junior champion at 15 and won the first of her five US Amateur titles when only 19. A powerful hitter, she won the US Open twice in the seventies.

1957, 1960, 1962, 1966 and 1968, and before that had been US Girls Junior Champion at the age of 15. Indeed she won the first of her five US Amateur titles at the age of 18.

Born in Kirkland, Seattle on 4 April 1939, she turned professional at 30 and had an equally distinguished career, winning a tournament in her very first season. She had earlier won an LPGA tournament in Miami while still an amateur. Her professional career has brought her $2.5 million in prize money and 42 official victories. She won the US Women's Open in 1971 and again in 1976. In 1987 at the age of 48, and by now known affectionately as 'Big Momma', Joanne tied for the US Open but lost the play-off to Britain's Laura Davies.

At 5' 7" and powerfully built, Joanne Carner was a forbidding opponent at every level at which she played – something of a Jack Nicklaus. With husband Don she travelled the tournament circuit often in a mobile home, and much of their spare time was spent fishing and sailing in the Bahamas from their 40-foot boat.

CARNOUSTIE

All the famous golfing coastlines of Scotland have their shrines. Ayrshire has Royal Troon, in East Lothian it is Muirfield; there is the Old Course at St Andrews in Fife, and in the case of Tayside, Carnoustie, the most northerly of the Open championship courses in Scotland.

In many respects it may be the most formidable, in the relentless challenge of its holes and a sequence building to the final five which may well be the most fearsome in golf. Open championships at Carnoustie have been won by the greatest golfers of the times – Tommy Armour in 1931, Henry Cotton in 1937, Ben Hogan in 1953, Gary Player in 1968. Since the victory of Tom Watson in 1975, the championship has not returned to Carnoustie, not because of any shortcomings of the course as a test, but because of the absence of hotel accommodation and the traffic situation in the area. Vigorous steps are being taken to deal with this and the expectation is that Carnoustie will be back on the championship rota before the end of the century.

Golf has been played in the area since the middle of the 16th century to our knowledge, and no doubt earlier. The first club dates from 1839, and Allan Robertson of St Andrews laid out an initial ten holes, made up to 18 in 1867 by Old Tom Morris. The famous James Braid, as successful and industrious a course designer as he was a championship player, modernised the course in 1926 to such an extent that only five years later it was ready for its first Open Championship.

The links at Carnoustie, the championship course, the adjoining Burnside and the Buddon Links, dating from 1981, have always been public and are used by half a dozen local clubs, the Carnoustie, Caledonian, Dalhousie, Mercantile, New Taymouth and Carnoustie Ladies, and are managed by the Carnoustie Championship Golf Courses Committee. Back in the 1930s, this committee was chaired by Dundee chartered accountant James Wright, a man of substance with extensive business interest in the United States, and a man of vision. He set about modernising the course, adapting the design, the placement of bunkers and so on, to accommodate the influence of steel-shaft golf. Wright's creed was, 'Quality rather than pure length has been our objective.'

The altered course was ready for the 1937 Open which Henry Cotton won, but Carnoustie Opens are forever spoken of and associated with Ben Hogan, and that great American's victory in 1953, the only Open in which he competed.

In simple terms, the course is flat, without the towering dunes of Birkdale or the magnificent seascapes of Troon or Turnberry. Although it is close by, the sea is never in view – rather like the Old Course at St Andrews. But there is a good deal of localised movement in the fairways and the course is without a weakness. No more than two successive holes run in the same direction and in any kind of wind, it represents a major challenge to the golfer. Among the outstanding holes are the sixth and the 16th.

The sixth, the 'long' hole, is

Long and forbidding, Carnoustie, the most northerly Open course, was left off the championship rota because of difficult access and shortage of accommodation in the Angus village. But early in the 1990s, strenuous efforts were being made to enable it to play host to the Open Championship once more.

a par-5 of some 517 yards. It is a straight hole, with an out of bounds fence running along the entire left side of the fairway. The right side of the fairway has serious rough and some drainage ditches. Two bunkers, one behind the other, are placed in the centre of the fairway 200 and 240 yards from the medal tee respectively. They dominate

HOLE	NAME	YARDS	PAR
CARNOUSTIE			
1	Cup	401	4
2	Gulley	418	4
3	Jockie's Burn	321	4
4	Hillocks	375	4
5	Brae	377	4
6	Long	521	5
7	Plantation	376	4
8	Short	149	3
9	Railway	427	4
OUT		**3,365**	**36**
10	South America	406	4
11	Dyke	367	4
12	Southward Ho	476	5
13	Whins	145	3
14	Spectacles	487	5
15	Luckyslap	424	4
16	Barry Burn	235	3
17	Island	438	4
18	Home	453	4
IN		**3,431**	**36**
MEDAL TOTAL		**6,796**	**72**
CHAMPIONSHIP		**7,200**	**72**

the hole, imposing the tactics of the hole on the golfer. The second shot to the green is best played from the left side of the fairway from a point past these bunkers. Thus the first question asked of the golfer on the tee is how to get to that point. Downwind – the hole runs almost due West – he may be able to carry them. But he had better be sure. He does not want to flirt with the out of bounds on the left. If he is trapped in either of these bunkers, he has no real shot out. If he is too far to the right of them, his second shot will have to be across rough, across a ditch, across bunkers, to a green set diagonally across the shot.

The 16th, 'Barry Burn', is just as demanding. It is a par-3 of 238 yards, playing to the North East. The green is mounded, like an upturned saucer which will tend to throw the ball off. It is long and contoured. There are a pair of bracketing bunkers 40 yards short of the green and a dip in the fairway short of the putting surface. There is a bunker short left and three along the right side, none of them hard against the putting surface, so that the golfer from there will have one of the game's most difficult shots – the long bunker shot. This, coming towards the climax of the round, is a very severe hole indeed, justifying the judgement of some critics that Carnoustie is the most severe of all championship courses.

CARR, Joe

Born 1922

Nationality Irish

When he became the first Irishman to be elected Captain of the Royal and Ancient Golf Club of St Andrews (1991–92), Joseph Boynton Carr of Sutton, Dublin, set the seal on one of the most remarkable careers in amateur golf. He was born in the clubhouse at Portmarnock, where his father was club steward, on 18 February, 1922, and from then on the world of golf seemed to fall at the feet of Joe. He won the East of Ireland Amateur Championship at the age of 19, the first of twelve successes. He won the South of Ireland three times, the West of Ireland twelve times over a span of 20 years from 1946, and he won the Irish Amateur Championship six times as well as being twice a beaten finalist.

His crowning achievement as one of the finest match players in history were his Amateur Championship wins in 1953, 1958 and 1960, at Hoylake, St Andrews and Portrush respectively, and his losing final against Michael Bonallack at Troon in 1968. Joe, a gregarious, outgoing type, was perhaps less effective as a team player, yet played an unbroken sequence for Ireland from 1947 to 1969. He took part in 11 Walker Cup matches from

One of Ireland's most famous golfing sons, the swashbuckling Joe Carr's light-hearted approach to the game brought an impressive collection of titles – three Amateur Championships, six Irish championships, Walker Cup and international matches galore.

1947, once as captain (1963), once as non-playing captain.

Joe held honorary memberships of more than 30 golf clubs, including Portmarnock, Killarney, Lahinch, Royal Portrush, Royal Lytham & St Annes, and in the US he was a member of the Augusta National and of Pine Valley. He reached the semi-final of the US Amateur Championship in 1961 at Pebble Beach (won by Jack Nicklaus) and was leading amateur in the Open of 1956 at Hoylake and of 1958 at Lytham.

CASPER, Bill

Born	1931
Nationality	United States
Turned Pro	1954
Majors	US Open 1959, 1966; US Masters 1970

Bill Casper, very much a contemporary of Arnold Palmer, was an outstanding competitor on the US Tour for twenty years. He was an exceptional putter, and this combined with a sound, undemonstrative tee-to-green game and a relaxed personality brought him much success. He had 51 official victories in all and from 1956 to 1971 inclusive he won at least one tournament each year. He became something of a butt for the media when certain allergies forced him to take up an unusual diet which included buffalo meat.

Bill Casper's long career has been marked by rather matter of fact play from tee to green, and marvellous putting. His first tournament win was in 1956 and he continues playing very successfully in senior golf.

Bill, born in San Diego on 24 June 1931, was not perhaps the most ardent of international players, travelling abroad only when invited, but he still listed the Canadian, Italian and Mexican Opens among his trophies. He also won in France and Morocco, and confessed in his senior years that he should have 'devoted more time' to the British Open.

His second US Open win, over Arnold Palmer at the Olympic Club in San Francisco, was one of the most dramatic in the history of the event. Casper was six strokes behind with nine holes to play, yet tied and won the 18 hole play-off, despite being strokes behind again with nine to play. He was runner-up three times in the US PGA Championship, leading money winner in America in 1966 and 1968, and was second to Arnold Palmer in winning more than $1 million in prize money. When he joined the Senior Tour, where he enjoyed continued success, he described it as 'kicking over stones and finding money'. It brought him a further $1.5 million prize money.

Billy had always been a portly figure, seldom weighing less than 200 pounds, and he became easily spotted at Senior Events by the voluminous plus-fours, or in American parlance 'knickers', which he took to wearing. He won the US Senior Open Championship in 1983. He was a Ryder Cup player eight times, from 1961, and was non-playing US captain in 1979.

CHARLES, Bob

Born 1936

Nationality New Zealand

Turned Pro 1960

Majors Open Championship 1963

The place of Robert James Charles is at least a footnote in the broad history of the game on two counts – he was the first New Zealander to win the Open Championship, and the first left-handed golfer to do so.

A devastating putting technique and placid temperament has given Bob a long and successful career in the game, stretching profitably into senior golf, and brought him the championships of Switzerland, Canada, South Africa and Scandinavia, as well as his Open Championship success in 1963 at Royal Lytham, when he won a play-off with the American Phil Rodgers with 140 against 148 over 36 holes.

Bob won his first New Zealand Open as an amateur in 1954, then again as a professional in 1966, 1970 and 1973. He played for New Zealand nine times in World Cup teams. The Senior PGA Tour provided him with a rich vein of tournament wins and more than $3.5 million in prize money, much more than the regular tour ever brought him.

Thirty years on - Bob Charles hoists the British Seniors Open trophy in 1993 at Royal Lytham and St Annes, where he won the Open Championship in 1963. He is so far the only left-handed golfer to have won the Open.

COLES, Neil, MBE

Born 1934

Nationality British

Turned Pro 1950

As Chairman of the PGA European Tour, Neil Coles presides over an organisation which presents almost 100 events each year, with £20 million in prize money. When Neil topped the PGA rankings for the British circuit in 1963, there were only 14 tournaments, and he earned £3,742!

Born in London on 26 September 1934, he turned professional at the tender age of 16 and his tournament career, lasting more than 30 years and taking him into senior golf, brought him a total of 28 wins, including the national Opens of Germany in 1971 and Spain in 1973. Between 1961 and 1982, he was never out of Europe's top 20 in the money list, and when he won the Sanyo Open in 1982 aged 48 he became the oldest man to win on the main tour. In senior golf, he took the British Senior title in 1987 and for four years, from 1985 to 1988, held the PGA Senior title.

Neil played eight times in the Ryder Cup, but an aversion to flying restricted his international appearances. In association with Brian Huggett, an old adversary, he has been active in golf course design.

COLLETT VARE, Glenna

Born 1903

Nationality United States

Glenna Collett was perhaps the greatest of all American lady golfers. She dominated the game there throughout the 1920s and 1930s, winning her first US Women's Amateur Championship at the age of 19 in 1922 and the last of her record six wins in 1935. Thus she was directly comparable to Bobby Jones. She did not start playing until she was 14, but developed into a fine free-swinging golfer who drove the ball a long way, and one with impressive concentration. She was a finalist in the 1929 and 1930 British Ladies Championships, and her 1929 final against Joyce Wethered has been considered a classic. Glenna played her first 11 holes at St Andrews in 41 strokes and had been five up in the match, but went down 3 & 1 to an inspired counter-attack from Joyce. Glenna died in 1989, aged 86.

As they were in the twenties - great champions, Glenna Collett (left) of the United States, and Simone Thion de la Chaume of France.

COLT, Harold

Harold Shapland Colt was a contemporary of Willie Park Jnr. and between them they made golf architecture a profession. Colt studied law at Cambridge where he captained the golf team, and practised as a solicitor for several years. He laid out the course at Rye, subsequently the 'home' of the Oxford and Cambridge Golfing Society, in 1894 when only 25 years old! When the new Sunningdale club in Berkshire was opened in 1901, he became its first secretary, a post he held until 1913.

During these years, he developed his talents as a golf architect, not only at home but in Europe and in the US, to which he was to make three separate extended visits. He expanded and lengthened Sunningdale to cope with the changes which the new Haskell ball brought, cleared much of the heather on its heathland, and planted trees extensively.

Harry Colt planned Stoke Poges in 1918, Swinley Forest in 1910 and 36 holes at St George's Hill in 1913. In that same year, he was invited by George Crump, creator of Pine Valley, to work with him. Colt helped with the routeing of the holes on the great New Jersey course. One of his greatest achievements was the Eden course at St Andrews for the Royal and Ancient club in 1912, no doubt a contract much sought after by designers at the time. From a flat and unpromising piece of land, cramped in places, Colt laid out a course quite worthy of St Andrews and which continues to give pleasure to this day.

Included in his carnet are the Wentworth courses and the remodelling of Muirfield; in Spain, Puerto de Hierro in Madrid and the Severiano Ballesteros home course, Real Club de Golf de Pedrena; in France, courses at Cannes and Le Touquet, and in Germany the Frankfurter and Hamburger courses. Prominent work in America was Sea Island in Georgia, the Country Club of Detroit and Burning Tree, near Washington. Harry Colt helped to train other leading architects in Dr Alister Mackenzie, CH Alison, JSF Morrison and John Harris.

Colt was probably the first golf architect who had not been a professional golfer, the first to use the drawing board extensively, the first 'tree-planter' and the first truly international designer. He died in 1951.

COMPETITION, Types of

The following types of competition, all variations on the basic 'lowest score wins' concept, are used by clubs for a number of reasons. In some cases the format of the competition speeds up play, in others it gives greater opportunities to high handicap golfers or increases the team play element. In some cases, of course, the variations are used just for fun.

GREENSOMES

A form of foursomes played off ³/₈ of the combined handicaps of the partners. Each player drives on every hole. They then select which ball they prefer to play and the other ball is picked up. If player B's ball is selected, player A then plays the second shot and the partners proceed playing alternate shots until the hole is completed. Penalty strokes do not affect the order of play.

STABLEFORD

A scoring system devised by a Dr Stableford of Wallasey in 1931, in which one point is awarded for a score of one stroke over the net par on a hole, two for net par, three for one under par, and so on. The game is usually played with full handicap allowance. The highest points scorer is the winner. Players who have played two shots more than the net par have no need to hole out.

AMERICAN FOURSOMES

A form of foursomes played off ³/₈ of the combined handicaps of the partners. Each player drives, then plays the second shot with the partner's ball. They then decide which ball they prefer to play and the other ball is picked up. If player A has hit the second shot with the selected ball, player B hits the third shot and the partners proceed playing alternate shots until the hole is completed. Penalty strokes do not affect the order of play.

CANADIAN FOURSOMES

A form of foursomes played off ³/₈ of the combined handicaps of the partners. Each player drives and plays a second shot. They then decide on which ball they prefer to play, and the other ball is picked up. If player A's ball is selected, player B hits the third shot with the selected ball and the partners proceed playing alternate shots until the hole is completed. Penalty strokes do not affect the order of play.

RYE FOURSOMES

A form of foursomes played off ³/₈ of the combined handicaps of the partners. Both players drive on every hole, but must declare in advance which of them will play second shots on an alternate hole basis. Player A for example, may elect to play second shots on the odd-numbered holes, player B on the even. The player nominated for the odd numbers will select the ball to be kept in play on hole number one – it may well be his own drive. The other ball is picked up and play continues on an alternate shot basis until the hole is completed. Penalty strokes do not affect the order of play.

TEXAS SCRAMBLE

A fourball team game played as a stroke event and usually played off ¹/₈ of the combined handicaps of the partners. All drive on every hole, then decide which ball is in the best position. The other balls are picked up, and all play second shots from within a club length of that best position. Play continues under that system until the hole is completed. If the ball in play is in a hazard or in the rough, the same procedure applies.

ECLECTIC

An eclectic score is the lowest gross score achieved at each hole on the course over a specified period of time – a week, a month, a year, in some cases quoted over an entire career!

CORNISH, Geoffrey

A Canadian born in 1914, Cornish took a BA degree from the University of British Columbia, followed by a Masters from the University of Massachusetts, both in agronomy. In 1935, the Winnipeg-born Cornish was hired to evaluate soil characteristics for the now famous Capilano course in Vancouver, designed by Stanley Thompson, the Scots-born Canadian designer famed for Banff and Jasper among many other fine courses. Cornish, invited to join Thompson's organisation, worked with him for four years. After serving overseas with the Canadian Army in the Second World War, Cornish became an associate of the Thompson firm, and worked there through the late forties. He was involved with the University of Massachusetts in developing turfgrass science, and in 1952 formed his own design company.

Cornish subsequently designed more courses in the New England area than any other architect, and also across Canada, from Prince Edward Island to British Columbia.

With William C Robinson, he wrote *Golf Design – An Introduction*, which was distributed by the US National Golf Foundation, and with Ronald E Whitten in 1981 published the definitive work *The Golf Course* which lists hundreds of courses throughout the world, with profiles of golf course designers and embracing the history of the profession.

COTTON, Henry

Born 1907

Nationality British

Turned Pro 1926

Majors Open Championship 1934, 1937, 1948

Sir Henry Cotton, knighted posthumously for his services to a game he loved, was a man born 50 years ahead of his time. It is difficult to imagine how much a talented extrovert like Cotton with plenty to say and a liking for the odd bit of controversy would have earned today. Suffice to say that he played his part in upgrading his chosen profession to the point where the modern stars can and do make millions. The great American professional Walter Hagen once said that he never longed to be a millionaire, just wanted to live like one. Cotton wanted to live like one but wanted to be one too – and never reached that status. Two generations later and he would have.

Still, his formidable wife 'Toots', his most loyal fan if sometimes his most severe critic, was a millionairess. It was she who harnessed the tremendous vitality possessed by Cotton, the most stylish and innovative player of his day. Cotton won two Open Championship titles before and one after the Second World War. In 1948 His Royal Highness King George VI came to watch him play because of who he was – a larger than life sports personality with drive and energy and shot-making

Henry Cotton, the mature champion, handsome, composed, at the height of his powers, just turned thirty, at Ashridge golf club. The portrait is by JAA Berrie.

skills that were the envy of most of his peers.

Behind most top golfers there is a woman driving or coaxing him on to ever greater glories. 'Toots' knew what she wanted for Cotton and invariably he followed her advice. They were a team.

He could not help but meet her when he headed off on one of his South American tours in the 1930s. When the ship arrived in Buenos Aires, 'Toots' was waiting for him although he had never met her nor did he know anything about her. She had made sure of meeting him by booking up every one of his pre-publicised individual instruction classes.

If his golfing goal was to win major titles, 'Toots' had a much simpler personal ambition – marriage. She got her man.

When as a teenager Henry Cotton, a public schoolboy, suggested to his father that he might wish to become a professional golfer, one can imagine the parental response – disbelief, disappointment perhaps. Shock certainly.

Professionals in the 1920s were not the prominent, well-paid superstars of sport they are today but Cotton's father decided to take his son to Royal Mid-Surrey Golf Club in Richmond near London to have the professional JH Taylor, one of the original golfing triumvirate, look him over. Taylor must have given Mr Cotton Senior sufficient grounds for believing his boy could make it because at the age of 17, when he might have been expected to head for the city and a career in banking or insurance, Henry Cotton turned professional.

Every golfer in Britain today should be thankful that Cotton chose golf. JH Taylor could have had no idea when he gave young Cotton the thumbs-up that he was letting loose on the game a pioneer, a man who would so effectively raise the status of the professional golfer at both club and tournament level and at the same time continue to promote and popularise it.

Cotton was not just a stylish golfer who had gone to the United States to learn how the Americans, dominating golf in the late 1920s and early 30s, managed to do things better, he was a communicator with distinctive ideas on how to play the game and a clear and precise manner of expounding his theories. In short, he was commercial.

Today's stars should remember that it was not the great Arnold Palmer and his lawyer friend Mark McCormack who invented contracts and endorsements. Cotton was the man who blazed that particular trail before the Second World War.

Always a believer that he would get more respect and become a bigger hero by leaving Britain, Cotton spent much of his early golfing life on the Continent – a decision that had its drawbacks. After having holed the winning putt on his debut in the 1929 Ryder Cup match, he was banned from competing for the next three matches because he had dared to leave the country to find fame and fortune in Belgium and in the south of France, where at his golf school pupils drove balls into the Mediterranean.

Angered at having to change for championships in the tent provided by the authorities because professionals were not allowed inside clubhouses in the 1930s, Henry and 'Toots' used to enjoy a champagne lunch from the boot of his Bentley car parked close to the front door of the clubhouse. It was all part of a determined plan to change

for ever the status of the golf professional. What happened at Sandwich in 1934 gave him the platform he needed to make his campaign more effective.

Outwardly he looked calm and composed that week. Inwardly he was nervous as he began his bid to end 10 years of American domination in the Open. Until 1934 the lowest score ever shot in an Open had been a remarkable 67 by the American golfing showman Walter Hagen in 1929. Cotton matched that in the first round and then shot a 65 in the second. That score stood as the Open record for 43 years until Mark Hayes of America shot 63 in the 1977 Open at Turnberry won by Tom Watson.

Even more remarkable is that Cotton's 1934 total of 132 for two rounds is still the record for the first 36 holes, although it was matched by Nick Faldo and Greg Norman in the 1990 Open at St Andrews won by Faldo. That gives a measure to the quality of Cotton's play. He single putted eight times and ended the record round by hitting a 2-iron to seven feet. Despite a bout of stomach cramps brought on by pressure and nerves, Cotton won the title that year by five strokes and afterwards the Dunlop Sports company produced their famous Dunlop 65 golf ball in recognition of his remarkable feat.

Cotton was news and through to the outbreak of the war he made the most of it. What Hagen had started, Cotton continued. The Englishman wrote well, he taught well, he even went on the stage to spread the word and proved so successful with his theatrical golf act, in which he hit soft balls into the audience, that he was asked back again. He not only popularised the game with the general public but worked hard to tear down

the barriers of elitism which had for so long surrounded the game in England and had threatened to stifle its growth and expansion. Cotton won the Open again in 1937 in the rain at Carnoustie – a victory he always considered was the best of his three title wins – and the third was the one watched by the King at Muirfield in 1948.

Despite the appalling weather there were 15,000 with Cotton when he came to the closing holes at Carnoustie on the final day and they – and the always loyal 'Toots' walking with them – willed him to what can still be described as one of the greatest of Open Championship victories. Not everyone appreciated Cotton's sometimes brash, always confident attitude in which everything was always black or white. He had no room for compromise and some people rather resented his determination to go it alone and do it 'his way' long before Frank Sinatra came round to singing about it.

The comparison in this respect between Cotton and Nick Faldo and his singular attitude today is obvious, but unlike Faldo who can make enough from golf and all the associated contracts to live a quiet life out of the public gaze when not at tournaments, Cotton had to work hard to make what was big money in those less commercial and certainly less hectic days when travelling the world was not as comfortable nor as easy as it is today.

The last man to win a top tournament playing hickory-shafted clubs, Cotton might have won more Opens than Harry Vardon (who collected six) but the war intervened.

Invalided out of the RAF, Cotton was awarded an MBE for his services to the Red Cross and after the war he continued playing, teaching and writing flamboyantly

about the game which he helped change so dramatically. He believed that the secret to playing well was in the hands. Strong hands were what he felt were needed to score well in golf and to strengthen his own he would scythe down the rough with a wedge on which he had sharpened the leading edge. He pioneered the use of an ordinary tyre to help his pupils strengthen their hands by hitting the club against it. No other teacher has followed suit but Cotton felt it helped.

He captained the Ryder Cup team that lost at Wentworth in 1953 when many felt he should have played, and in 1956, by now 50, he finished sixth in the Open, underlining how good he still was. He made his nostalgic farewell appearance in the 1977 Open at Turnberry and retired to Penina on the Algarve where he had built a golf course out of a rice field.

Having stayed at one stage in his career in a penthouse in the Dorchester Hotel and then in fashionable Eaton Square, Cotton moved latterly to Portugal where he had a staff of five serving him in a cottage beside the five star Penina Hotel into which he and 'Toots' latterly moved. Cotton was always ready to meet and talk golf with anyone and frequently enjoyed telling a risque or ribald story at just the wrong time! Golf for Henry was always fun and that word perhaps sums up his hectic and adventurous life in golf with 'Toots.' Believe it or not they had fun even on the day when at a pro-am 'Toots' warned Henry that if he put her in the rough she would turn and hit the ball back towards the tee. He did, she did and they still won!

Writing regularly for the *News of the World* and for golfing magazines allowed Cotton to air his thought-provoking, stimulating opinions quite fearlessly while building up long-lasting friendships with the press. If he felt it needed to be said, he said it, irrespective of the consequences. Twice captain of the Professional Golfers Association, the man who took the profession out of the cloth-cap era, Cotton was justly proud when he was made an honorary member of the Royal and Ancient Golf Club of St Andrews.

Sir Henry Cotton's name is revered the world over for what he achieved in a personal sense and for what he did for his fellow professionals. The many books he left, the records and standards he set and the courses he built are tangible legacies.

It is what you do not see, however, that is most important. Above all, he gave the golf professionals pride in their profession. He may have got a great deal out of the game himself, but he put a great deal more into it right up to his death at the age of 80.

CRENSHAW, Ben

Born 1952

Nationality United States

Turned Pro 1973

Majors US Masters 1984

In almost every memorable victory in a major championship, one shot stands out as 'the shot that won it'. In recent years, Sandy Lyle's 7-iron shot from the bunker at the 72nd hole of the 1988 Masters, which clinched the title, would be

Ben Crenshaw, outstanding champion (US Masters 1984), golf historian and collector of golfing impedimenta.

the memorable shot there, despite the fact that his birdie putt on the 16th – slick, downhill 15 feet and breaking a good six inches – was just as critical.

It is an innocent if inconclusive game which all golfers play, like the selection of 'player of the year' in a team game, and not to be taken seriously in a championship in which a man might play 280 shots over a period of four days.

Yet if there is one single shot accepted as turning the tide of a championship, it was Ben Crenshaw's putt on the 10th green of the Augusta National Course in the 1984 US Masters, Crenshaw's first major championship win. He was 60 feet below the hole of the sloping green, the putt breaking as much as eight feet. Crenshaw rolled it preposterously into the very middle of the hole, and said later, 'Couldn't do that again

in a thousand tries.' It kept him in front of the field, an advantage he held to the end.

For many people, the wonder was that Ben's major breakthrough had taken so long. He had chances to win the Open Championship at St Andrews in 1978, when Jack Nicklaus beat him by two strokes, and at Royal Lytham and St Annes in 1979, when Severiano Ballesteros beat him by three. In that same year of 1979 he was to lose a

play-off to David Graham in the US PGA Championship.

Crenshaw, from Austin in Texas, had been an outstanding amateur, winning national honours when with the University of Texas team in the early 1970s. And he won the very first tournament he entered as a professional, the San Antonio-Texas Open in 1973. His golf has been distinguished by a long, rhythmic but powerful swing and an immaculate putting technique. He has been one of the best-loved and most popular players in the game, mainly because of his equable personality and easy smile.

'Gentle Ben' was judged to be the superstar who would follow the line of Palmer, Nicklaus and Watson, but that did not quite materialise. In 1982 everything seemed to go wrong for Ben, on and off the course, and at 83rd in the rankings he left the Tour and went home to Austin to revamp his game. After much toil and sweat, and advice from his old teacher Harvey Penninck, he tied for second in the 1983 Masters and in the same year won the Byron Nelson classic. Ben was back. Ben Crenshaw lists his other interests as fishing, bird watching, country music and golf artefacts and architecture. He is something of a golf historian and an ardent buyer of old clubs and golf books.

CROOME, Arthur

Arthur Capel Molyneux Croome was a sporting aristocrat. At school (Wellington) he excelled at cricket, rugby and athletics and after graduation from Oxford University he became expert in golf, curling and billiards. When he was a teacher, housemaster and athletics coach at Radley School, he took up golf with

such dedication that he was soon competing in the Amateur Championship and other major events. With John L Low and RG de Montmorency, he formed in 1898 the Oxford and Cambridge Golfing Society which sent a team on tour to the United States where they played matches against American universities. The architect CH Alison was one of the early members.

While at Radley, Croome wrote articles on golf for the London newspapers, the *Evening Standard* and the *Morning Post*, and when he retired from teaching he wrote on golf and cricket for *The Times*. A meeting with the architect JF Abercromby introduced him to some of the mysteries of golf course design, and Croome was fascinated by the business. Among Abercromby's many notable courses were Worplesdon and Coombe Hill. After the First World

War, Croome became a partner in the firm of Fowler, Abercromby, Simpson and Croome – impressive company for Arthur.

If his contribution was mainly as business manager and publicist for the group, he did design at least one course entirely on his own. It was Liphook, opened in 1922 and a gem on sandy heathland on the Hampshire border. Many critics consider it to be in the Sunningdale category. Ill health in his later years much curtailed the work of Arthur Croome.

CRUMP, George

In the early years of this century a group of golfers from the Philadelphia CC at Bala, its original nine holes designed by 'Young' Willie Dunn, would often take a Reading Railroad train to the Atlantic shore, to play over the Atlantic City CC course

Arthur Croome, talented exponent of cricket, Rugby, athletics, curling, billiards and golf - and a golf course architect to boot.

which in turn had been laid out by that other equally famous early Scottish architect, Willie Park Jnr. The leader of the group was George Arthur Crump, the wealthy owner of the Colonnades Hotel in Philadelphia.

Crump was an enthusiastic hunter, fisherman and golfer, good enough to be a finalist in the 1912 city championship. He had been one of the founders of the Philadelphia Country Club and had always carried the notion that one day he might create his own golf course. It appears that on one of these journeys across New Jersey, Crump spotted a stretch of ground near Clementon which looked suitable for his ambition and he and a colleague, Howard Perrin, who was to become the first president of the Pine Valley Golf Club, spent several days walking over the property. The ground was essentially virgin scrub, sandhills overgrown and heavily forested with pines, of course.

A syndicate of friends, whom he had convinced of the merits of the project, was formed and Crump sold his hotel in the city, bought 184 acres of the land, and set about building what many knowledgeable in these matters think of as the world's finest golf course, or certainly the world's most penal golf course. Famous now as the amateur golf architect who built only one course, Crump had a bungalow built on the property and moved in to spend the last six years of his life – and some $250,000 of his own money – in making his vision a reality. Many professional architects came to look at Crump's work and the land. Only Harry Colt, the British designer of Sunningdale, for instance, was invited to contribute. He made minor changes, one of the most notable being to extend the 5th hole, a par-3 over water from a mid-iron to a full wood shot of 210 yards; and the 15th was stretched to 520 yards to move it up from a par-4 to a par-5.

When George Crump died suddenly in January 1918, 14 holes had been completed. It took some time to raise the last capital needed. Hugh Wilson, yet another amateur designer who was responsible for Merion, Philadelphia, completed the work, helped by his brother Alan and with contributions from another British architect, CH Alison. The completed Pine Valley Course was opened in 1918, and since then has been acclaimed as a landmark in golf architecture and a place of pilgrimage for designers to this day.

CURTIS CUP

The Curtis Cup match between the women amateurs of the United States and Great Britain & Ireland had its origins in 1905 when Frances Griscom of Philadelphia got together a group to travel to Cromer in England, where the Ladies Amateur Championship was to be played. Eight women travelled, four of whom were or would be United States champions, including the remarkable Curtis sisters, Harriot and Margaret. Miss Griscom and Georgianna Bishop had been champions in 1900 and 1904 respectively.

Harriot Curtis won the 1906 US Championship and in defence of her title reached

the final in 1907, only to be beaten by sister Margaret, 7 and 6. The following year, with a Miss Evelyn Sears, Margaret won the women's doubles at the US Tennis Championships and is the only American to hold titles in both sports at the same time. She also won the American golf title again in 1911 and 1912.

Before that Cromer championship in 1905, an informal match between a British team and the visiting Americans was held, and although the home players won comfortably, the exhilaration of international competition and the goodwill expressed by all remained, particularly with the Curtis sisters. After the First World War, as happened with the Walker and Ryder Cups, interest in international golf was revived and over the years the Americans talked with the British Ladies Golf Union and the French Federation on the subject. Finance, as ever, was a problem. In 1927 the Curtis sisters gave the prospect a push by donating a cup for an international match, a rose bowl with an inscription, 'To stimulate friendly rivalry between the women golfers of many lands'.

In 1928 the USGA's Women's Committee had a sub-committee looking into the possibility of financing an international team, and when that committee disbanded, Glenna Collett went ahead and arranged for a group of amateurs to play in Britain in 1930, as they had done in 1905. The USGA undertook to finance a match and the cup donated by the Curtis girls was accepted as the trophy. So the series began in 1932, with the US travelling to meet the British and with the proviso that the French, and any other nation for that matter, might join in whenever they could. In the event, it has remained a

THE CURTIS CUP

Year	Venue	Winner	Margin
1932	Wentworth	Marion Hollins (US)*	5½ - 3½
1934	Chevy Chase	Glenna Collett Vare (US)	6½ - 2½
1936	Gleneagles	Glenna Collett Vare (US) tied Doris Chambers (GB)*	4½ - 4½
1938	Essex (Mass)	Frances Stebbins (US)*	5½ - 3½
1948	Birkdale	Glenna Collett Vare (US)	6½ - 2½
1950	Buffalo	Glenna Collett Vare (US)*	7½ - 1½
1952	Muirfield (Scotland)	Lady Katherine Cairns (GB)*	5 - 4
1954	Merion	Edith Flippin (US)*	6 - 3
1956	Prince's (Sandwich)	Zara Bolton (GB)*	5 - 4
1958	Brae Burn	Virginia Dennehy (US)* tied Daisy Ferguson (GB)*	4½ - 4½
1960	Lindrick	Mildred Prunaret (US)*	6½ - 2½
1962	Broadmoor	Polly Riley (US)*	8 - 1
1964	Royal Porthcawl	Helen Hawes (US)*	10½ - 7½
1966	Hot Springs	Dorothy Porter (US)*	13 - 5
1968	Royal County Down (Newcastle)	Evelyn Monsted (US)*	10½ - 7½
1970	Brae Burn	Carol Cudone (US)*	11½ - 6½
1972	Western Gailes	Jean Crawford (US)*	10 - 8
1974	San Francisco	Allison Choate (US)*	13 - 5
1976	Royal Lytham & St Annes	Barbara McIntire (US)*	11½ - 6½
1978	Apawamis	Helen Sigel Wilson (US)*	12 - 6
1980	St Pierre	Nancy Syms (US)*	13 - 5
1982	Denver	Betty Probasco (US)*	14½ - 3½
1984	Muirfield (Scotland)	Phyllis Preuss (US)*	9½ - 8½
1986	Prairie Dunes	Diane Bailey (GB)*	13 - 5
1988	Royal St George's (Sandwich)	Diane Bailey (GB)*	11 - 7
1990	Somerset Hills	Lesley Shannon (US)*	14 - 4
1992	Royal Liverpool	Liz Boardman (GB)	10 - 8

* non playing Captain

US/GB&I match.

The first Curtis Cup match was played over the East Course of the Wentworth Club, resulting in a win by America, and the pattern of results was to follow strangely those of the Walker and Ryder Cup series. In 1936 the match at Gleneagles was halved, but victory went relentlessly America's way until the fifties. Then, the home team won in 1952 at Muirfield, again in 1956 at Prince's, Sandwich, and the 1958 match at the Brae Burn Club in Massachusetts was halved.

After a desperately close match at Muirfield in 1984, when America won by one single point, the Great Britain & Ireland team had a stunning victory at Prairie Dunes in Kansas, their first on American soil. And they retained the Curtis Cup next time out, at Royal St George's, Sandwich. Indeed these last eight years were

somewhat freakish, for out of the blue came victories in the Walker Cup, Ryder Cup and Curtis Cup for the old countries, all at the same time.

But regardless of the dominance of the American players over six decades, the true meaning of the Curtis Cup has never been lost on the players. The matches have been played in an outstanding spirit of sportsmanship. When the 1982 match marked the 50th anniversary of the competition, the USGA invited all past players and officials to Denver for a Golden Jubilee celebration. More than 125 attended, including 47 past players and captains. And four members of the original 1932 teams were present – Dorothy Higbie, Maureen Orcutt and Glenna Collett Vare from the American side, and Enid Wilson representing Great Britain & Ireland.

CYPRESS POINT

The story of Cypress Point, the beautiful course at the southern tip of the Monterey peninsula 100 miles or so south of San Francisco, is linked with that of Marion Hollins and Dr Alister Mackenzie. Marion Hollins of the Westbrook Golf Club in New York was clearly a powerful lady among a group of fine American women golfers of the First World War years, and into the 1920s. She played a prominent part in the founding of the women-only 'Women's National' club at Glen Head, New York. In the US Women's Amateur Championship final of 1913, she lost to Gladys Ravenscroft, an English girl who had been British champion in 1912. But in 1921, Marion beat the famous Alexa Stirling of Atlanta in the final to prevent her making it four championships in a row.

When Marion first set eyes on Monterey and the area, she fell in love with it, and was soon resident there, selling real estate for the Del

CYPRESS POINT		
HOLE	YARDS	PAR
1	421	4
2	548	5
3	162	3
4	384	4
5	493	5
6	518	5
7	168	3
8	363	4
9	292	4
OUT	3,349	37
10	480	5
11	437	4
12	404	4
13	365	4
14	388	4
15	143	3
16	231	3
17	393	4
18	346	4
IN	3,187	35
TOTAL	6,536	72

Monte Company, owners of Pebble Beach and much besides. With Byington Ford, a former mayor of nearby Carmel, and one Roger Lapham, who was in shipping in San Francisco, she paid the Del Monte property company $150,000 for Cypress Point's 175 acres. Seth Raynor, a partner of Charles Blair Macdonald, was invited to design the new course. He had trained as asurveyor and worked on the site of Macdonald's famous National Links course in Long Island. He had also done some work at Pebble Beach, but he died unexpectedly of pneumonia in 1926. Dr Alister Mackenzie took over, and created a masterpiece.

Cypress Point opened in 1928. Unlike Pebble Beach, which can be described as a 'clifftop' course with six or seven holes flirting dramatically with the ocean, Cypress Point has but three. But what a trio they are. The course is built through a pine forest which sweeps down to the ocean past an area of heaving sand dunes, to the cliffs. The three clifftop holes which Mackenzie created are superb and dramatically beautiful, making a thrilling climax to the round. The middle hole, the famous 16th, is reckoned to be the most photographed hole in the golf. The green of this 231 yards par-3 is set out on a headland. For the brave, the direct drive is across an inlet of the Pacific Ocean usually seething with surf. The fairway skirts this bay to the left, giving the cautious player an open target, which leaves him with a pitch to the small green and the hope of a single putt. Thus the hole

Cypress Point on the Monterey peninsula, California, one of the world's most beautiful courses.

provides options, the hallmark of strategic design.

The 15th hole, at 143 yards, is simply a short pitch along the cliffs, over a slight inlet, but to a green protected by six bunkers, with typical egg-plant rough and a bank of

cypress trees behind. The third 'cliff' hole, the 17th, a par-4 of 393 yards, carries yet another challenge on the drive. The hole bends to the right around an ocean bay, and the trick for the golfer is just how much he dare cut

off. A drive to the left will find lots of space, but a longer, more demanding second shot. Mackenzie elsewhere marches his course through the forests and among the sand dunes. Cypress at best is only 6536 yards but perhaps its greatest single defence lies in the design of the greens. Mackenzie has made them raised, mounded, split level, tilted, and very difficult. The course has successive par-5s in the 5th and 6th holes, successive par-3s in the 15th and 16th. This matters little.

When Bing Crosby moved his famous Pro-Am from Los Angeles to Monterey, Cypress Point was one of the courses used. But in general, the club has never sought to stage tournaments or championships. It is a private club of 250 members drawn from all over the United States. They did think it right and proper, however, to stage the 1981 Walker Cup matches.

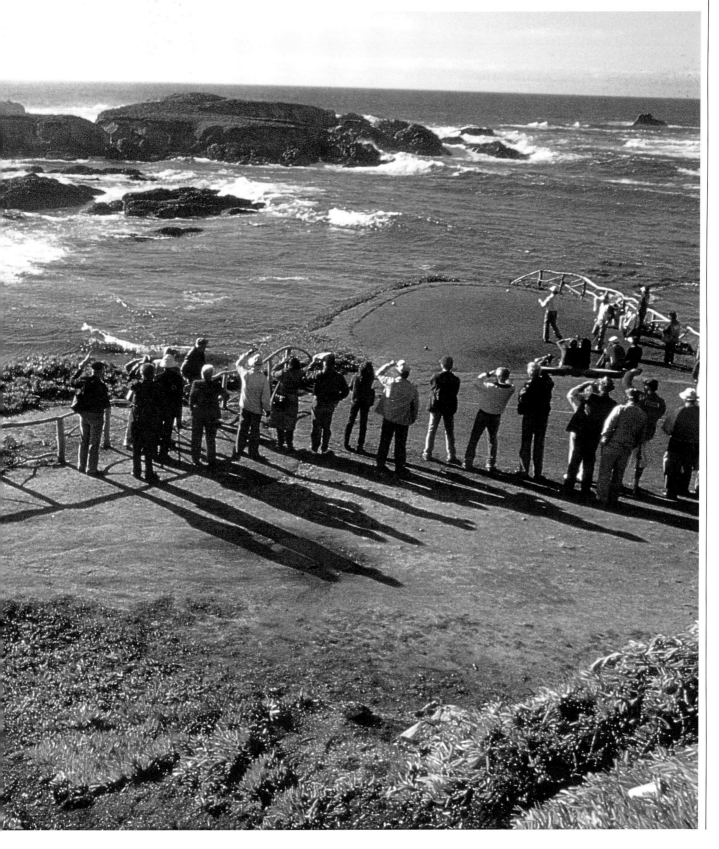

D

DARWIN, Bernard

Generally considered to be the first, and in the judgement of many the finest, of golf writers, Bernard Richard Meirion Darwin, grandson of Charles Darwin, was born in Kent in September 1876 and died in Sussex in 1961. From 1907 until he retired in 1953, he wrote on golf in *The Times*. His first article was something of a milestone in journalism and in the attitude of newspapers to the coverage of sports. Before Darwin, this had amounted to not much more than results and statistics at the bottom of the page. Indeed *The Times* called this 'Sporting Intelligence'. After Darwin, things were never the same. Bernardo, as his friends chose to call him, was an essayist of the first order. He was above all a man of his age, a product of his times which were essentially the high noon of the British Empire.

He was also, it could be said, a product of his class. He was educated at Eton College, always calculated to put a mark on a man, and at Cambridge University, where he qualified in law. He practised it until he joined *The Times* in 1907 and found his metier writing about golf. He was a talented player of the game, if not of the highest class, who first played for England against Scotland in 1902, and for a further 20 years thereafter. He was to reach the semi-finals of the Amateur

Championship in 1909 and 1921. In 1922 he played in the Walker Cup match at the Country Club, Brookline, Massachusetts, and in 1924 won the President's Putter. He was Captain of the Royal and Ancient Club in 1934-35 and thus had touched on the game at virtually every level. His Walker Cup experience was singular – attending the matches as 'Our Golf Correspondent', he was hauled into the team when the captain, Robert Harris, fell ill, and he won his singles match handily against Bill Fownes. It may well be, of course, that in Darwin's mind none of the above compared to the fact that he had played golf for Cambridge, indeed had captained the University team.

In the years of his prime, of course, the Amateur Championship was of first-rank importance. The Amateur Championship, the Open Championship, the England v Scotland match, Oxford v Cambridge, and as the years passed the Walker Cup matches, were of prime importance, indeed comprised the golf season. There was not then the torrent of events, week after week, that we know now.

Through all these long years, Darwin wrote a Saturday essay on one or other aspect of the game. They became widely known and praised. He wrote regularly on golf for *Country Life* and 'fourth leaders' for *The Times* on a wide range of topics. Few men knew more about the work of Charles Dickens than did Bernard Darwin. It was said that he could quote whole passages of *Pickwick Papers* verbatim. He was certainly widely read, a man of great learning. Yet he was quite obsessed with the game of golf and in action, this kind, charming man suffered an almost total personality change. He would talk to himself,

admonish himself, encourage himself in the third person, be quite abusive of playing partners beyond the point of rudeness, and had a tigerish temper. He became aware of this and expressed his personality change in one of his more notable essays 'Hydes and Jekylls'.

Darwin could be rude, partial, romantic, emotional, paranoid, impish, eccentric, partisan, the latter particularly with anything concerning Cambridge University, and one supposes him to be an arch-conservative. But essentially, he was a late Victorian English gentleman. In a broad sense, he could be snobbish. His various pieces and essays, not all about golf, were collected in a dozen books but sadly, some of his writing, and in particular his journalism, has not carried well across the years. Darwin's time was a simpler, slower, more relaxed time than the intense, complicated years of the last quarter of the 20th century. Yet his greatest achievement lay in sustaining his output of work, which was never less than erudite and seldom less than charming, over half a century.

DAVIES, Laura

Born	1963
Nationality	British
Turned Pro	1985

The outstanding British lady golfer of the moment, Laura Jane Davies, born 5 October 1963 in Coventry, has won both the British (1986) and American (1987) Open Championships. At 5' 10", blonde Laura is a big girl who strikes the ball powerfully and far, and even as a teenager it was clear that she could have an outstanding career in the game. She was

English Intermediate Champion in 1983 and played in the Junior European Team Championship and the Curtis Cup in 1984.

Laura turned professional in 1985 and has since played

The finish of another big drive by Laura Davies, the leading British lady professional who is having a splendid career both in Europe and the US. She is one of the few winners of both US and British Opens.

at Dalmahoy, Edinburgh, she inspired the Europe team to an unexpected victory by winning all three of her matches.

DEY, Joseph C Jnr.

Joe Dey was one of golf's most influential administrators. During 35 years with the United States Golf Association, first as executive secretary then as executive director, he came to personify the authority of the governing body of the game in America. Above all, he made himself an expert on the Rules of Golf, which he applied without favouritism and very firmly. In 1969 he left the USGA to join the Tournament Players' Division of the American PGA as commissioner, where he guided the tournament players to the independence they sought from the PGA and saw the separation achieved without rancour on either side.

Joe was born in Norfolk, Virginia on 17 November 1907, but spent much of his childhood in New Orleans, then Philadelphia, where he became a sports writer on the city's *Evening Bulletin*. In 1934, a friend of the USGA Executive Committee asked if he would be interested in the job of executive secretary of the organisation. Joe said yes, and by December was installed in the USGA's New York headquarters. He always considered that the single most important event

of his career was when the USGA and the R & A in 1951 agreed on a uniform code of rules, which has been sustained ever since and which is constantly under review by a joint committee. The only difference remaining between the two governing bodies in 1951 was the size of the golf ball. Joe Dey retired after five years, leaving the structure of the US Tour in place, and was thrilled to be elected captain of the R & A in 1975. He considered that his greatest honour. Only one other American, Francis Ouimet in 1951, had been so honoured.

DUNCAN, George

Born	1884
Nationality	British
Turned Pro	1902
Majors	Open Championship 1920

As much as anything else, George Duncan from the little village of Methlick in Aberdeenshire is recognised as the leader of a generation of golfers that emerged to challenge and succeed the 'Great Triumvirate' of Harry Vardon, James Braid and JH Taylor. Duncan was part of the large family of the village policeman, and he made the traditional start to the game for such a boy, by caddying. He learned to play by imitation, and his talents led him eventually to the post of assistant professional at the Hanger Hill club in North London. It was the start of a road that was to lead him to victory in the Open Championship of 1920, the first to be played after the First World War.

Duncan had made his mark before that. His first Open was Muirfield in 1906, when he finished eighth. Over the next seven years, he finished in the top ten half a

extensively and successfully on the US LPGA tournament circuit, where she has recorded a personal best round of 62. She won the US Open Championship before becoming a member of the US LPGA Tour, which

amended its constitution to give her an automatic membership. In the Solheim Cup match of 1990 between the women professionals of the United States and Europe, Laura won two points out of three and in the 1992 match

and although it is seldom acknowledged, a fine teacher of the game.

At the end of the Second World War, he was asked to 'restore' Royal Dornoch, and did a good deal of course design work, often associated with James Braid and Abe Mitchell. He designed the Mere Club in Cheshire in the 1930s, in association with Braid, and became the professional there. He also had a spell as professional to the Wentworth Club. George Duncan was above all a confident Scot whose play would be either quite brilliant or downright rubbish. All told, he emerges from the years as the type of fellow anyone would enjoy an hour with, in the 'snug'.

DUNN, Willie (Young Willie)

Born	1865
Nationality	British
Turned Pro	1883
Majors	US Open 1894

In the 19th century two remarkable families emerged from Musselburgh, one of golf's earliest hotbeds, and in each case, the patriarch was not a golfer. The 'founding father' of the Park family was a farmer, and of the Dunn family a plasterer, yet their descendants over two or three generations had profound effects on the development of golf as teachers, champions and course designers. The brothers Dunn, 'Old Willie' and James, his twin, had played in a famous money match for £400, a vast sum in 1849, against Allan Robertson and Old Tom Morris of St Andrews. The

dozen times, including fourth to Ted Ray in 1912. In the Match Play Championship of 1910, he beat Braid and Taylor before going out, and in 1913 had the audacity to beat James Braid in the final, on his ground, at Walton Heath.

When the First World War started, George was 30 years old. He was to serve in the Royal Flying Corps, and no doubt it cost him golden golfing years. But he took the Open at Deal in 1920 when his friend and contemporary Abe Mitchell suffered a third round collapse with an 83 and from leading after 36 holes finished fourth. Two years later, Duncan chased Walter Hagen all the way to the last hole of the championship at Royal St George's when the flamboyant American won

the first of his four titles. Playing a brilliant last round, the Scot came to the final hole needing a par four for a 68 and a tie. He missed the green with his second shot, was short with his chip, missed the putt and missed the tie, scoring 69. But rounds under 70 were quite unusual in those days.

Hagen was to become a regular adversary of Duncan. Like Tommy Armour, he could match Walter in confidence and in chatter. They each played in the preliminary matches between the professionals of their countries, at Gleneagles in 1921 and at Wentworth in 1926, where Duncan beat Hagen 6 and 5. They were both prominent Ryder Cup players, and opposing captains in 1929. With Abe Mitchell, Duncan toured the

US in 1921, 1922 and 1924, George finishing 8th in the US Open of 1921 and 6th in 1922.

George Duncan was an altogether dashing golfer, going about his work so briskly that he was dubbed 'The Flying Scotsman', and his one book was quite properly titled *Golf at the Gallop*. But there was nothing slapdash about it all – George was a lovely golfer with a grip and swing that looked entirely natural. He was a majestic fairway wood player, a part of the game that seldom challenges modern champions, and George Duncan of course was a hickory shaft player, a pre-steelshaft player. He had a very positive personality, was a lively talker, opinionated, disputatious in argument, full of theories,

Musselburgh men lost. Old Willie's sons, Tom and 'Young Willie', 16 years his junior, trained as professionals and greenkeepers, and Tom was professional at Wimbledon in 1870. Young Willie spent some time at Westward Ho!, then laid out the Chingford course in London. On design and construction, the brothers worked together and Tom was the most prolific architect of the day, albeit none too imaginative. His courses were cheap and simple, his forte simply to throw cross-bunkers all across the fairways to be carried. He worked extensively in England.

Young Willie was the first of the family to descend on the New World. He did it with a vengeance and in the highest of company, and became the first US Open Champion, unofficial, in 1894. He had been tempted to the US in the first place by WK Vanderbilt. The American millionaire spotted Dunn at Biarritz, where he was professional to the club which he and his brother had built, and invited him to find an appropriate piece of ground for a course on Long Island. The result was Shinnecock Hills, with 12 holes opened in 1891, built for the Vanderbilt syndicate. Willie built the course with a crew of 150 Shinnecock Indians, none of whom had ever heard of golf or golf courses, but it was to be considered the first great American 'links' course, still good enough in 1986 to stage the US Open Championship which Raymond Floyd won.

Willie Dunn remained there as professional for several years. As a designer, as in other things, he was innovative, one of the first to work with lateral rather than cross bunkers. He experimented with the notion of steel shafts and around the turn of the

century was attempting to insert slim steel rods into cane shafts. He also devised a paper tee peg, and was concerned with one of the first indoor golf schools.

His brother Tom's two sons, John Duncan and Seymour, were both in golf and both moved to the United States as young men, and they too, with Willie, were involved in many designs across the country. They both made frequent trips back to the UK. Willie eventually moved west and found his way to California, where he worked on several courses with his nephew John Duncan. He returned to England in 1940, and spent the rest of a long life there.

DYE, Paul 'Pete'

Small greens, railway sleepers holding up banks and marking the edge of greens, greens placed on islands in lakes, swales, pot bunkers, areas of rough sand along the side of the fairways, the impish use of water – little wonder that Pete Dye has been called the Picasso of modern golf architecture. He has certainly been the most controversial American designer in the later decades of the 20th century, returning to his courses much of the naturalness of the early Scottish links.

He was born in a small town in Ohio, and after university in Florida, worked in Indianapolis as a life insurance salesman. He became a fine amateur golfer, winning the Indiana State Amateur Championship in 1958, after being runner-up in 1954 and 1955. As chairman of the greens committee of the Country Club of Indiana and as a friend of William Diddel, his interest in design was aroused. Diddel, who lived to be 100, had won the state

championship five times, and designed dozens of simple, inexpensive courses throughout the Mid West. He told Dye that there was a course in Cincinnati to be done. He would not do it because they insisted on installing a watering system and he was against that. It was an example to Dye that traditionalists have to come to terms with the new.

Pete Dye was sufficiently successful in the insurance business to be able to retire in 1959, and he laid out his first course that year. He worked for a short time with golf architect William Newcomb, learning more of the business. In 1963, Dye and his wife Alice, a championship golfer, made an extensive trip to Scotland, played all the championship courses, and were fascinated by the basic and timeless elements which these courses displayed – the railway sleepers at Prestwick, the swales of St Andrews, the plateaued greens of Royal Dornoch, the revetted bunkers of Muirfield, the pampas grass fringes to the bunkers at Turnberry.

He put all of these into practice on his return. At a time when the fashion in the US courses – it still persists – was for vast acreage of rolling fairways, huge greens, extra long tees and spacious parkland developments costly to construct and maintain, Dye went for narrow, undulating fairways and small-tiered or fiercely sloping greens. None of this was entirely new to America, it had all been done in the early days of golf there. But because it contrasted to the fashion in American design largely set by Robert Trent Jones and developed over several decades, Dye was dubbed a radical.

In 1964, the Crooked Stick course in Indiana illustrated the shape of Dye things to come, but it was the Harbour

Town Golf Links on Hilton Head Island in South Carolina which made Dye's reputation. Jack Nicklaus, beginning an interest in design, collaborated with him there, in 1969. If one word could define a Pete Dye course, it might be 'rugged'. Nowhere was this more evident than at his Kiawah Island course, on the Atlantic seaboard 20 miles from Charleston, again in South Carolina. The island is ten miles long, a mile and a half across. On this property, Dye fashioned a links-type course with, on each hole, the ocean on one side and marsh on the other. 'The finest piece of ground I've ever had to work on,' he said. He raised the level of much of the course by six feet so that the sea was visible from more holes, and built up sandhills. He installed a drainage system which recycled 300,000 gallons of irrigation water each day. He built a dramatic golf course. Nothing like it had been built in the US for years.

It was not universally praised. Many felt that Pete Dye had gone 'over the top'. The greens had very severe movement in them. They were hard and quick and difficult to hold. There were long tracts of sand, Pine Valley style, running the entire lengths of some fairways. There were deep swales in front of greens perched high, leaving players still on the putting surface but unable to see the bottom of the flagstick. But Dye, the avant garde composer, probably had the last laugh when the course was rushed into use for the 1991 Ryder Cup match. It turned out to be the most thrilling of the entire series, going down to the last putt of the last match on the last day, when the US team beat the European team by one slender point.

E

EQUIPMENT

During the week of the Open Championship of 1992, various auction houses held sales of golf memorabilia. At the Phillips sale, an early gutta percha ball, dated at 1849, was bought for £17,500. At the Sotheby's sale, a rake iron dated from the early 17th century was bought for £84,000 on behalf of Jaime Ortiz-Patino, the wealthy owner of Valderrama Golf Club in Southern Spain. The explanation for these exceptional prices is simply that these artefacts are antiques and rare, and because there is a growing interest among golf enthusiasts for past times, in this ancient game.

The earliest clubs back in the 15th century no doubt had a plain strong shaft, a heavy head and a handle wrapped around with animal hide of one kind or another. But by the beginning of the 18th century, golf clubs had a more crafted, more sophisticated look, and were being designed for specific purposes. Clubheads were generally made from apple, pear or cherry wood, later dogwood or beech, and finally, before the man-made compounds of today, of persimmon, a particularly strong, cross-grained American wood. Shafts were of ash or hazel until finally, before steel shafts appeared towards the end of the 1920s, hickory was found to be perfect. These shafts would be sanded and rubbed down, then spliced to the heads, the joint glued, then wrapped in twine. In the 18th and 19th centuries, clubs became quite elegant, fashioned by skilled makers such as Simon Cossar of Leith (1766–1811), Hugh Philp (1782–1856) and Douglas McEwen (1809–1886), both of St Andrews. Their finished wooden club heads would be rubbed down with keel, a red ochre substance which gave them a brilliant, grainy finish.

A golfer then might carry anything between eight and a dozen clubs. The playclub, the driver of the day, was long in the shaft, long in the nose, straight-faced and from a flat swing would give a low, running flight to the ball. A selection of spoons for use from the fairway would vary in shaft length, and in loft. The wooden putter, a speciality of Philp, would be shorter in the shaft, straight-faced, and upright in lie. The head would be broader, shorter and by comparison, heavy – the putter could be used from 100 yards short of the green.

Early iron clubs were bludgeons with thick shafts and squared-off heads, clubs designed to rescue the golfer from dire trouble in heather, for example. They too became more sophisticated, the heads modified for specific tasks such as the 'track iron' for playing out of ruts and tracks in the ground, and the 'cleek' for long fairway shots from tight lies. By the 1850s, there was also

Peter Senior of Australia demonstrates his technique with the long 'broom-handle' putter.

a driving iron. All of these iron heads were hand-forged, with the shaft inserted in them.

The earliest golf balls were no doubt made of wood, but the first 'standardised' golf ball was the 'featherie', made from strips of cowhide sewn together and stuffed with feathers. The resultant ball was stitched up, hammered into shape, and painted.

The arrival of the Gutty ball had a definite impact on club design and manufacture. It was firmer and heavier than the feathery, and demanded more powerful clubs. The long-nosed elegant woods had to become shorter, broader, deeper in the heads and less destructive of the new ball than they had been with the feathery. The

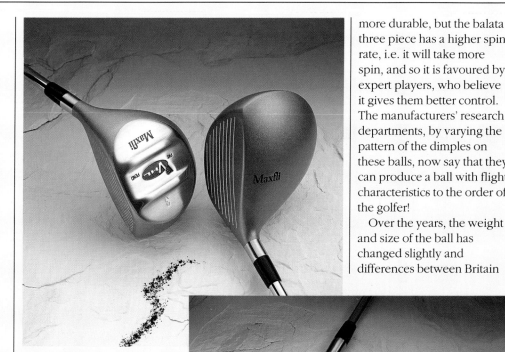

Metal 'woods' (above) and carbon shafted clubs are all part of the modern player's armoury.

woods that were left, driver, brassie and spoon, had inserts in a variety of materials put into the face, to resist this more demanding ball.

All the game's equipment advanced, as did playing techniques and indeed the condition of the courses. The first golf bags – clubs had previously been carried under the arm or by a caddie – appeared in the 1880s. And at the turn of the century, the gutty ball, after 50 years, succumbed to the Haskell ball, just as the feathery ball, a leather cover stuffed with feathers, a ball that had been used for centuries, had succumbed to the gutty.

Modern golf balls give the golfer ample choices. The one piece ball is what it says it is, made out of one sphere of Surlyn, a substance developed by the Du Pont company, with dimples moulded on it. It is inexpensive, very durable, but flies less far than any other ball because of its low compression and so is widely used at driving ranges. The two piece ball has a large resin core and a cover of Surlyn. It is almost impossible for the average golfer to cut or damage it, and since it gives good distance, it is the most popular ball. Three piece balls, either with Surlyn or balata cover, are the most sophisticated golf balls, constructed of a core, thin rubber windings and a cover. The core can be of almost any substance – ball bearings have been tried – but in the main it is of liquid or resin. Since Surlyn is a tougher material, that ball is more durable, but the balata three piece has a higher spin rate, i.e. it will take more spin, and so it is favoured by expert players, who believe it gives them better control. The manufacturers' research departments, by varying the pattern of the dimples on these balls, now say that they can produce a ball with flight characteristics to the order of the golfer!

Over the years, the weight and size of the ball has changed slightly and differences between Britain and the US in major competitions have been eliminated. The modern ball must have a diameter of not less than 1.68 in (43mm) and must weigh no more than 1.62 oz (46g). Ball manufacturers often make strong claims, supported by sophisticated research, as to the particular characteristics and performance of their products.

In the same way, technology has been applied to the development of golf clubs. By the later 1920s, steel shafts, which had been under experiment 20 years earlier in Britain, were in common use in the United States. They were approved by the R & A in 1929. The matched set quickly followed, with a limitation to 14 on the number of clubs which could be carried. As shaft material, steel has resisted to a large extent challenges from graphite, aluminium, titanium and boron-graphite blends. Clubhead material has seen greater change. As persimmon wood fell into short supply, so steel and more recently graphite has been used for clubheads, so much so that these paradoxically named 'metal woods' now command 70% of that market.

Modern golf balls: similar in appearance, different in manufacture from their predecessors.

EUROPE, Golf in

The beginnings of golf in Europe consisted essentially of resort golf. It may be ironic to consider that 100 years on, European golf's recent tremendous expansion has also been substantially in resort golf.

The first course on the Continent was at Pau in the French Pyrenees. It dates from 1856 and the Duke of Hamilton of the day was prominent in forming the club. Pau was and is a pleasant resort town, and it is

Bernard Gallacher with the Ryder Cup that was to be lost on Kiawah Island, South Carolina, in 1991. Undoubtedly the popularity of the tournament has grown since Europe have been truly competing, rather than merely taking part.

said that Scottish regiments involved in the Peninsular War were stationed there. At any rate, Pau probably has the longest continuous history of any club outside Scotland. The spread of the railways in France, as in Britain, brought the resorts of the Channel and Atlantic and Mediterranean coasts within comfortable reach of the great population centres. And as in England, golf enjoyed its first 'boom' in the 1880s as courses were opened at Dinard (1883), Biarritz (1888) and Dieppe in 1887. On the Riviera, Cannes-Mandelieu dates from 1891, Valescure from 1895. Names now world famous continued to appear – Baden Baden in 1901, Ostend and Montreux in 1902, Lucerne 1903, Vichy 1904, Monte Carlo 1910. The great cities of Europe had to have their courses, too. Royal Antwerp was one of the earliest in 1888, Compiegne near Paris, and Berlin-Wannsee, where Percy Allis was professional thirty years later, date from 1895. Madrid had its La Puerta de Hierro in 1904, Hamburg its Falkenstein in 1906 and Wien (Vienna) Golf Club came in 1901.

The oldest course in Italy, Roma, was founded in 1903 in a unique setting bordering the ancient Appian Way, beside the famous

The inclusion of European, rather than just British, golfers in the Ryder Cup teams facing the United States brought about greater interest, and greater success. One of the most popular players on the enlarged team in 1991 was Jose Maria Olazabal, seen here in a bit of bother still some way from the green.

Aquasanta spring and overlooked by a Roman viaduct. Italy perhaps epitomised golf in Europe in the first half of the 20th century. Then, it was in the main an aristocratic affair. Not for the Europeans the commonality of Scotland, where golf, the people's game, was cheap, available to all and, it could be said, under-capitalised. Thus the Scots enjoyed excellent, natural courses, but too often clubhouses and off-course facilities which were primitive. In Europe the golf club was a place for the aristocracy, the privileged people who rejoiced in elitism since they *were* an elite and their courses and clubhouses reflected that.

As in so many other elements of the sport, in the middle of the 20th century the coming of jet travel and television had had a prodigious effect on the development and the democratisation of the game in Europe.

The jet aircraft opened up holiday horizons, in particular winter holidays in the sun of Spain and Portugal and their islands, for the northern Europeans of Scandinavia, Germany, Holland and the UK. And television's coverage of major golf championships throughout the world brought the game to the attentions of millions. Thus airlines, resort hotels and resort property developers saw golf as an exceptional marketing tool, and were quick to use it. Guadalmina in 1959 was the first course on the Costa del Sol. In 1964,

the developers of Sotogrande, a quality property development near Gibraltar, felt able to ask the renowned American golf architect, Robert Trent Jones, to design his first course there, to entice the house purchasers. Since then, dozens of courses have been built in Spain, particularly along its Mediterranean coasts. The emergence of Spanish international champions Severiano Ballesteros and Jose-Maria Olazabal, both oddly enough from the north of Spain, has helped make that country a major player in all

of golf's great events. By 1966, Henry Cotton had built Penina, the first major course on the Algarve, and the first of many.

As at Wentworth in the past, property developers have increasingly seen the golf course as a core element in selling land and houses, and not only by the sea – Saint-Nom-la-Breteche, near Paris and St Mellion in Cornwall, with its Jack Nicklaus golf course, are examples.

In the past decade there has been a marked expansion of courses in Germany, France and

Sweden. By the start of the nineties, stimulated by the championship successes of Bernhard Langer, Germany had 260 golf clubs and more than 100,000 golfers; France had 300 courses and 150,000 players, but most remarkable of all was the development of the game in Sweden where, despite its long winters and short season, there were 200,000 golfers and 230 courses.

F

FALDO, Nicholas

Born 1957

Nationality British

Turned Pro 1976

Majors Open Championship 1987, 1990, 1992; US Masters 1989, 1990

When Nick Faldo hit a 3-iron safely onto the 18th green at Muirfield on 19 July 1992, he did much more than win the Open Championship for a third time. He scaled a golfing Everest.

Not since Henry Cotton, winner of the Open in 1934, 1937 and 1948, had Britain produced a three-times champion, or a golfer of such single-mindedness.

Indeed the solitary successes of Max Faulkner (1951), Tony Jacklin (1969) and Sandy Lyle (1985) bear testimony to the psychological pressures as much as the physical demands of winning the Championship. Faldo, however, has been uncompromising in his quest for stardom. His craving for universal respect caused him to sacrifice friendships for fame. His obsessive individualism drove him into a punishing work routine where application and discipline became bywords. But this blinkered approach

Golf's famous double act – Nick Faldo and his caddie, Fanny Sunesson, now almost as well-known as her boss.

drove him steadily towards fulfulling his principal ambition – that people would one day look back and say, 'I saw Nick Faldo play.'

In essence, Faldo achieved that with his triumph at Muirfield. In 1989 and 1990 he had emulated the great Jack Nicklaus by winning successive Masters titles. He was the number one player in the world by a comfortable margin, and his 27 victories on the PGA European Tour to that point included a record four PGA titles. Yet his third Open victory in no way lessened his desire. 'My goal has always been to be able to say to myself when I retire that I gave it 100 per cent,' he said. 'I don't want to sit back when I'm 45 and say that I could have done more. There is surely no harm in trying to get the best out of yourself.'

Faldo, born on 18 July 1957, was an only child so perhaps he was prepared for a lonely passage through life. He was an excellent all-round sportsman, swimming for his county and winning road races as a cyclist, and his yearning to become a champion was transparent. 'I never liked team sports because it so annoyed me that even if you did your bit you could still go home a loser.'

Golf, an examination of individual strength, skill and stability, provided the medium in which Faldo could escape from the pack. Even so, it happened by accident. He was at home during the Easter holidays of 1971 when, changing channels on television, he came across Jack Nicklaus playing in the Masters. He was transfixed. Golf became his obsession. After five years he came to the professional game with exemplary credentials, a staggering self-confidence and a forthright outlook. As an amateur, he was a Boy international in 1974 and a Youth

international in 1975. That year, he won in addition the Youths' Championship and the English Amateur Championship. Turning professional in 1976, he became Rookie of the Year in 1977 and that year won his first tournament and played in his first Ryder Cup match, winning singles against Tom Watson, the Open Champion of the day, and with Peter Oosterhuis winning his foursome to make it a clean sweep.

By the early eighties he had won three PGA championships in four years and was the golden boy of British golf. But Faldo wanted more than that. He wanted to win the Open. He wanted to win the Masters. He wanted to win the Grand Slam, to be the best golfer in the world. At the end of 1984, he decided to rebuild a swing which he reckoned was not good enough to serve him at those levels. He accepted the theories of a then little-known teacher, David Leadbetter. They agreed that while the swing was attractive to the untrained eye, it would never withstand the extraordinary pressures which develop over the final nine holes of a major championship.

What Leadbetter possesses is the eye to detect a fault, and the ability to rectify it. Faldo played his part by responding to all the instructions. But as more than three years passed without a win, he more than once questioned his own judgement in deciding to change. But success came at Muirfield in 1987 when, with 18 relentless pars in the final round, he won his first Open Championship.

He has since become regarded as the most complete player since Ben Hogan. His ambition to be recognised as the true champion has driven him to indiscretions at times, but he

Nick Faldo hoists the Johnnie Walker World Championship trophy which he won at Tryall, Jamaica in 1992

has succeeded in setting a standard which will have future generations remembering him.

He can be brittle, but then he is essentially a shy man, and no doubt has decided that his best method of defence is attack. His golf game, however, is admired by all. And he can be generous with his time and money. He gave his winnings from the 1989 World Match Play Championship – £100,000 – to charity. Nick Faldo is leaving his imprint on the game. He is the role model he yearned to become, because he has demonstrated to young people everywhere that dedication can bring fame and glory.

FAULKNER, Max

Born 1916

Nationality British

Turned Pro 1933

Majors Open Championship 1951

When Max Faulkner was walking towards the tee to begin the last round of the 1951 Open Championship at Portrush, a man asked him to autograph a ball 'for my son. He's 12.' Faulkner obliged. Then the man said, 'Put down 1951 Open Champion – you're bound to win.' Max said, 'Oh, hold on, hold on.' But all of a sudden he agreed with the man. He had scored 71, 70, 70 and was six strokes

ahead. He obliged again, wrote 1951 Open Champion, and went out and won it.

Max Faulkner was that kind of man. The more preposterous the ploy, the more likely Max was to be the ringleader. He affected striking ensembles of canary or purple or whatever, with plus-twos and matching stockings and shoes at a time when the rest of golf was inclined to be grey in the rationed Forties after the Second World War. Max had spent six years in the uniform of the RAF – never again would there be sombre clothing for him. Max was the personality kid.

A powerful top-of-the-backswing position – Max Faulkner, Open Champion of 1951.

His golf had something of the same bravado. From a rather wide stance, he went through the ball at lightning speed, hitting it far and true. He had immensely powerful hands and in particular was always very fit. That developed from his war service as a physical training instructor, and the strength of his hands came from long hours of filing, rasping, and sandpapering clubhead blocks and shafts as a young professional. His father Gus had been a professional, an assistant to James Braid at Walton Heath for a time, and when Max turned professional at 17 (he was born on 29 July 1916 at Bexhill in Sussex), he was put to clubmaking.

Faulkner was one of the earliest tournament players in the sense that he never did have a club professional's job. Before the war, he was an assistant to Henry Cotton at Royal Mid-Surrey, where Henry paid him precisely nothing. He earned £1 a round playing with a member, and ten shillings (50p) for an hour's lesson. This gave him a base, a place to practise and he played in every event he could reach. Max was a master of ball control and shotmaking. He could fly it high or low, fade or draw, stop it, let it run. The power in his hands made this possible.

He was apt to appear with a putter carved out of driftwood. It was never a problem for Max to talk to the gallery as he walked along. He'd call everyone guv'nor and they loved it. His caddie for many seasons, 'Mad Max', was even more eccentric, in his dress which anticipated Oxfam, and in his ways. They were made for each other.

Faulkner's time was the late 1940s and the 1950s. When he went to Portrush in 1951, he just knew he was going to win the

Championship. He had finished sixth to Bobby Locke in the two preceding years, 1949 and 1950. He went on to win three Spanish Opens, a Portuguese Open and a dozen other tournaments. He played on five Ryder Cup teams without, it should be said, too much distinction. The responsibility of being a team player did not seem to sit comfortably on Max's psyche.

FLOYD, Raymond

Born 1942

Nationality United States

Turned Pro 1961

Majors US PGA 1969, 1982; US Masters 1976; US Open 1986

Only the British Open Championship stands between Raymond Loran Floyd and a place in the small company of golf's 'Grand Slam' winners, and despite the fact that Floyd is qualified to play on the US Senior Tour (he was born on 4 September 1942), it would be a brave man to say that he cannot do it.

One of the greatest names in the game, Floyd first impressed American golf when he won the National Jaycees Junior Championship at Waterloo, Iowa in 1960 by five shots. His father, a professional golfer, encouraged him in all sports, and that same year, he had to make the choice between baseball, with a contract offered by the Cleveland Indians Club, and golf. He chose golf, and after only four months on the tour won the St Petersburgh Open to become the youngest winner, at 20 years and four months, for 35 years. And in 1986 when he won the US Open, at 43, he became the oldest winner

since Ted Ray in 1920 (Hale Irwin, winner in 1990 at 45, now holds that record).

Raymond in fact was to win tournaments in each of four decades, as only Sam Snead had done before him. In his twenties, he had something of a playboy image, at one time being part-owner of a 'topless' nightclub. After his marriage in 1973, Floyd settled down to become one of the most charismatic figures in the game and to put together an exemplary career. It was graced with bursts of staggeringly low scoring. When he won the Masters in 1976, he tied Jack Nicklaus's record of 271 with rounds 65, 66, 70, 70. His first 36-hole score and his 54-hole score remain records. He won by eight shots. In winning the US PGA Championship six years later, his opening rounds were 63, 69. He led from beginning to end.

His first PGA Championship win in 1969 had seen Floyd, paired with Gary Player, get through the two final rounds under armed guard, as militants demonstrated against Player simply for being a South African. Not surprisingly, Floyd's final round of 74 remains the highest last-round score by a winner.

Five years earlier in the US Open of 1964, Floyd had partnered Ken Venturi, the winner, over the final 36 holes in Washington's mid-summer 100 degree heat. Venturi almost died from dehydration, and Floyd was almost overcome by the man's bravery. It proved to be the last time that the third and fourth rounds of the US Open were played on the same day, and it had given the young Floyd a telling insight into the demands and stresses of major championship play.

Raymond Floyd has always had a very distinctive swing, which seems to start off flat,

then goes quickly up to a very upright top-of-the-backswing position. He has always been an outstanding driver of the ball and an excellent putter. When he won his US Open Championship at fabled Shinnecock Hills, coming from three shots behind Payne Stewart with six holes to play, his putting totals for the championship were 25-29-29-28. Surprisingly, in 1990 when he seemed to have a second Masters title secured, he dropped strokes over the closing holes, tied with Nick Faldo and lost on the second play-off hole.

His first Ryder Cup appearance was in 1969 and he played on seven teams. He captained the 1989 team which played in the tied match at The Belfry, then was selected by the American players as a 'wild card' for the thrilling 1991 match at Kiawah Island, which the US won by just one point, and in which Floyd was a tremendous corner stone for the US team. Now he shares another distinction with Sam Snead. Only they have won events on both the US PGA Tour and the Senior Tour in the same year.

FOWLER, Herbert

Herbert Fowler was a large, wealthy, rather intimidating Londoner who was an exceptional cricketer in his early years and did not begin to play golf until he was in his mid-thirties. Typically he became a scratch golfer, a member of the R & A and of

Herbert Fowler, designer of Walton Heath and many other fine courses, was also a fine player - here at Ranalagh, with Mrs Lionel Jackson.

the Honourable Company of Edinburgh Golfers, and a tough competitor who more than once made inroads in the Amateur Championship. He formed a strong desire to design golf courses, and in the event became one of a group of talented architects, JF Abercromby and Harry Colt among them, who followed Willie Park Jnr in

seeing the merits of the sand-based stretches of heathland around London for golf course construction.

Fowler got his chance when his in-laws, Sir Cosmo Bonsor and his son Malcolm, headed a group which bought a property at Tadworth in Surrey, and invited him to lay out a course on it. Walton Heath was a great, heather-strewn expanse 600 feet above sea level, with stirring views of London to the north. Fowler spent two years covering the entire heathland, often on horseback, establishing sites for greens and working backwards from them,

defining fairways and tees. His course opened in 1904 to immediate critical acclaim and it has remained one of the outstanding London courses ever since. In 1907, Fowler laid out a further nine holes, then in 1913 extended that to 18, giving Walton an Old and New Course. Experienced judges find it difficult to declare which is better.

Herbert Fowler remained associated with the club for the rest of his life, eventually becoming a director, but his success at Walton Heath set him off as a full-time course designer. Fowler's architecture created many

very fine courses, among them the Berkshire's Blue and Red, Cruden Bay in Scotland, with extensive changes made to Royal North Devon at Westward Ho! and Royal Lytham and St Annes. He spent most of the First World War in the United States and worked on several courses there, particularly in California. In the 1920s, back in England, he worked variously in association with other architects JF Abercromby and Arthur Croome, and in partnership with Tom Simpson. He died in London aged 85.

THE FOWNES, HC and WC jnr

The 'Fownes of Oakmont', father and son, have a particular place in the history of American golf. They are the creators of Oakmont, the course near Pittsburgh which

WC Fownes, son of Henry C, founder of the famous Oakmont course at Pittsburgh. Bill spent his life improving it.

is rated one of the most difficult in the United States. Henry Clay Fownes (1856-1935, pronounced as in 'phones') was a Pittsburgh man who worked in the local iron and steel industry, and in time formed the Carrie Furnace Company there, with his brother William C Fownes. In 1896, the company was bought by the huge Carnegie Steel Corporation, and Henry Fownes at 40 was wealthy. He immediately put aside executive labours, although taking directorships of various companies, including banks, and concentrated on his golf, becoming good enough to play more than once in the US Amateur Championship and get through a round or two.

He had been introduced to golf at the Pittsburgh Field Club, then moved to the Highland Country Club which had a nine hole course of no great distinction; by the turn of the century, Fownes and his friends began to think of creating a new club with a full 18 holes of golf.

His son William Clarke Fownes Jnr (1878-1950), who had been named after his uncle, followed his father into the steel business and into golf, and became an even better player, winning state amateur titles and the US Amateur Championship of 1910 at the Country Club, near Boston. 'WC' pulled together a group of top amateurs, the young Bobby Jones included, to travel to Britain in the first of many substantial American invasions. They beat a British team comfortably on their 1921 visit at Hoylake. Bill Fownes went on to captain the US team in the first Walker Cup match, at the National Links on Long Island a year later, and was President of the US Golf Association in 1926.

Henry Fownes, just as Charles Blair Macdonald was at the National Links and as George Crump was to be at Pine Valley, was the lead personality in purchasing the land, pulling a membership together, and designing the Oakmont course. For the rest of his life, he constantly changed and improved and tinkered with the course as did his son after him, until Oakmont became one of the most respected and difficult courses in America, generally considered to be the first of the great American parkland courses from which so many others took a lead.

FUJITA, Kinya

One of the outstanding and critical personalities in the growth of golf in Japan is Kinya Fujita. The son of a wealthy banking family, after university in Tokyo he became a graduate student at the University of Chicago and then Columbia University in New York. He worked in the family banking business for a spell but on returning to Japan he started an import-export company. Excelling in sports, he became a fine golfer and his interest in course design arose when he met CH Alison, who was laying out the Tokyo club's course in 1914. After the First World War, Fujita travelled to Britain, as Charles Blair Macdonald of the National Links and Hugh Wilson of the Merion Club had done, to study the British championship courses and discuss further with Alison golf design techniques.

Back in Japan, he organised the creation and launching of the Kasumigaseki Club, some 25 miles from Tokyo, and its first course, which came to be known as the East, opened in the 1920s. It was to become a milestone in the development of the game in Japan. In time, Kinya became the club's secretary, champion three times, captain and chairman of its board of directors. He built a second course at Kasumigaseki and invited Alison to inspect it. The Englishman made few changes but did put in some deeper bunkers.

Immediately before the Second World War, when Japan had a military government, golf was frowned upon to some extent as being too 'foreign', but Fujita designed many courses in the post-war boom. Kasumigaseki was his love, and as its patriarch, he died on the property at the age of 80, when planning even more refinements.

G

GALLACHER, Bernard

Born 1949

Nationality British

Turned Pro 1967

When Bernard Gallacher went down to the great Tom Watson, Open Champion, by 2 and 1 in the last match on the last day of the 1983 Ryder

The Ryder Cup, 1991, and Bernard Gallacher, the non-playing captain of the European team, relaxes with some putting practice.

Cup at the PGA National Club in Palm Beach Gardens, it turned the match in favour of the US by $14\frac{1}{2}$ to $13\frac{1}{2}$ points. And when Bernhard Langer's putt on the final green in the final match on the final day at the 1991 match in Kiawah Island failed to drop, captain Gallacher's team went down to the USA by the same slender margin, surrendering the Cup held since 1985. But for Bernard Gallacher, the Ryder Cup had not been all disappointment. In the first of his eight successive appearances, in 1969, he was the youngest player selected to that time. His record shows singles victories over Lee Trevino, Jack Nicklaus and Lanny Wadkins. And as vice-captain to Tony Jacklin, he contributed greatly to the European team winning and retaining the Ryder Cup in the 1980s.

Bernard was born in Bathgate in Scotland on 9 February 1949 and was

bound for golf from an early age. He won the Scottish Open Amateur Championship when just 18, and played in the Home Internationals against England, Ireland and Wales in that same year, 1967. He promptly turned professional and was Rookie of the Year in 1968 and leader of the Order of Merit in 1969!

Physically compact at 5' 9", he spread his tournament successes – 14 on the European Tour and seven others – over 15 years from 1969 to 1984 with the seventies being his most fruitful decade. Following his appointment as senior professional at the Wentworth Club, one of the most prestigious in Britain, his tournament appearances have been reduced. Bernard's golf was always characterised by a certain Scottish determination, which suggested that he preferred the old Scottish game of match play golf.

GLENEAGLES HOTEL

In June 1924, the *Morning Post* announced the formal opening of the Gleneagles Hotel by describing it as 'The Scottish Palace in the Glen – The Playground of the Gods'. And SL (Sam) McKinlay, in his time editor of the *Glasgow Evening Times*, Walker Cup player and golf essayist, and a man who knew his golf, wrote, 'The golfer who has not seen the Gleneagles Hotel courses is like the medieval traveller who had not seen Avignon in Papal times – he has seen nothing.'

Such Olympian endorsements may seem somewhat overdone, but the

The wide open expanses of the Gleneagles Kings course; large greens and large bunkers are features of the course.

fact is that there is nothing like Gleneagles Hotel and its courses anywhere in the UK, indeed anywhere in the world, in quality, in scale, in the particular and majestic beauty of the setting. Its creation arose from the example of the Turnberry Hotel early this century, built on the Ayrshire coast by the Glasgow and South Western Railway Company. Donald Mathieson, general manager

GLENEAGLES HOTEL KING'S COURSE			
HOLE	NAME	YARDS	PAR
1	Dun Whinny	362	4
2	East Neuk	406	4
3	Silver Tassie	375	4
4	Broomy Law	465	4
5	Het Girdle	167	3
6	Blink Bonnie	476	5
7	Kittle Kink	429	4
8	Whaup's Nest	170	3
9	Heich o' Fash	354	4
OUT		3,204	35
10	Canty Lye	450	4
11	Deil's Creel	233	3
12	Tappit Hen	399	4
13	Braid's Brawest	451	4
14	Denty Den	266	4
15	Howe o' Hope	460	4
16	Wee Bogle	135	3
17	Warslin' Lea	531	5
IN		3,299	35
MEDAL TOTAL		6,503	70

of the Caledonian Railway which served the Highlands, was not a man to be outdone, and he resolved to go one better. Having found the site, a wide moorland a dozen miles south of Perth, he commissioned James Braid to design the 18 holes King's Course and the (initially) nine holes Queen's course. Work began in 1908 and was finished by 1914, Braid having Major CK Hutchison as a collaborator. Hotel construction was interrupted by the First World War but by 1924 all was in place, with the Queen's course extended to 18 holes and an additional 'Wee Course', a par-3 of nine holes, added. Such was the demand for Gleneagles golf that in 1974, the Wee Course became the 18 holes Princes, and in 1980 a completely new Glendevon course was needed. These two latter courses were consumed by the grand design of the 'Monarch' course, the first Jack Nicklaus course in Scotland, which opened in 1993 and sweeps and rolls its wide fairways across the Gleneagles moorland.

From a plateau some 600 feet above sea level, these courses are surrounded by a magnificent landscape – the Ochil Hills to the east and south, the peaks of the Trossachs to the west, and the Grampians to the north. The turf is firm and crisp, an inland links. The immediate environment is one of heather and pine, bracken and fir and birch. A long ridge runs through the King's course and Braid directed his holes along the valleys, sometimes over the ridge, so that the golfer most of the time plays in splendid isolation, but has to tackle huge, sloping greens. All told, the Gleneagles courses are a great challenge to the average golfer, although they are never overbearing, never monstrous. And when

conditions are still and the courses soft, the modern tournament professionals love it – in winning the 1992 Bell's Scottish Open Championship, Peter O'Malley won with a final round of 62 and an aggregate of 262, 18 under par.

GOLF FOUNDATION, THE

The Golf Foundation was founded in 1952 to promote the development of junior golf in Britain. It had become clear that unless young people had a parent or parents interested in the game, it was very difficult for them to get started, both with the proper tuition and in achieving membership of a golf club. The Foundation's Coaching Scheme for Schools and Junior Groups subsidises instruction by qualified PGA professionals to students in schools, universities and other places of higher education, and to junior members of golf clubs who are in full time education.

Over the years, its activities have expanded to sustain young people's interest in the game from junior through to adult level. It awards vouchers for individual tuition; sponsors coaching sessions during school holidays; encourages the formation of schools golf associations; operates a film and visual aids service; organises national championships; and recently initiated a coaching awards scheme for school teachers who play golf, whereby qualified PGA professionals will prepare them to teach children.

The Foundation covers a vast range of teaching activities, and is funded wholly by donations from clubs, ordinary club golfers, governing bodies, and

equipment manufacturing companies.

GRAHAM, David

Born 1946

Nationality Australian

Turned Pro 1962

Majors US PGA 1979, US Open 1981

The first Australian to win the US Open Championship, David Graham probably started in life with fewer advantages than almost any other successful champion golfer, with the exception perhaps of Lee Trevino. Born in Windsor, near Sydney, his early family life was troubled and less than privileged, but from the time he found an old golf club in a garden shed, he was intrigued with the game. When he was 12, he found weekend work in the pro shop at nearby Wattle Park, a nine-hole course. At 14, when he told his father that he was leaving school for a full-time job in golf, they were estranged and remained that way.

He went to work for George Naismith, the professional at the Riversdale club near Melbourne. Young David played left-handed. Naismith made him a right-handed player. After four years, he was fired allegedly for being too informal with the members, and he took a job in Tasmania as a head pro. Three years later, knowing nothing about stock control or accountancy, he was in debt, and demoralised. Tom McKay, a local businessman,

David Graham of Australia overcame a hard beginning to succeed in the United States, with US Open and PGA titles.

helped him clean up the mess. Back in Sydney, he found a job in the PGF clubmaking factory and combined that with tournament play wherever he could. So determined was young Graham that by the age of 20, he had made himself a solid player, earning enough money to have thoughts of Europe and eventually the US Tour.

The year 1970 was important. It brought his first major breakthrough, with victories in the French Open and the Thailand Open. He also met Bucky Woy. Woy was managing the affairs of Lee Trevino at that time, and offered to sponsor David Graham on the US Tour. At the age of 23, the Australian thought that here at last was a gift from the gods who had been less than kind to him, and signed in double time. Next he learned that Trevino was suing Woy for mismanagement, and Woy was counter-suing. When Graham checked the small print in his own Woy contract, he discovered that Woy was taking 50% of the gross, with all expenses coming out of Graham's half. He had to buy his way out of the situation and in his own words, 'The whole thing cost me three years.'

It affected his net worth, but not his play. In 1971 he won the Japanese Open. In 1972 he took the Cleveland Open, his first US success, and in 1977, his own Open, the Australian, in Sydney.

In winning the 1979 US PGA Championship, he holed long putts for halves on the first two play-off holes against Ben Crenshaw, then another for a birdie on the third hole to win it. When he won the US Open at Merion in 1981, his performance was masterly, his last round 67 being one of the finest closing rounds the championship had ever known. And in 1985, he was

within one shot of tying Sandy Lyle in that year's Open Championship at Royal St George's.

David Graham's golf swing was orthodox and unremarkable. But his golf game mirrored his personality as plainly as could be – determination, defiance of all the odds, intense concentration, never say die. With two major championships and the Opens of France, Thailand, Japan, Australia, New Zealand and Mexico behind him, perhaps David Graham has finished one up on fate.

GREEN, Hubert

Born 1946

Nationality United States

Turned Pro 1970

Majors US Open 1977; US PGA 1985

Closing in now on the US Seniors Tour, Hubert Green, born on 28 December 1946 at Birmingham, Alabama, was one of the outstanding players of the 1970s and early eighties. He won the US Open at Southern Hills in Tulsa, and the US PGA Championship at Cherry Hills in Denver, so he seemed to enjoy the West. All told, Hubert won 19 American tour events despite having a style that was unorthodox, verging on the bizarre. At address, he crouched over the ball, knees bent, hands in front of the ball. His backswing was short and steep, his through swing fast. In putting, he crowded even more over the ball, his hands apart. He was invariably close to contention at major championships, and in the US Masters of 1978, when Gary Player had a final round of 64, Green missed a three foot putt on the last green to tie him.

H

HAGEN, Walter

Born 1892

Nationality United States

Turned Pro 1910

Majors Open Championship 1922, 1924, 1928, 1929; US Open 1914, 1919; US PGA 1921, 1924, 1925, 1926, 1927

'I never wanted to be a millionaire. I just wanted to live like one'.

That was the creed of Walter Hagen, repeated every time anyone talks of him, writes of him, even thinks of him. He certainly succeeded. Hagen was a larger than life character, the first great American professional who took the world as his oyster. He won 11 major championships, a total of 60 tournaments and played in 1500 exhibition matches which took him around the world in a career spanning 30 years, and which had him at one time listed among the top ten best-dressed men in America! When he first travelled to Britain to play in the Open Championship at Deal in 1920, he stepped off the boat train in London with four trunks full of clothes. He played golf with Lord Northcliffe on his private estate at North Foreland. Wherever Walter went, it was the best suite in the best hotel for him. When he travelled, it was first class all the way. He wore silk shirts, alpaca sweaters, camel polo coats, two-toned shoes – the last word. And he was apt to give his first prize cheque to his caddie.

Henry Cotton wrote of him: 'The Haig, as the press called him, loved to do himself well and I do not think I have met anyone who had the capactiy and the health to enjoy so much what most of us call "a good time".'

Walter Hagen was a magnificent showman. He realised early in his life that Americans love success, love a winner, love a show. Walter saw that professional golf was show business, and he was the one to put on the show. He dominated the professional game on both sides of the Atlantic throughout the 1920s, and much of his success was due not only to his undoubted ability and personality, but to his philosophy. Hagen believed that in the course of any round, even the finest golfer would play a few bad shots, and the thing to do was to dismiss them from the mind immediately. It was his temperament, his equanimity, which was Walter Hagen's greatest asset. Tommy Armour wrote of him: 'Making a million, or having the return of his laundry delayed by fiscal factors, nothing bothers Hagen. He could relax sitting on a hot stove.'

Walter Hagen pitches to Troon's 'Postage Stamp' hole, the 8th, in the Open Championship of 1923.

Yet no man can win 11 major championships without a core of steel. When he knocked in a ten foot putt on the last green at Hoylake to win the 1924 Open, a journalist said to him, 'You seemed to take that putt very casually – did you know you had it to win?'

'Sure I knew I had it to win', Walter said, 'but no man ever beat *me* in a play-off.'

His resolution was best illustrated by perhaps his greatest golfing achievement, his sequence in the US PGA Championships from 1921-1928, all at match play. In the 1921 final he beat Jim Barnes by 3 and 2. He did not enter in 1922. He lost to Gene Sarazen at the 38th hole in 1923. He then won the title for four successive years beating Jim Barnes again, two holes; Bill Melhorn, 6 and 4; Leo Diegel, 4 and 3; and Joe Turnesa, one hole. Over six championships, he lost only one match in 30, when Sarazen beat him in that 1923 final.

Walter Hagen, born in Rochester, New York, emerged from modest beginnings, the only son in a family of five children. The Hagens were of German descent, the father working in the local railroad repair yards. As a boy, Walter caddied at the nearby Country Club of Rochester, a haven of the city's privileged. By the age of 14, he had left school and was working in the pro shop there; and when the professional Andrew Christy moved on, Walter, aged 19, got the job. By then he had grown to six feet and become a fair golfer. When the 1913 Open came around, Walter, now 21, spent his savings on a tilt at the championship at the Country Club, near Boston, arriving at the course to tell his compatriots that he was here to help them 'take care of the English cracks' (Vardon and

Ray). He finished fourth behind Francis Ouimet, Harry Vardon and Ted Ray. The next year, impressed with his work at Boston, a club member paid all his expenses, and those of a friend, to the US Open at Midlothian, near Chicago. Despite stomach trouble on the eve of the first round, Hagen opened with a 68 and went on to win the championship. He repeated in 1919, beating Mike Brady in a play-off.

In technique, he was no fashion plate. From a very wide stance, his swing, in the words of one observer, 'started with a sway and finished with a lunge', with the left foot pointing to the hole. Walter saw no reason to dispute this. His was not the relentless, repetitive shot-making game that some later champions displayed. He did of course play most of his career with hickory shafts. If his long game was occasionally wayward, that gave him the opportunity to bring off, with considerable brio, recovery shots that he made look immensely difficult.

His short game was quite brilliant. His bunker recoveries with a thin-bladed niblick – no sand wedge in Walter's time – were exceptional and above all, Walter Hagen was a truly great putter. He practised much more than he admitted, happy with the myth he sustained of his roistering the night away and arriving the next day on the tee still dressed in a tuxedo and scoring 68. Walter Hagen was a giant of the game, a professional who liberated his fellow pros from the caste system which forced them, certainly in the UK, to 'change your shoes in the pro shop' and keep out of the clubhouse.

Gene Sarazen wrote in his *Thirty Years of Championship Golf,*

published in 1954:

'Golf had never had a showman like him. All the professionals who have a chance to go after the big money today should say a silent thanks to Walter Hagen each time they stretch a cheque between their fingers. It was Walter who made professional golf what it is.'

HANDICAPS

The popularity of golf owes much to the appliance of handicapping which, as an objective at least, allows players of widely ranging abilities to compete on the same course at the same time and on equal footing.

Such devices, which allow for a deduction at the end of a round of up to 28 strokes for men and 36 for women, never have been and never will be perfect. There will always be scope for argument that some players' handicaps are too high while others, in the top categories in which figures are regarded as passports into open scratch competitions, are too low.

The search for true equity continues relentlessly and systems are constantly evolving. There are two in use in Great Britain, the men's which is administered by the Council of National Golf Unions (CONGU) and the women's by the Ladies' Golf Union (LGU).

The men's system takes into account playing conditions in every round while the women's system does not. In the spirit of handicapping, it might be simpler to have just one system so that men and women can compete together in medal competitions.

This is impossible as things stand because the two methods are incompatible, though the CONGU system is

in wide use throughout Europe for women as well as men. Tradition is probably the biggest hurdle on the road to union, but that is another matter.

Under the CONGU system, a player obtains a handicap by submitting three cards to his club's handicap committee. Scores of more than two over par at any hole are adjusted to two over par and the handicap allotted, subject to discretion, is the difference between the standard scratch score (SSS) of the course and the score for the best of the three rounds.

In a medal or qualifying competition, a player's handicap is reduced if his net score (gross score less handicap) is lower than the competition scratch score (CSS). The CSS was introduced in 1988 and allows for a reduction of the SSS by one and a rise of up to three. This is determined by the scoring of all entrants in the competition with the best players having the most influence.

There are four handicap bands: up to 5, 6 to 12, 13 to 20, and 21 to 28. For every stroke under the SCC, handicaps are reduced according to band by 0.1, 0.2, 0.3 and 0.4 respectively. The use of decimal points means that players have both exact handicaps and playing handicaps which are rounded up or down. For example, an exact handicap of 12.5 gives a playing handicap of 13, while 12.4 goes down to 12.

Net scores which are the same as the CSS, or just over, are in what is termed the buffer zone and handicaps remain unaltered. Until 1993 this zone was one or two shots more than the CSS for all bands, but has now been changed to one, two, three and four over in respect to the above bands.

Net scores higher than the buffer zone will cause handicaps to rise by 0.1 in all bands, whether they are one over or 20 over, unless the CSS is calculated as a non-counter for handicap increases. The general practice is for increases to be made at the end of a month while reductions take effect immediately.

Beyond this arithmetic, handicap committees have the power, under Clause 19 of CONGU's 1983 booklet 'The Standard Scratch Score and Handicapping Scheme', to reduce a player's handicap further if they have reason to think it is too high, though permission of the area authority or home union must be given if this takes it below 5.5. The committee also has the power to increase handicaps, though this is rarely done.

By 1996 it is expected that British courses will have been re-rated according to difficulty as well as length in an operation in which the Scottish Golf Union is leading the way, and a slope value given which will mean that a player's club handicap can go up or down on an away course depending on its slope value in relation to that of the player's home course.

To obtain a handicap under the LGU system, a player must submit at least four cards. Handicaps are awarded in five categories : E (36 to 30); D (29 to 19); C (18 to 10); B (9 to 4); A (3 and under).

In category E the handicap is the difference between the player's best score and the SSS of the course; in category D the handicap is the average of the two best differentials; in category C it is the average of the four best differentials; in category B it is the average of the six best differentials in competition; in category A it is the average of the 10 best differentials of

which at least four must have been scored away from home on a minimum of two different courses.

Handicaps, unlike in the men's system, can be lapsed if the minimum number of cards are not submitted in any year. The minimum is four for categories E, D and C, six for B and 10 for A.

Stableford and bogey competitions also affect both men's and women's handicaps, and the latter system was amended in 1993 so that incomplete scores count. In other words, players can now pick up at the point at which no Stableford points can be scored at any hole, or if a hole is lost in a bogey competition, which, incidentally, has been renamed a par competition because the meaning of the word has changed over the years.

Although women play off forward tees, their SSS on any course is usually higher than men's. When men and women do play together in non-medal competitions such as in pro-am teams, or men versus women matches, a common practice is to allow women players courtesy strokes based on the difference between the standard scratch scores of the course.

The best scores produced by the two systems are monitored during the summer months in the Glasgow-based newspaper *The Herald*, from club returns throughout Scotland, representing around 12,000 rounds of medal golf each week. Often the best score is ten or more lower than the CSS with an equal likelihood of the winner being either a man or woman.

These figures suggest that the system to outlaw what are known colloquially as 'bandits' has yet to be invented, and in all probability never will be.

THE HAWTREES

The Hawtree family of three generations, father, son and grandson, represents the longest continuous practice in golf course architecture, and one which has made a very distinctive contribution to the discipline, from 1912 to the present day.

Frederick G Hawtree (1883–1955), born in Ealing, London, started in life as a greenkeeper and began designing courses a couple of years before the onset of the First World War, in which he served with the British Army. After the war, he took up his practice again and in 1922 formed 'Hawtree and Taylor', the Taylor being 'J H', one of British golf's great triumvirate of Vardon, Braid and Taylor. George Gunn, of Taylor's clubmaking company, was a shareholder. Taylor's function was essentially one of promotion and public relations, meeting clients and the like, while Hawtree, as managing director, got the work done. All in all, the company built some 50 courses and remodelled just as many, including Royal Birkdale. Fred Hawtree ventured abroad too, with courses in Lisbon, Monte Carlo, Italy, Sweden and Ireland to his credit.

His son 'Fred W' was born in 1916, and joined his father as 'Hawtree and Son' in 1938 after graduation from Oxford, but was soon caught up in the Second World War. He served in the Royal Artillery in the Far East, survived being a prisoner of the Japanese, and came back to become one of the most prolific golf architects that the game has known. Holding fast to his creed that 'the golf course should be suited to the site, not the site to some preconceived notion of what a course should be', he was involved in more than 100 courses all over England

and in Belgium, El Salvador, France, Iran, Ireland, Morocco, Holland, Northern Ireland, Portugal, Scotland, South Africa, Spain, Wales, and Zimbabwe. As his father had been involved in the foundation of the British Golf Greenkeepers' Association, so Fred was a founder member of the British Association of Golf Course Architects.

His son Martin, the third Hawtree, prepared for the family calling by taking an arts degree at the University of East Anglia, and a masters in Civic Design at the University of Liverpool. He spent three years researching the history of town planning at Liverpool before joining the firm in 1973, and becoming actively involved.

HILTON, Harold

Born 1869
Nationality British
Majors Open Championship 1892, 1897

The Royal Liverpool Golf Club is credited with having launched the Amateur Championship, first played in 1885 over its Hoylake course, and was clearly then, as it is still, prominent in the evolution and administration of the game. And Hoylake was also to be the proving ground for two quite exceptional players who could be said to have dominated the amateur game from the late 1880s right up to the outbreak of the First World War.

John Ball won eight Amateur Championships and was runner-up once. Harold Hilton won four and was three times a beaten finalist. In addition, both were Open Champions, Ball at Prestwick in 1890, Hilton at Muirfield in 1892 and again at Hoylake in 1897.

Harold Horsfall Hilton was

born at West Kirby, a few miles from Hoylake, on 12 January 1869. By persistent practice and experiment, he became a quite outstanding player. Even if he lunged somewhat through the ball, his long game with fairway woods and his punched-out iron shots were notable features of his play. He won two Open Championships before he recorded his first Amateur Championship win in 1900 at Sandwich. His first Open win, at Muirfield in 1892, was the first played over 72 holes. He became the first, indeed to date the only, British player to win the Amateur Championships of Great Britain and the United States of America in the same year, 1911. His American victory, over Fred Herreshoff, was dramatic in the extreme. Six up with 15 to play, he was taken to the 37th hole of the Apawamis course in New York, where his spoon shot rebounded from a bank on the right of the green down to the putting surface, guaranteeing him a par four, good enough to beat an unnerved Herreshoff.

Hilton was invariably seen with a cigarette in his mouth and was said to consume 50 in the course of a day's golf, a record later challenged by Bobby Jones. They also shared the pleasures of a restorative 'cup' in the evenings after play. If Harold Hilton was on the small side, only 5' 7" tall, he was powerfully built and his shot-making was rich in subtleties. He could fade and draw the ball, and hit it straight, with all the clubs (with hickory

Harold Hilton, the most scientific of golfers. He is the only British player to have held both US and Amateur Championship titles at the same time (in 1911).

shafts of course) in a career that embraced both the gutty and the new wound Haskell ball.

He wrote extensively on the game and was the first editor of *Golf Monthly* magazine, a post which he held right up to the First World War. As such, Hilton was loquacious – in the early 1920s he was moved to write, 'There can be no doubt that the American player of the game has somewhat rudely annexed that presumptive hereditary right of ours…American players of the present day are better golfers than their British cousins.'

HISTORY OF GOLF

Six hundred years ago, an edict from Edward III 'to the King's sheriffs' proscribed football, handball, cockfighting and other leisurely pursuits, including 'cambuca'. The last of these was played with a ball and curved stick, and is thought to have derived from the Roman 'paganica', played with a bent stick and a ball of leather stuffed with feathers. This edict of 1363 is probably the first documentary evidence that an activity of at least some kinship with golf existed. Another decree, in the 14th Parliament of James II of Scotland, banned golf more specifically in 1457. These pastimes, it seems, were keeping the lieges from their archery practice.

The evolution of the game as we know it at the end of the 20th century has been reasonably well documented, but its origins remain fabled, almost mystic. What is certain is that the simple act of hitting a stone with a stick seems instinctive to man as much as throwing a stone or running and jumping. Nevertheless the Scots, if not entirely the 'inventors' of golf, have created the structures of the game, developing the idea of the golf course, designing and making golf clubs and balls, establishing rules, structuring the early societies which became famous and influential golf clubs, and excelling at playing and teaching the game.

The early game there was played crudely on public or common ground, mainly on those stretches along the shore between the beach and the beginning of arable land – the 'machair' of bent grass, whins and heather, used otherwise for drying clothes, mending fishing nets or general recreation. And the east coast of Scotland was garlanded with stretches of machair – at Dornoch, Aberdeen, Montrose, St Andrews, Leith, and Musselburgh. Prohibitions on the playing of golf relaxed with the passage of time. The interest of the Stuart kings was to be important. When James VI of Scotland went to the court at Greenwich to become James I of a United Kingdom in 1603, he was said to have had golf clubs with him. He certainly played over the adjoining Black Heath, where the Blackheath club was supposedly formed in 1608.

As the 17th century wore on, the game became more popular. It had, incidentally, spread to the American colonies this early, and there are records of golf clubs in Pennsylvania, West Virginia, Georgia and the Carolinas importing clubs from Scotland. Groups who played regularly began to define their 'courses' more clearly. The links at Leith had five holes, those at North Berwick seven, St Andrews had 12 and Montrose 25! In the same way, the rules under which the game was played were entirely local, varying from place to place. Yet at the end of the 17th century, the game remained casual.

There were no golf clubs as we know them, no clubhouses – these were likely to be adjoining taverns. There was no medal play, no handicapping system, no professionals, and the game was one of matches, with rules agreed in advance between the two or four players concerned. The early clubs were in fact societies, for wining and dining as much as golf. In 1744, the Company of Gentlemen Golfers was formed at Leith, forerunner to the Honourable Company of Edinburgh Golfers, now housed handsomely at Muirfield. The Edinburgh men played over Leith Links, then the city's principal open space. They were confident enough to petition the Edinburgh City council for a trophy for competition, and the city fathers obliged. It was first played for in April 1745, and has been ever since. It was clear that a proper organisation was needed so the Leith golfers became the first golf club as such. Their claim has been contested by Royal Burgess, which was formed in 1735 but has no documentary evidence to sustain that claim, and by Royal Blackheath, whose claim is tenuous in the extreme. In any event, the Edinburgh golfers, in addition to organising themselves and their play more definitively than any others, also made a massive contribution to the advancement of the game by laying down the first comprehensive Rules of Golf, the famous '13 Articles', most of which are still relevant to this day.

Leith Links, used by all and sundry and particularly the military for training, became progressively more crowded, and many of the golfers had taken to crossing the Firth of Forth to St Andrews for more comfortable play on what was a better if still unpolished piece of ground. Thus ten years after the Edinburgh men had formed their club, some 'Twenty-two noblemen and gentlemen' formed 'The Society of St Andrews Golfers', later to become the Royal and Ancient Golf Club of St Andrews. With a few minor changes, they adopted the 13 Articles from Edinburgh. The St Andrews Society prospered. They had 12 holes of golf, playing out and back a round of 22 holes, sharing the 'out greens' with the 'in greens', but in 1764 they combined four of these holes quite arbitrarily, giving a round of 18. The example of St Andrews spread around the world. More and more clubs adopted their rules, as the Edinburgh men went into decline. Indeed early in the next century, the Edinburgh golfers shut up shop and suspended their existence for a time before recovering in 1836, when they moved to Musselburgh. St Andrews became 'Royal' in 1834 when King William IV granted the title and became its patron.

From 1825, railways became a fact of life in Britain and transformed the economy as well as the landscape. They hastened the formation of clubs within reach of the growing cities – Liverpool, Manchester, Glasgow, Belfast, and Dublin. In 1851 the Prestwick club was formed and in 1860 it instituted what was to become the greatest single competition in golf – the Open Championship. In 1869 came Royal Liverpool at Hoylake, which in 1885 started the Amateur Championship amid an enormous expansion in the number of clubs. Significantly, ten years later

William St Clair of Roslin, captain of the Company of Gentlemen Golfers in 1761, 1766, 1770 and 1771. The portrait is by Sir George Chalmers. The Gentlemen Golfers later became the Honourable Company of Edinburgh Golfers.

One of golf's classic paintings, prints of which hang in golf clubs throughout the world. The elegant figure is William Innes, captain of Blackheath circa 1790.

the first club in Europe, although golf clubs and balls had been exported from Leith to Bordeaux as early as 1767. The Army, the Empire and trade took golf to the far places of the world.

The year of 1848 was critical in the history of the game. It was the year of the 'gutty', the ball which transformed the playing and the cost of golf and made it possible for thousands of people to take up the game. It took the aristocracy out of the game and made it available to the common man. Before the arrival of the gutty ball made from gutta percha, the gum of a Malaysian tree, the golf ball had been made of leather covers filled with feathers and stitched tightly together – the 'feathery'. These were hand made, and expensive. A good day's output by a skilled worker might be no more than three balls. The gutty ball by contrast could be made in a mould, virtually mass-produced, and was inexpensive. It flew further, lasted longer and was unaffected by rain. It brought changes in the golf swing, changes in the design of clubs and all told, the gutty ball may well have been the greatest single revolution in the story of golf.

The gutty lasted for 50 years until another of golf's revolutions came in the shape of the Haskell ball, developed by Coburn Haskell in Ohio. It had a rubber core wound around with thin strips of rubber and

the United States Golf Association was formed and the US Open and US Amateur inaugurated. By 1830, golf was established in Calcutta – Royal Calcutta is the oldest golf club outside the British Isles. In Bombay and New South Wales there were golf clubs by 1842. In 1856 at Pau in France, close to the Spanish border, came

encased in a rubber cover, and was much more resilient than the gutty. It was easier to hit off the ground, easier to drive off a tee, flew much further and was much kinder to the golfer. Within the first few years of the 20th century, it was in universal use.

Just as the number of golf clubs and golfers grew with these new travel and implement developments, so the administration of the game expanded. In the 1880s the Irish and Welsh Golf Unions were formed. In 1897, the clubs acknowledged the R & A as the rulemaker and its Rules of Golf Committee was formed. After the First World War, in 1919, the clubs again proposed that the R & A should take over the management of the Amateur Championship and the Open Championship, which had formerly been done in each case by the host club. The Rules and Championship Committees were to include outside representatives. In 1920 the Scottish Golf Union was formed, in 1924 the English Union and in that year all four unions recognised the R & A as the 'ruling body' of golf. A joint advisory body was set up to supervise the systems of standard scratch scores and handicapping, and other common interests such as greenkeeping, research and fixture co-ordination.

The R & A became the governing body of golf in the British Isles and the Commonwealth countries. In Europe and elsewhere, the other countries formed golf federations to govern their own affairs, but looked on the R & A as their law giver and mentor. Not so the Americans, who preferred to be independent. The R & A had standardised the ball size and weight at 1.62

inches and 1.62 ounces in 1921. The Americans decided that their particular playing conditions demanded a larger and lighter ball that would be easier to hit, so they opted for a 1.68 inch ball. They legalised the use of steel shafts in the twenties, long before St Andrews did, and all told, coming up to the Second World War, relations between the two bodies had deteriorated. In 1951, a joint meeting of the Rules Committees took place; a joint body was established and has met regularly and successfully since. In the 1960s, the British tournament professionals elected to play the 1.68 inch ball exclusively; the R & A followed by allowing its use in the Open Championship, and the smaller 1.62 inch ball is now confined to history.

Since the Second World War, the game has retained its essential character, but dramatic advances have been made in technology and materials in the manufacture of clubs and balls, and in greenkeeping and the preparation and maintenance of courses. In the United States and Japan in particular, the game has expanded furiously. In the 1980s, it seemed to be Europe's turn, with a great increase in the number of courses in all Western countries, and with the southern coasts of Spain and Portugal in particular experiencing an explosion of courses and golf-related developments.

Much of the history of the game is caught up with champions and championships, from the early St Andrews men in the mid-19th century, Allan Robertson, Old Tom Morris and Young Tom, on up through Vardon, Braid and

Taylor to Hagen, Jones and Cotton, then Snead, Hogan, Nelson and the vast numbers of hugely talented tournament professionals of more recent years in Palmer, Player, Nicklaus, Watson, Trevino, Ballesteros and Faldo. The pattern was that the Scots were the original teachers and winners, the English ruled up to the First World War, then for fifty or more years the Americans dominated world golf, amateur and professional, men and women. More recently, the European players and the Australians have found places in the sun. The huge advances in telecommunications and the myriad of television channels have brought champions and championships from around the world within the experience of everyone and made the televised game a powerful medium for product exposure and corporate involvement.

As the end of the 20th century approached, as far ahead as could be seen golf's problems might be a shortage of land to satisfy the demand for courses, and costs. Even in Scotland, where golf has been historically cheap to the extent of being under-capitalised, the cost to the average player was increasing considerably.

Golf Illustrated, *the oldest golf magazine, reflected the growing interest in the game, with a king (Edward VIII) on the cover.*

No. 1766.—VOL. CXXIV. SATURDAY, FEBRUARY 1st, 1936

HIS MOST GRACIOUS MAJESTY KING EDWARD VIII

HOGAN, Ben

Born 1912

Nationality United States

Turned Pro 1931

Majors Open Championship 1953; US Open 1948, 1950, 1951, 1953; US Masters 1951, 1953; US PGA 1946, 1948

William Benjamin Hogan, born in Dublin, Texas on 13 August 1912, is one of the three or four greatest golfers in the history of the game; ranking certainly with such as Harry Vardon, Bobby Jones and Jack Nicklaus by general acclaim, and in the judgement of several of the game's most perceptive critics, the greatest golfer of all time.

His entire life had the stuff of legend, and Ben Hogan duly became an American hero. He was born, if not into poverty, then into a world without privilege. His father, a motor mechanic plagued with ill health and money worries, committed suicide when the boy was nine years old, trauma enough for any child. Young Ben sold newspapers, hustled, and caddied at the nearby Glen Garden Club, as did his contemporary Byron Nelson. He turned professional at 19, took nine years, many of them years of extreme hardship, before he won his first tournament, and just as he had established himself as a major figure in American tournament golf, surrendered two and a half years of his life to the US Army Air Corps in the Second World War.

Returning to golf in 1946, he played 32 events, won 13 and was second seven times. Hogan was back with a vengeance to challenge

The incomparable Ben Hogan in his seventies - still hitting practice shots.

Nelson, Snead and the others. Much of 1947 was taken up with a swing change. Hogan, at a mere 135 pounds, had to lash through the ball to keep up with the big fellows and make the prescribed carries from the tees. His swing, flat and furiously fast, often saw him finish with his back to the hole, and he was very prone to hooking the ball. He

worked on cutting down his backswing, finding a more upright plane, and fading the ball slightly for more accuracy. In 1948 came the first of his four US Open wins, and he was leading money winner again for the fifth time.

Then in February 1949, he was terribly injured in a car crash in West Texas. With a double fracture of the pelvic

bone, a broken ankle, rib and collar bone, he was two months in hospital during which time he had surgery on his leg veins to eradicate blood clotting. He weighed 95 pounds when he was discharged from hospital. Yet from the spring of 1949 until the end of that year, Hogan, his legs encased in supportive bandages from hips to ankles, forced himself

back to fitness. First there were the few faltering steps around the living room, then more around the garden. By the autumn, he was visiting the Colonial Club, chipping a little, putting a little, playing a few holes, and finally 18 holes. In September the medical people allowed him to travel to Ganton as US Ryder Cup captain – needless to say, the US won.

His accident had touched the hearts of the American public, not just the golf fans. The stages of his recovery were widely reported, but when he sent in an entry for the Los Angeles Open in January 1950, this was a national news story with a vengeance. Considering his condition – he walked with a perceptible limp and had to soak his legs in a hot bath for a while after every exertion – his scoring of the Riviera course in 73-69-69-69 for 280 was all but miraculous. It tied him with Sam Snead of all people, to whom he lost a delayed play-off. But from then on, Ben Hogan, like it or not, was a national treasure.

In the summer of that same year, he won the US Open, still scheduling 36 holes on the last day, and he needed to win an 18 holes play-off against George Fazio and Lloyd Mangrum to do it. Hogan was on the front page of every newspaper in the US and on many others around the world. A film was made of his life, with the actor Glen Ford playing Hogan.

In 1951, the US Open fell to him again for a third time. Now he was concerned only with the majors. Between the US Open of 1952 (he finished third to Julius Boros) and the Masters of 1953, he played no competitive golf. But 1953 was to be his annus mirabilis, entirely comparable to the Bobby Jones Grand Slam of 1930. He entered six events and won five. He won the US Masters by five shots, beating the course record by five

shots. He won the US Open by six, with Sam Snead in second place. And finally, he won the Open Championship at Carnoustie.

His performance there revealed Hogan at his peak, and at the peak of an incomparable year. Hogan at Carnoustie was a sustained public demonstration of the golfer in complete control of himself, on and off the course, with the small ball and on a course and in weather quite foreign to him. His preparation was meticulous. He arrived ten days in advance. He played two or three balls on every hole during his solitary practice rounds, hitting shots to both sides of the fairways, both sides of the green. In the evenings, he walked the course backwards in the long summer light. In the championship, he scored 73-71-70-68 for 282 and victory by four shots. At the time, Bernard Darwin wrote, 'One felt that if he had to do a 64, he would have done it.' Masters, US Open, British Open – there was a Grand Slam to rank with any. Hogan was given a ticker-tape welcome in New York, as had Bobby Jones in 1930.

In the US Open of 1955, Hogan lost a play-off to Jack Fleck, who had birdied two of the last four holes to tie him in the championship proper. Putting became a torment for Ben. Yet at the age of 54, he scored a 66 in the 1967 Masters with an inward half of 30. In retirement, he wrote with Herbert Warren Wind, the American golf writer, *The Modern Fundamentals of Golf,* a classic analysis of the golf swing and a profound instructional manual. He was content to return to Fort Worth and concentrate on developing the Ben Hogan Company, which manufactured clubs and balls. Ben Hogan no longer sought centre stage. In 1965,

the American golf writers voted him 'The greatest professional of all time'. Allan Robertson, Old Tom and Young Tom, Vardon and Hagen might all have agreed.

THE HONOURABLE COMPANY OF EDINBURGH GOLFERS

Golf has been played on Leith Links, one of Edinburgh's earliest open spaces, certainly since the 15th century. Until the 1740s there was no sign of the formation of any type of club or society. Then the 'Company of Gentlemen Golfers' was formed, taking their refreshments after play at Luckie Clephan's Tavern. Luckie was both innkeeper and clubmaker. He died in 1742, and it was the house of his widow that became the Company's first headquarters. One of the earliest members, and very possibly a driving force behind the creation of the club, was Duncan Forbes, Lord President of the Court of Session, Forbes of Culloden.

On 7 March 1744, Edinburgh Town Council presented to the Company, no doubt with its prompting, a silver club to be played for annually. With a change of name to 'The Honourable Company of Edinburgh Golfers', the members claimed that date as the beginning of the club's records (carefully maintained ever since) and existence, supported by the minutes of the Town Council. Royal Blackheath, and another Edinburgh club, Royal Burgess, claim to be older but have no documentation to prove it. The 'Hon. Coy.' insists that it is the oldest golf club in the world in continued existence, now in 1994 for 250 years.

With a fine silver club to play for, rules were required.

The Hon. Coy. produced the famous 'Thirteen Rules', the first Rules of Golf, and so precise and comprehensive were they that many people believe that they have been little improved since. They are virtually identical to the rules adopted by the 'Gentlemen Golfers of Fife' when they became the Royal and Ancient Golf Club of St Andrews, ten years later.

The club membership has always been ripe with the landed gentry and the professional classes – its list of captains is sprinkled with lords, earls and knights, colonels, captains and surgeons – and above all it has been a club of the Edinburgh legal establishment, with judges and advocates galore forming a significant element in the membership. It has never seen the need for a club professional or a shop on its premises, and foursome golf, the original match play game, has always taken precedence in its fixtures.

In the early 19th century, Leith Links became unsatisfactory for the company's golf. It was a public expanse, invaded by cattle, the general public and the military. During the Napoleonic Wars and later, it was used for training purposes. Increasingly, members were drifting away to Musselburgh, further from the city and more spacious, for their pleasures until eventually their Golf House was sold and the club suffered some lean years.

It moved to Musselburgh in 1836 and remained there for 50 years before moving, for the same reason – public pressure over the Musselburgh Links – to Muirfield in 1891 and developing a private course that was to become famous throughout the world, and an outstanding venue for the Open Championship.

I

IRWIN, Hale

Born 1945

Nationality United States

Turned Pro 1968

Majors US Open 1974, 1979, 1990

There is a saying in American golf that no one wins three US Opens without winning a fourth. For Hale Irwin, despite being the oldest winner at 45 when he won his third in 1990, there may still be time. But even if he didn't, Irwin would still be seen as one of the finest players of his times, a golfer who sustained his talents over a quarter of a century. Only Jack Nicklaus has won US Opens over a longer period than Irwin's 16 years.

His game has been distinguished by a certain steadfastness and consistency. He has won his national championships at great, classic, demanding American parkland courses – Winged Foot in New York, Inverness at Toledo and Medinah in Illinois. In other American events he has won over such fine courses as Habour Town, Pebble Beach, Pinehurst No. 2, Riviera in Los Angeles and Muirfield Village. From early in 1975 to the end of 1978, Hale played 86 tournaments without once missing the 36 holes cut. He said he felt less than comfortable playing links courses because the absence of trees meant there was less definition of the target areas, yet in 1979,

when he was US Open Champion, he led by one stroke going into the last round of the Open Championship at Royal Lytham & St Annes. He was partnered by Severiano Ballesteros, who found only one fairway with his driver, and missed all of the last six fairways – but won the championship. Irwin, who was shattered by all this, said 'I cannot believe that anyone can drive as badly as that and still win an Open.' Then in 1983, at Royal Birkdale, Hale had an 'air shot' on the 14th green, reaching over the hole to pop the ball in, and missing. He finished one shot behind the winner, Tom Watson.

Hale Irwin was a player to be reckoned with on tight courses where par would represent fine play, but despite saying 'I am not much of a birdie man', he has shown a competitive spirit that can inspire him to thrilling scoring. He played the second nine holes of the final round in the 1990 US Open in 31 strokes, five under par for a 67, including a 50 foot birdie putt on that last green, to tie with Mike Donald. And he won the play-off with a birdie on the 19th hole.

Irwin had not won a tournament in the previous five years, but his rational thinking, his long game, fairway woods and long irons had always made him a threat on US Open courses, stretched and severely trapped, with punishing rough and lightning fast greens as they always are.

Born in Joplin, Missouri, in the very heart of America, on 3 June, 1945, Hale went to the University of Colorado

Hale Irwin, relentless, methodical, three times winner of the US Open Championship.

on a football scholarship, but he soon decided that he was not big enough or fast enough for that game, and

turned his attention to golf to such an effect that he was voted No. 1 collegiate player in the US in 1967. Twice a

winner of the World Match Play Championship, beaten in the final in 1976 as he went for an unprecedented three-in-a-row at Wentworth, he has also won events in South Africa, Australia, Japan and Brazil.

Perhaps the highlight of Hale Irwin's five Ryder Cup appearances was his halved match with Bernhard Langer at Kiawah Island in 1991, which meant that the US recovered the trophy from the European team.

J

JACKLIN Tony

Born 1944

Nationality British

Turned Pro 1962

Majors Open Championship 1969, US Open 1970

When Tony Jacklin won the Open Championship of 1969 and the US Open Championship of 1970, he was the first British player since Harry Vardon 70 years earlier to hold both titles simultaneously, and the first British player in 50 years, since Ted Ray in 1920, to win the US Open. The consequences for British and in time European golf have been inestimable.

At the peak of his powers, Jacklin was a beautiful, rhythmic ball striker, with a flowing, balanced swing, a fine putter and with a confidence that often seemed close to cockiness. This was never more clearly illustrated than on the 72nd hole at Royal Lytham & St Annes in 1969, when he split the fairway with his drive, then hit a 7-iron 12 feet from the hole to give him a perfect par and his two stroke Open Championship win over Bob Charles of New Zealand. The win was the first by a British golfer in 18 years, since Max Faulkner won at Royal Portrush in 1951. Tony

Tony Jacklin, a Ryder Cup captain, talks to the Press.

Jacklin was 25. This was to be his first great contribution to the rise of European golf – a few months later, at Royal Birkdale, the British Ryder Cup team was sufficiently inspired to play a tied match with the Americans. The second came in the eighties with Jacklin's successful captaincy of what had become Europe's Ryder Cup team.

He was not exactly born to golf. Scunthorpe is a long way from being a golfing mecca. But the boy Tony, taken to a golf course at the age of eight by his father, was instantly obsessed with the game. At 13, he won the Lincolnshire Junior Championship. At 15 he was in the England Boys team which played Scotland at Dalmahoy, Edinburgh. In the same year, he won the Lincolnshire Open against the professionals. He wanted to turn professional then, but was obliged to take a job in the local steelworks. Eventually he did clinch an assistant's job at the Potters Bar club in Hertfordshire, starting in January 1962. The following year he had his first crack at the Open Championship, at Royal Lytham of all places. He finished 30th. Arnold Palmer, defending champion, finished 32nd. Young Jacklin reckoned he had beaten the great man.

He won the Assistants' Championship in 1965 and with help from the club members, he was able to play on the tour and make overseas trips. By the middle sixties, a flurry of wins graced his progress – Pringle and Dunlop Masters at home, New Zealand PGA and South African events abroad.

But Jacklin quickly realised that if he wanted to be the best, he would have to beat the best on their own ground. That meant America, then with a tour vastly greater than the slender UK

and Europe version. He broke through there by winning the Greater Jacksonville Open (repeated in 1972). When he won at Royal Lytham, he said he could never have done it without the American experience. The Jacksonville success marked the start of five golden years for him. In 1970, he won the US Open by six shots! Defending his Open title at St Andrews, he played the first nine holes of the first round in 29 strokes, but the round was interrupted by a violent rainstorm. He finished fifth. In 1971 and 1972, he finished third each time, after having winning chances. In 1972, he had the title 'stolen' from him by Lee Trevino. Towards the end of the third round, Tony was a handful of strokes ahead, but Trevino birdied all of the last five holes including holing a bunker shot on the 16th, and a chip shot from behind the 18th green. Then on the final round, he holed another chip shot from the side of the 17th green. All of this knocked the stuffing out of Jacklin, as he later confessed. He was never again a serious Open Championship contender.

There were still events to be won, of course, but the Italian, German and Venezuelan Opens and other tournament wins throughout the seventies, could not compare to the majors.

The first of Tony's seven successive Ryder Cup appearances as a player came in 1967, but it was his appointment as captain for the 1983 matches which brought the series back to life, particularly for the American television public, and provided an enormous stimulus for the European Tour and its expansion. He took on the job on condition that everything concerning his team and its preparation would be first class. They would travel Concorde

across the ocean. Their accommodation would be first class, so too their equipment. In particular, he leaned heavily on the counsel of Severiano Ballesteros, who had already succeeded in the majors, having won the Masters, knowing the American scene, the American players; and above all he harnessed Ballesteros' ambition and determination to prove that European golfers were now a match for the best of the Americans.

Jacklin's first match as captain was at the PGA National Golf Club, at Palm Beach Gardens in Florida. Europe lost by one slender point in 28. The 1985 match, played at the Belfry in Sutton Coldfield, was won by Europe, handsomely, 16½–11½. The Americans had been defeated, for the first time since 1957. The 1987 match at Muirfield Village, the course created by the US captain Jack Nicklaus, was won by Europe 15–13 and was the first time an American team had lost 'at home'. And in 1989, back at the Belfry, Jacklin's team tied 14–14 with Raymond Floyd's team, allowing Europe to retain the trophy. As in the early seventies, so in the eighties, Tony Jacklin had enjoyed a golden spell at the summit of the game. And as he handed over to Bernard Gallacher, succeeding him as captain, perhaps he was not finished with golf. Born on 7 July, 1944, Tony may well have been pondering a spin around the Senior Tour.

JACOBS, John

Born	1925
Nationality	British
Turned Pro	1947

If golf historians of the future should seek a 'Renaissance Man' for the second half of the 20th century, it might well be John Jacobs. He has touched and graced the game at every conceivable level – as club professional, tournament professional, tournament winner; Ryder Cup player, Ryder Cup captain; television commentator and prolific writer; managing director of a company developing driving ranges and par–3 courses; as a quite brilliant teacher of the game at personal level, on video and through a chain of golf schools in the US; and perhaps most far reaching of all, as the first and inspirational Director General of the PGA European Tour.

John was born at Lindrick Golf Club in South Yorkshire, where his father was professional, his mother stewardess. After service in the RAF, he became an assistant and professional at the Hallamshire club near Sheffield in 1947. Success in local and regional events came along in time, but in September 1949, Jacobs made one of the most important moves in an eventful career. He went to the Gezira Sporting Club in Cairo as head professional, aged 24, and spent most of the next three years teaching a rich, enthusiastic and somewhat aristocratic membership. Much of his subsequent success as a teacher was as a result of his experiences at Gezira. In the winter of 1952–53, installed as professional at the Sandy Lodge club in Northwood, Middlesex, his teaching appointments book was soon as full as it had been in Egypt. And he was able to play tournaments to the extent that he played in the 1955 Ryder Cup match at Palm Springs. In 1957, he took both the South African Match Play and Dutch Open championships.

His reputation as an instructor was what got him invited to teach national amateur teams and Walker Cup teams. Golf federations on the Continent – Spain, Italy, France, Sweden – invited him to help their young players, both amateur and professional, and their national teams, as the game gradually increased in popularity there. He made winter trips to South Africa and, with such young Turks as Peter Alliss and Bernard Hunt, to the United States. They were the leaders of a faction among tournament players who felt that the meagre tournament schedule of the time could be greatly extended by sensible management and marketing expertise.

Jacobs left Sandy Lodge in 1963, extending his activities in writing, teaching and television and as managing director of Athlon Sports, developing driving ranges and par–3 courses at Sandown Park, Dublin and Newcastle. But still he was seen by the tournament players as the man who could lead them to the promised land of a greater professional tour, self-government and independence from the PGA. They succeeded after almost 20 years of resolutions, 'revolts' at annual meetings of the PGA, the formation of committees and sub-committees, politicking, and personality clashes. A whole new generation of players was to benefit when John Jacobs, on 1 October 1971 became the first Director General of the PGA's Tournament Division. Yet such was the strength of the opposition in the PGA with its membership of club professionals, that it was almost five years before the players were completely independent as the PGA European Tour, with their own organisation and headquarters at Wentworth.

Their new boss had extensive contacts on the Continent. Jacobs saw that the way ahead lay substantially in Europe. And he had another important card in Tony Jacklin, Open Champion in 1969, US Open Champion in 1970. Everyone wanted Jacklin for their tournaments. Jacobs arranged a modus operandi with Mark McCormack, Jacklin's manager, for the player's appearances which kept all parties happy.

The rise and eminence of John Jacobs as a world renowned teacher of golf has been reflected in the John Jacobs Practical Golf Schools throughout the United States. There, where there is warm, sunny weather somewhere in the huge country at all times in the year, the golf school provides quality accommodation over a period of days, or a week, with first class instruction. The phenomenon is widespread. Such is the affluence of the American economy that Jacobs and his partner Shelby Futch, by the end of the 1980s, were servicing some 10,000 students each year with locations in Hawaii, Florida, and Arizona, with as many as 32 Jacobs-trained instructors. These schools, although little known in the UK, have been hugely successful in the US.

Jacobs has collaborated with Gary Player in the design of the Edinburgh course at Wentworth. Can there be other fields for John Robert Maurice Jacobs to conquer?

JANZEN, Lee

Born	1964
Nationality	United States
Turned Pro	1986
Majors	US Open 1993

Lee Janzen, US Open winner in 1993, was the unknown champion, at least to the world at large if not to his peers among the American tournament professionals. And the impression that the world at large had from its television screens was of a young man, austere and silent, withdrawn under the peak of a baseball cap, tight-lipped, cold-eyed, walking the fairways of Baltusrol's

rich parkland as though entranced. But he scored like a champion, all four rounds under 70 (67-67-69-69 for 272), like those of the British Open champion Greg Norman in the same year. And playing with his principal challenger, the experienced and hardened Payne Stewart, on the final round, Janzen never once looked like being overawed.

Having turned professional in 1986, he played successfully on the US mini-tour, being leading money winner there in 1989. At the end of that year, he joined the 'big' tour, aged 25, and over the next three years he improved his position progressively from 115 to 72 to 9 in the rankings. In that last year, 1992, he won his first tournament. Even then, he was considered just one of a score of talented young players on the circuit, but despite the fact that he described his success at Baltusrol as an 'over-achievement', many judges were convinced that with his all-round abilities and his intense powers of concentration, Lee Janzen would certainly win more major championships.

Lee Janzen and caddie celebrate a vital chip shot holed for a birdie on the 16th hole in the last round of the US Open, Baltusrol, 1993.

Johnnie Walker World Championship

Until the inaugural Johnnie Walker World Championship at the Tryall Club in Jamaica in December 1991, there had not been a World Champion of Golf. True, there were other events with 'world' in their titles - the World Match Play Championship, the World Cup - but none in which all of the world's finest players were gathered in one place, in one championship, to

It's well known that weather conditions influence golf. In the Johnnie Walker World Championship it is often the heat that affects players. This is up-and-coming Scandinavian Jesper Parnevik taking local relief during the 1993 tournament.

establish the game's supremo for the year.

The World Championship was made up of 26 players who qualified by winning one of 29 designated tournaments worldwide. To allow for duplicate winners and absence through sickness or whatever, the championship's International Advisory Committee retained the right to select four players to round out the field.

The first event was a resounding success, and a thrilling climax to the year in golf. The immediate appeal of the Johnnie Walker World Championship was reflected in the fact that 34 countries around the world took television coverage of the event, either live, or tape-delayed. And in 1992 and 1993, that increased to more than 80 countries each year, with news coverage reaching 130 countries around the world. Johnnie Walker of

defending, was out of sorts, and his opening 77 put him out of the race. Tom Kite, Tony Johnstone, Craig Parry, Steve Elkington and David Frost had rounds in the sixties. Nick Faldo's third round 65 gave him a five shot lead over Greg Norman, but wonder of wonders, the big Australian produced a staggering final round of 63 to catch him, before losing

on the first play-off hole.

Yet the 1993 championship was perhaps even more astonishing. Larry Mize, the 1987 US Masters champion, was invited to take the place of Greg Norman, who declined his invitation. Mize promptly astonished the rest of the field, and the world of golf, by destroying Tryall, wind and all, in 67, 66, 68, 65, for a total of 266, eighteen under par, and ten shots ahead of the second placed Fred Couples. It was one of the greatest achievements in world golf in 1993, fittingly, at the game's World Championship.

course had had a considerable presence in golf even before 1991, with some $18 million invested in sponsoring tournaments in Australia and Asia, and in sponsoring the Ryder Cup matches.

The course, on Jamaica's North Shore, normally played at 6,407 yards, but was stretched to 6,849 making Tryall much more than your average resort course. The fairways were narrowed, the rough stiffened, and with a taxing inward nine in particular it was a testing 34-37 par 71. And Tryall's winds compounded the problems.

But that first year Fred Couples of the US, with a stunning closing round of 66, finished on 281, three under par and four shots clear of the next man, Bernhard Langer of Germany. Couples was rewarded with a cheque for $550,000 from the tournament total of $2,550,000.

The action in the 1992 event was even more dramatic. Fred Couples,

Larry Mize, holding the trophy won in stunning fashion in the 1993 Championship.

JONES, Bobby

Born 1902

Nationality United States

Majors Open Championship 1926, 1927, 1930; US Open 1923, 1926, 1929, 1930; Amateur Championship 1930; US Amateur 1924, 1925, 1927, 1928, 1930

The game of 'Who was the greatest…' this, that or the other is a pleasant diversion, but little more. An even more pointless if nonetheless pleasant pastime is trying to assess achievements in sport, as in other things, over a century or more of time. The most that can be said is that a man is the best of his time. Yet in the history of golf there have been a handful of men who have left their marks on the game in a way that is timeless – Harry Vardon, Francis Ouimet, Walter Hagen, Ben Hogan, Arnold Palmer, Jack Nicklaus. And one must say Coburn Haskell, the creator of the rubber wound ball, and in the field of golf course design, Donald Ross and Robert Trent Jones.

And then there is Bobby Jones, of whom rational men will say 'the finest golfer the game has ever known'.

Robert Trent Jones Jr, Bob Jones as the Americans called him and as he preferred to be known, won the Amateur Championship once, the Open Championship three times, the US Open four times and the US Amateur Championship five times. He won at least one of these championships every year from 1923 to 1930. In 1926, he won both Open Championships. In 1930 he won all four, both Opens and both Amateurs, then retired at the age of 28. This latter 1930 achievement, known as the 'Grand Slam' of golf, is considered the greatest single feat by any player and

one which can never be repeated. There are many reasons for this claim, but the most significant is probably the fact that at that time, the best of amateurs could still match the best of professionals. Francis Ouimet won the 1913 US Open from the English 'cracks', Harry Vardon and Ted Ray, Jerome Travers won it in 1915 and Chick Evans won it in 1916. All three were amateurs.

The 1920s was a decade of affluence in America. Between the end of the First World War and the depression of the early thirties, it was boom time in America. And American amateurs were men of substance, of privilege if not of aristocracy – Travers first played golf on his father's 'estate' on Long Island, and such Jones contemporaries as Jess Sweester, Jesse Guilford, Bob Gardner and Bill Fownes were far from being impoverished. Their like was also to be found, of course, in England, where Roger Wethered, Cyril Tolley, Lord Charles Hope, and Sir Ernest Holderness were to be found in Walker Cup teams and championships. Moreover, the American professional tour scarcely existed. The professionals then had but a handful of events in comparison to the scope and sophistication of the present PGA Tour, which has vast attraction for today's amateurs who are now tempted to turn professional in their early twenties. Yet Jones still had to wrestle with great professionals in assembling his championship record – Walter Hagen, Gene Sarazen, Leo Diegel, Tommy Armour, Johnny Farrell and Macdonald Smith were considerable players.

If the twenties was the Jones decade, he had lean times before breaking

through with the US Open of 1923. And a desperate business that was, at the Inwood club in New York. He led after three rounds, but took a two-over-par six on the very last hole. Bobby Cruikshank, a determined little Scottish professional, birdied the last hole to tie him. It took a masterful 2-iron shot from Jones, from rough and over a lake guarding the last green, to give him a play-off victory, 76 to 78. And in his first British Open Championship win, at Royal Lytham in 1926, he found himself in a fairway bunker at the 71st hole, tied for the lead with his playing partner Al Watrous. Al played his second nicely to the front of the green. Jones was 175 yards from the green with a mass of rough and bunkers ahead of him. But he hit one of golf's historic shots, as his ball carried all the way to the green finishing inside the Watrous ball. Al was shattered, took three putts and Jones had won his first British Open. To this day, a plaque in that bunker commemorates the shot. Then in his US Open of 1929, he scored seven twice on his last round and had to hole a 12 foot putt to tie Al Espinosa – then won the 36 holes play-off by 23 strokes!

Bobby Jones was a prodigy. He was born on St Patrick's Day, 17 March 1902, in Atlanta, Georgia, the son of a successful attorney. The child had a digestive ailment which meant his early years were sickly. His father was a member of the famous Atlanta Athletic Club, which had a golf course at nearby East Lake, a small community since overwhelmed by the spread of Greater Atlanta.

To help build up his son's health, Jones senior took a summer cottage by the golf course, and when his parents played golf the child would follow with a cut-down club. And when Stewart Maiden

from Carnoustie followed his brother as the East Lake professional, young Bob imitated the Maiden swing. When he was seven, he was allowed to play the full course. In 1913, he read about Francis Ouimet and his US Open win, and saw the same Harry Vardon and Ted Ray play an exhibition over East Lake. That same year, he scored his first 80 round the course. At the age of 13 he won the club championship, and at 14 he could drive a ball 250 yards. That year, 1916, he played in the US Amateur Championship at Merion. He won a couple of rounds, received national press attention for club throwing as much as anything, then was soundly beaten by Bob Gardner, the defending champion.

During the First World War, Jones played a long series of exhibition matches for charity around the country with Alexa Stirling and Perry Adair, both talented Atlanta amateurs; and in 1919, more matured and physically more powerful, he reached the first of his seven US Amateur finals. All through the period of his successes, Jones was very much a true-blue amateur. He studied mechanical engineering at the famous Georgia Tech for three years. He studied English at Harvard, law at Emory University, and went into practice in Atlanta.

Throughout the 1920s, he played very little golf apart from championships – a modern player, amateur or professional, would find this unthinkable.

Bobby Jones was a perfect Southern gentleman,

Young Bobby Jones and old Ben Sayers, at St Andrews in 1921. It was the 19-year-old American's first appearance at the home of golf.

gracious to opponents, modest in victory. He was a stickler for the rules. He called penalties on himself in the US Opens of 1925 and 1926, the first when he said his ball had moved in the rough, then when he said it had moved on the green. No one else could have seen these incidents. His swing was rather slow, rhythmic, almost poetic. His stance was strangely narrow, but he had a wide arc from a big shoulder turn, and went through and up to a high finish. In retirement, he was largely responsible for the creation of the Augusta National club, its super course and the US Masters event which emerged from it. Some people claim this as a greater memorial to him than his championship victories.

He was made an honorary member of the Royal and Ancient Golf Club, and in 1958, visiting St Andrews for the last time as captain of the US Eisenhower Trophy team, he was given the Freedom of the Burgh. The only other American so honoured was Benjamin Franklin. In his middle forties, Jones was stricken with syringomyelia, a crippling disease which he bore with great courage for the rest of his life. He died on 18 December 1971, aged 69.

JONES, Robert 'Trent'

Golf course architects are probably the least considered personages in the panoply of the game. The average golfer gives little thought to the layout of his course, and the whys and wherefores of its slopes, bunkers and hazards, any more than the average office worker gives to his building, its services and its creator.

Golf courses evolved from play over common ground, but the expansion of the game towards the end of the 19th century and on, in various countries, into the 20th, has required designers. The earliest were professional players – first Old Tom Morris, then James Braid, laid out dozens of courses between them. But the two most significant golf course architects have probably been Donald Ross and Robert Trent Jones, generally known as 'Trent' to distinguish him from that other RT Jones – 'Bobby'.

Trent Jones was taken to the United States from England at the age of five, and his family settled in Rochester, New York. In primary school there, he sat beside Walter Hagen's sister when they were 12 years old. She said that her brother was professional at the Country Club of Rochester and it would be a good place to go to make some money, caddying. Soon Trent was there, caddying for 25 cents a round. And he began to play, with the effect that he was a pretty good scratch player in his teens. When he broke the course record at the age of 16, playing in a city championship, he was offered a job at another golf club in the area. It produced enough to pay for him through college. Although he finished top amateur in the Canadian Open of 1927, won by Tommy Armour, he had already decided on being a golf course architect, and resolved to get quite specific training to equip him for the career. He enrolled at Cornell University, selecting the relevant subjects such as engineering, surveying, landscaping, hydraulics and architecture, but also art and literature. Thus Trent could be said to be the first properly trained and qualified golf course architect, in contrast to most of his predecessors who were in the main untutored, capable golfers who worked from their own playing experience only.

His education finished, Trent joined Stanley Thompson, a first class Scottish-born Canadian designer who remodelled the famous Banff course in the Canadian Rockies. They were very influential in having the concept of strategic design adopted in North America. Jones came to see that golf courses had been reacting to the development of equipment, and that improved golf balls and steel shafts were simply stretching courses indiscriminately. The Jones philosophy developed as having the course determining how the game should be played. He would build courses and holes at which it would be difficult for the expert to score birdies, but easy for the average player to score bogeys. One illustration of the effect of improved equipment came with the sand wedge, developed by Gene Sarazen. A bunker is placed on a golf course to impose a penalty, for strategic reasons, for cosmetic reasons, or perhaps a combination of all three. Before Sarazen, playing a 9-iron shot from sand was very difficult. After Sarazen and the coming of his heavily flanged wedge, bunkers as hazards became less intimidating, so conversely, water hazards had become more important. In his later years, Trent Jones was accused of using water in an excessively punitive way. He was also accused of the wanton spending of clients' money in moving vast amounts of material, excavating huge artificial lakes, diverting streams, moulding vast, sweeping fairways – in short, overwhelming the landscape.

To some extent, the criticism rang true, but what is often overlooked is that after the Second World War, an explosion of interest in golf meant that many new courses were needed, and quickly. Trent Jones had by this time the capability of designing and constructing, the knowledge of how to build a course with proper drainage and ease of maintenance, and of the hundreds which he created, many were on unglamorous, unprepossessing sites.

In his work, he held greens to be critical and like Donald Ross before him, Trent never forgot the example of the Old Course at St Andrews, and the contours of its greens, and how the fairways flow into these greens. The shot into the green he held to be of the greatest importance, which is why he was inclined to build large greens with several pin positions established. If golf, like all other sports, was to be one of attack and defence, then the designer must produce a course which could defend itself against the attacks of the players.

As Trent became the patriarch of golf designers, he could look at a vast body of work achieved. He was often called by the US Golf Association to modernise and stiffen US Open courses. Bobby Jones asked him to make some changes at Augusta National. His original work, throughout the United States and more than a score of countries, has left some magnificent and very beautiful golf courses – Spyglass Hill at Pebble Beach, Bellerive in St Louis, Peachtree in Atlanta, I Roveri in Turin, Pevero in Sardinia, Sotogrande in Spain, and Ballybunion 2 in Ireland.

Robert Trent Jones, revolutionary golf course architect.

KASUMIGASEKI

In one sense, the Kasumigaseki club's East course is the pride of Japanese golf. Not the oldest club in the country – it was opened in 1929 – nevertheless Kasumigaseki is held in singular affection as the venue for the Canada (now World) Cup of 1957, won by Japan in a victory that was the first indication that Japan was to be a major force in world golf.

The Japanese team of Torakichi (Pete) Nakamura and Koichi Ono won from an international field which included an American team of Sam Snead and Jimmy Demaret, and such

KASUMIGASEKI		
HOLE	YARDS	PAR
1	388	4
2	374	4
3	422	4
4	158	3
5	532	5
6	372	4
7	220	3
8	474	4
9	532	5
OUT	3,472	36
10	180	3
11	433	4
12	468	4
13	375	4
14	593	5
15	433	4
16	173	3
17	349	4
18	483	4
IN	3,487	36
TOTAL	6,959	72

international players as Roberto de Vicenzo, Dave Thomas and Gary Player. They became overnight heroes and sparked off a golfing boom that has continued uninterrupted for more than 30 years.

The East course is laid out through nicely wooded country with gentle contours. It has several stiff par-4s, one monster par-5, the 14th at 593 yards, and has almost none of the water hazards and indulgent decoration that have featured in more recent courses in Japan. The one exception is the short 10th, which has two tees, two greens, and virtually two lakes. The shot is 180 yards over water, to side-by-side greens, and the explanation lies in the Japanese climate. All Kasumigaseki holes have two greens, one for summer play, one for winter. The natural Korai grass, a very strong Bermuda strain, thrives during the hot summer weather but goes dormant in winter. Then, the climate will support rye or bent grass. Thus two greens for every hole, almost always side by side, with different grasses.

This has led to some complications for the designers in coping with shots onto the greens in either summer or winter play. In most cases it has been resolved simply, with a separating bunker or mounding. A second course, the West, was needed to accommodate Kasumigaseki's 2000 members.

KITE, Tom

Born 1949

Nationality United States

Turned Pro 1972

Majors US Open 1992

Up to the spring of 1993,

Tom Kite had won more tournament prize money than any other golfer in history, with more than $8 million in a 20-year career. In 1992, he won $957,445 and his lifetime total at the end of 1992 was $7,612,918. After five events in early 1993, two of which he won, he had added $515,761.

He had won the Nissan Los Angeles Open by three strokes and the Bob Hope Chrysler Classic at Palm Springs by six, then at the Masters in April he found himself playing through back pain severe enough to make him miss the 36-holes cut. The condition was diagnosed as herniated discs in the spine, and Kite was ordered to rest from golf indefinitely.

For years, Tom Kite was written off as a fine player who could win nothing but money, a reference to a lack of success in any of the major championships. It was said that he found the pressure of these events too much to handle and examples were trotted out in support of the argument. Challenging Ben Crenshaw with seven holes to play in the 1984 Masters, Tom took six strokes at Augusta's treacherous par-3 12th hole. Then in the 1985 'Sandy Lyle' Open Championship at Royal St George's, Kite scored six on the 10th hole when leading the field by two. Worst of all perhaps, he was three strokes in the lead in the 1989 US Open at Oak Hill, but hit into a creek on the 10th hole to squander his chance.

That all ended in June 1992 when Tom Kite at last won a major championship, his own US Open, fittingly on one of the great golf courses in the world. At 5' 8" and 11 stone Tom has never been a power golfer. Relentless efficiency with all the clubs, intense concentration and consistency have been his qualities. His vast winnings

have been amassed in spite of no more than a score of tournament victories. And with his stature, he has never been considered a foul-weather player, but his performance on the final round at Pebble Beach gave the lie to that.

For three days the weather over the Monterey Peninsula had been still and misty. On the final day, it broke and the wind got up to as much as 35 mph. But Kite played beautifully controlled golf. On the 12th hole when he holed a 40 foot birdie putt, he was four shots ahead and he must have known that at last a major championship was his. He won in the end by two strokes, never over par in any of his four rounds of 71–72–70–72 for 285.

The world of golf was genuinely delighted that Tom Kite had done it at last, aged 42 or not. Born in Austin on 9 December 1949, he was a member of the University of Texas golf team and shared national collegiate honours with Ben Crenshaw in 1972. He finished second to Lanny Wadkins in the US Amateur Championship of 1970, and played in the Walker Cup match at St Andrews in 1971, winning both singles. He turned professional in late 1972 and was voted 'Rookie of the Year' in 1973. Tom won the 1980 European Open at Walton Heath, and was a stalwart of US Ryder Cup teams throughout the eighties.

Tom Kite – the greatest money winner of them all, and at last a 'major' winner in 1992 with the US Open Championship at Pebble Beach. He played in both Walker and Ryder Cup teams and was a European Open winner.

L

LAHINCH

The pretty village of Lahinch, on Liscannon Bay on the Atlantic coast of County Clare in the Republic of Ireland, has been dubbed the 'St Andrews of Irish Golf', which is inevitably unfair to both places. What is certain is that few communities – Pinehurst in North Carolina, as well as St Andrews, might be another one – are so totally immersed in the game. And it has been that way at Lahinch since the club was formed in 1893.

It appears that officers of the Black Watch, stationed at Limerick forty miles away, had founded the Limerick Golf Club, one of the oldest in Ireland, in 1891 and played on a course of sorts set out on the local racecourse. But searching around for something better, they came upon the sand dunes of Lahinch, ideal for a 'Scottish', links-type course. Sir Alex Shaw and Rex Plummer, Limerick members among others, originally saw a course at Lahinch as an extension to the Limerick club, but that idea was abandoned and on Good Friday 1893 they negotiated a lease on a large tract of land from the local farmer, Dan Slattery.

Old Tom Morris was brought over that same year, and for a fee of one guinea (£1.05) a day 'and expenses', paid by Shaw, he laid out the original course and declared modestly that it was 'one of the five best courses in the British Isles'. Not much is left of Old Tom's course, but the

LAHINCH		
HOLE	YARDS	PAR
1	385	4
2	512	5
3	151	3
4	428	4
5	482	5
6	155	3
7	399	4
8	350	4
9	384	4
OUT	3,246	36
10	451	4
11	138	3
12	475	4
13	273	4
14	488	5
15	462	4
16	195	3
17	437	4
18	533	5
IN	3,452	36
TOTAL	6,698	72

Lahinch in the West of Ireland. Courses were less well-groomed in the 1890s!

ground remains – magnificent linksland, huge sand dunes, valleys running between them, heaven-made for fairways, clifftop tees and greens and, of course, stunning seascapes and views to the Aran Islands in Galway Bay and the cliffs of Moher to the north.

The course has been much revised, changed and improved over the years. Gibson, a Westward Ho! professional, extended the course early this century to accommodate the more lively 'Haskell' ball. In 1927, Dr Alister Mackenzie, later to win fame for creating such courses as Cypress Point, Royal Melbourne and Augusta National, was called in and made extensive changes, driving fairways deep into the sandhills and declaring as modestly as Old Tom that Lahinch 'might come to be regarded as the finest and most popular

course that I, or I believe anyone else, ever constructed'. His exuberance has scarcely been confirmed by history, but Lahinch, more than 60 years on, remains a magnificent test of the

golfer's game, and his temperament.

With the coming of the steel shaft, other architects have been involved – John Burke, Bill McCavery and more recently Donald Steel –

and now the course can stretch to 6,700 yards. So popular had Lahinch become as a holiday golfing venue that a second 18 holes of 5,345 yards on the landward side of the Old Course was designed by John Harris and opened in 1975.

Only one hole of the original Old Tom Morris design remains on the Old Course, the sixth, a par-3 of 156 yards. The tee shot is blind, played over a huge sandhill to a wide but narrow green, backed by another tall sandhill. The hole is named inevitably 'The Dell', and has been the subject of much controversy over the years, damned as an antique. No doubt it was modelled on the 'Himalayas', the sixth hole at Prestwick, a par-3 of 200 yards which demands a blind tee shot over a ridge of sandhills. Old Tom Morris laid out much of the course there also. Yet whenever there has been a cry of 'unfair' or 'obsolete' over the Dell at Lahinch, the conservatives have won. It remains.

And of course, there are Slattery's goats, one of the oft-told stories in golf, but always good for one more recital. In the fine modern extension to the Lahinch clubhouse, an old barometer has been retained. It is without hands, but bears a notice 'See Goats'. A small herd of goats is allowed the free run of the course. When the weather is fine, they are to be seen far out on the course. When the weather is foul, or about to be foul, they will be huddled in the lee of the clubhouse. Lahinch, as you see, is a relaxed place.

LANGER, Bernhard

Born 1957

Nationality German

Turned Pro 1974

Majors US Masters 1985, 1993

As the first truly international golfer to emerge from Germany, Bernhard Langer has not only made a profound impact on the development of the game in his own country, but has established himself as one of the top ten golfers in the world.

At the end of the Second World War, his father, a Czech, escaped from a Russia-bound train and eventually settled in Anhausen, Bavaria, where Bernhard was born on 27 August 1957. He became a

Bernhard Langer of Germany, twice a US Masters champion, lets rip with a big drive.

professional at his local course at the age of 16, and started to play in local and regional events. He first announced himself to the world of international golf in 1979, when he won the Cacharel Under-25s Championship in France by no fewer than 17 strokes. From then on, he won at least one tour event each year.

The first peak of his career came when he won the 1985 US Masters tournament, finishing ahead of Curtis Strange, Severiano Ballesteros and Raymond Floyd, and shrugged off all the intense media pressure which follows it by winning the next week the Heritage Classic. He led the European Order of Merit in 1981 and 1984, and a wide-ranging career has brought him the championships of Germany, Italy, France, Holland, Spain, Austria and Ireland, some

more than once, and beyond Europe he has won in Colombia, Japan, Australia, Hong Kong and South Africa.

Highly rated by his peers as one of the most analytical and tactical thinkers about courses and tournaments, Langer has displayed great tenacity and determination in his career. No fewer than three times he has completely 'lost' his putting. Other great players – Snead, Hogan, Vardon – have

suffered this, but never at the heights of their careers. But three times, by experimenting with the grip, with putters, and with techniques, Langer has overcome this and made himself as capable as any on the greens.

The fact that he was faced with the critical putt in the 1991 Ryder Cup match at Kiawah Island was ironic. It was perhaps an eight-footer, twisting from left to right, on the last green of the last match, Langer v Hale Irwin, with a huge gallery, and television audience, watching. Langer missed, Irwin won the match, the United States won by one point. Severiano Ballesteros said, 'No one could have holed that putt.'

Langer's powers of recovery and of sustained concentration were illustrated yet again when in the very next week, he won the German Masters Championship. One of his unlikeliest successes came in 1990 when he and fellow countryman Torsten Gledeon, essentially a club professional, won the World Cup for Germany. But he may come to regard his greatest achievement as his second victory in the US Masters of 1993. He scored 68-70-69-70 for a 277 total. He three-putted only twice during the four rounds and had only six bogeys. And nowhere did Langer's resolution, his domination over himself and his game, better illustrate the man than at his playing of the par five 13th hole on the final round. His drive found position A round the corner of the dogleg. His 3-iron shot was nailed to the flag all the way, finishing 20 feet above the hole. His putt dropped right into the centre of the hole. Langer's 1993 Masters was an immense performance.

LEITCH, Cecil

Christened Charlotte Cecilia Pitcairn, 'Cecil' Leitch burst onto British women's golf like a firecracker and remained sparking for the rest of a long life. Born at Silloth in Cumbria on 13 April 1891, she was a semi-finalist in the British Ladies Championship at 17, at St Andrews if you please, and dominated women's golf for two decades or more.

Cecil was one of five daughters of a Scottish doctor in practice at Silloth, and she learned her golf on the lovely links there, on the southern shore of the Solway Firth. She won the French Ladies Championship in 1912, repeated in 1914, and took the English and British titles to make it a hat-trick that year. What she might have achieved had there been no Great War is not hard to imagine, despite her youth. In 1910, aged 19, she had not been able to resist the challenge of Harold Hilton, who offered to take on any lady golfer and give her half-a-stroke a hole, i.e. a stroke every two holes. Hilton had already won two Opens and two of his four Amateur

Cecil Leitch at Sheringham, 1920.

Championships. Cecil took him on, and beat him 2 and 1 over the prescribed 72 holes.

After the war, she picked up where she had left her marker by winning the English Ladies in 1919 and the British and French championships in 1920. In all, she won the English in 1914 and 1919, the French in 1912, 1914, 1920, 1921 and 1924, and the British in 1914, 1920, 1921 and 1926. It is an impressive record. She also won the Canadian Ladies Championship in 1921. Her four victories in the British were matched only by Joyce Wethered, her perennial opponent whom she was seldom able to beat. She did so in 1921, in the British final at Turnberry, by 4 and 3, and then the very next year at Princes, it was Miss Wethered's turn in the final, by 9 and 7. Cecil also lost the English final of 1920 to her, at Sheringham by 2 and 1.

British Ladies golf belonged to Leitch and Wethered, but they were an oddly contrasting pair. Tall, slim, fragile and shy, Joyce Wethered would not be seen after a match; she would simply vanish until the next starter's call, be polite to her opponent on the tee, play and vanish again. Cecil Leitch by contrast was strong, tough, energetic and talkative with an outgoing personality, a natural leader liable to stand out in any company. Her game was one of power, her swing not particularly pretty. It was quite flat and she used a two-fisted 'baseball' grip with the right hand very much under the shaft. She punched out her iron shots with dash and vigour, and all told, brought power to ladies' golf. Not for Cecil the long, flowing, rather willowy swings that had been the fashion before her.

The Wethered-Leitch British Ladies Amateur Championship final at Troon in 1925 was an epic. It went to the 37th hole after Joyce Wethered had scored the big links course twice in 75 strokes. This quiet, almost ethereal girl won in spite of huge stampeding Scottish galleries, who found the clash of these two great players irresistible. Cecil Leitch won it the following year, for the fourth and last time. She lived the rest of her life just as she had tackled golf, looking it straight in the eye, and until she died at the great age of 86, was a regular attender at golf's major occasions and a steadfast critic of authority.

LEMA, Anthony

Born 1934

Nationality United States

Turned Pro 1959

Majors Open Championship 1964

When Tony Lema won the Open Championship at St Andrews in 1964, after arriving late, with only one day to 'learn' the course and never before having played a links course at all, it seemed that a star was born. Lema had everything – he was tall, slender, handsome; he had a flowing, elegant swing; his name had a Latin flavour, a touch of the Mediterranean; his habit of breaking out the champagne to the journalists after a victory earned him the soubriquet 'Champagne Tony'. It seems exactly right.

Lema was from San Francisco, of Portuguese origin. Born on 25 February 1934, he had been a caddie, a US Marine in the Korean War, then had worked in the professional's shop at the San Francisco Golf Club before trying his luck on the tournament circuit. It took three years of effort before he broke through with three tournament wins in 1962, and the following year, in his first appearance at the Augusta Masters, he finished second to Jack Nicklaus by one slender stroke.

He won his Open at St Andrews by five strokes from Nicklaus, scoring 73-68-68-70 for 279. Lema always insisted that Tip Anderson, Arnold Palmer's regular caddie, won it for him. Palmer did not compete in that Open and recommended Anderson to Lema, who said he simply did what Tip told him.

In defending his title the following year at Royal Birkdale, Lema led by two strokes after 36 holes. This was the last year in which the two final rounds were played on one day. Lema was paired

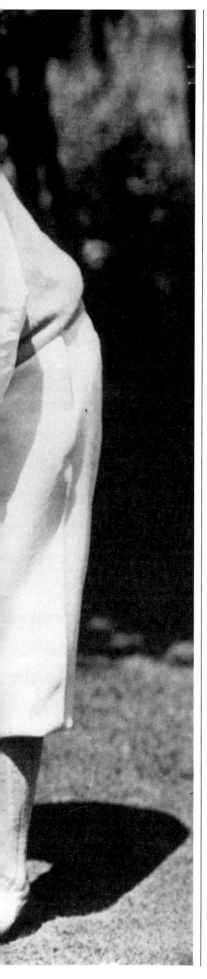

with Peter Thomson, and they spent part of the lunch-break watching the England-Australia Test Match, with Thomson trying to introduce the Californian to the mysteries of cricket. In the event, Lema finished fourth as Thomson took his fifth Open Championship.

It remained an eventful year for the American. Over that same Royal Birkdale course, he won four of his five matches in the Ryder Cup. And at Wentworth in October, he was six up after 18 holes on Gary Player in the Piccadilly World Match Play Championship, then seven up with 17 to play – only to lose on the 37th hole. Nevertheless, Tony Lema looked certain to be the one who would crack the hegemony of Palmer, Player and Nicklaus which ruled the 1960s. It was not to be. Lema and his wife Betty, glamorous figures both, died in 1966 in a light aircraft when it crashed on making an emergency landing.

LITTLE, Lawson

Born 1910

Nationality United States

Turned Pro 1936

Majors US Open 1940

Californian Lawson Little has a secure place in golfing records as the amateur who did what even the great Bobby Jones could not do – win the Amateur Championships of both Great Britain and the United States in successive years. In doing it, in 1934 and 1935, he recorded 31 consecutive victories in match play on both sides of the ocean. In

The young Lawson Little, soon to be an exceptional amateur champion on both sides of the Atlantic.

the first of them, in which he beat Jimmy Wallace at Prestwick by 14 and 13, the biggest winning margin on record in a final, he scored 12 threes in the 23 holes played, scoring 66 on the morning round. Vast Scottish crowds had poured in to see the Scot against this American wonder golfer, but the late arrivals had only five afternoon holes to see.

That same summer, in the Walker Cup match at St Andrews, Little and Johnny Goodman, the reigning US Open Champion and the last amateur to win it, beat the experienced Cyril Tolley and Roger Wethered by 8 and 6. Little beat Tolley in the singles by 6 and 5. Tolley was an immensely long hitter, but Little was always a good ten yards past him.

Lawson Little, born on 23 June 1910, was the son of a colonel in the US Army medical corps and came to consider the golf course as a battlefield on which he could beat anyone. He was immensely strong physically, and as a golfer, played right through the bag. At a time when a golfer could have an unlimited number of clubs, Little would often carry as much as half a dozen niblicks. In his best years, he was a deadly rap putter.

After his four amateur championship successes, he turned professional in 1936 and won the Canadian Open that year, but his career from then on saw rather limited success. He did win the US Open Championship in 1940, in a play-off with Gene Sarazen. He died in February 1968.

LITTLER, Gene

Born 1930

Nationality United States

Turned Pro 1954

Major US Open 1961

When a man wins the US Amateur Championship at the age of 23, wins a PGA Tour event while still an amateur, then turns professional and in his very first pro year finishes second in the US Open by only one stroke, you can be sure you are looking at an exceptional player. Gene Littler, born in San Diego, Southern California on 21 July 1930, was certainly that.

In 1953, he won the US Amateur Championship at Oklahoma City, beating Dale Morey one-up in the final. That same year he played on the winning US Walker Cup team in the match at the Kittanset Club in Marion, Massachusetts. The next year, still an amateur, he won his 'local' San Diego Open against all the top professionals and promptly turned professional himself. Then in the 1954 US Open at Baltusrol, incidentally the first to be televised nationally and the first to have the entire course roped off, he led after 36 holes with rounds of 70 and 69. His total of 285 was only one behind that of the winner, Ed Furgol – and Littler missed a putt of eight feet on the very last green to tie. However, seven years later his time came when he took the 1961 US Open at Oakland Hills near Detroit with a total of 281, one ahead of Bob Goalby and Doug Saunders.

One of the classic swings in golf – elegant, poised, controlled – brought Gene Littler a proud career. From 1954 to 1977, he won 30 events, He tied for the 1970 Masters, but lost the 18 holes play-off – it was the last of its kind at Augusta – to Billy Casper. He won the 1965 Canadian Open, tied Lanny Wadkins for the 1977 PGA Championship and again lost a play-off. Indeed his play-off record could have been better: in his career he won four but lost 10.

If Gene Littler lacked the passion of an Arnold Palmer, the ice-cold calculation of a Jack Nicklaus, his swing and his life purred along as smoothly as one of the Rolls-Royce cars he collected, indulging his interest in classic automobiles. But in the spring of 1972, when he had to have surgery for cancer in the lymphatic system, he showed the calibre of his character by being back in competition in the autumn, and in winning a tournament the very next year.

In 1981 he embraced the Senior PGA tour and promptly started winning tournaments and prize money. By the end of 1992 his regular career earnings of $1.5 million had been surpassed by a Senior total of $1.9 million. 'Gene the Machine', as the American writers dubbed him, was a regular Ryder Cup player throughout the 1960s and into the seventies, seven times in all.

LOCKE, Bobby

Born 1917

Nationality South African

Turned Pro 1938

Majors Open Championship 1949, 1950, 1952, 1957

Arthur D'Arcy Locke, for so he was christened, was known to the world of golf as 'Bobby', for so he dubbed himself as a boy because of his hero-worship, at a distance, of the great Bobby Jones, his idol. Locke was the outstanding international

A slender Bobby Locke in action before the Second World War. After service with the South African Air Force, his shadow grew larger.

golfer of the 1940s and 50s. He won the Open Championship four times, and was second twice, in 1946 and 1954, thus finishing six times in eleven years as either first or second. And in the United States, he won the first tournament he entered, four of the first six he played, and eleven in all in a four year span.

Bobby was something of a boy prodigy, and his career had an almost inevitable progression from the time he won the South African Boys' Championship in 1931 at the age of 14. In 1935 and again in 1937, he won both the South African Amateur and Open Championships – he was to win the South African Open a total of nine times. With his record very much preceding him, he made his first visit to the UK in 1936, but in his first appearance in the Amateur Championship he was beaten in the very first round by Morty Dykes, an ebullient and powerful Glasgow golfer, whose

achievement pitched him into the Walker Cup at Pine Valley. Locke was leading amateur in the Open at Carnoustie in 1937, which was won by Henry Cotton, and when Locke turned professional in 1938 he set about dethroning King Cotton. Head-to-head challenge matches were something of the order of the day, but Cotton, king of the golfing castle at that time, saw no profit in possibly being defeated by this talented youngster. Eventually a four-ball challenge over 72 holes, at £500-a-side over Walton Heath, proved too tempting for him. Partnered with the 1938 Open Champion, Reg Whitcombe, Cotton had to play brilliantly to put away Locke and his fellow South African partner, by a mere 2 and 1.

As a pilot in the South African Air Force during the Second World War, Locke flew Liberators, mainly in the Western Desert and the Mediterranean theatres. By 1947, he was ready for his first tilt at America. That year he finished third in the US Open, second leading money-winner and with four tournaments to his credit, against such opposition as Byron Nelson, Ben Hogan, Sam Snead and Jimmy Demaret.

So successful was Bobby in America that, to their lasting shame, the US PGA sought to suspend him and ban him for playing there – for no reason but that he was a foreigner taking their money. He won a tournament there in each of four yearly visits, but by 1950 had turned his attention to Europe and the rest of the world, winning variously the open championships of New Zealand, Canada, Germany, Switzerland and France, and in the UK a dozen or more commercial tournaments. Locke was a careful man. He invested much of his large

earnings and winnings in Johannesburg property.

He could be dry, even sardonic. He would say to a young player, 'Great round son, what did you score?' or 'Tell me about your round, start at the 18th.' As slender as a Zulu spear in his youth, he became more and more portly as the years passed and would amble down the fairway like an Edwardian bishop, clad always in his distinctive uniform of white shoes, white socks, white shirt and tie (of all things) and grey or navy plus fours, when the fashion was for exotic sports shirts and slacks. The Americans never quite knew what to make of Locke, calling him 'Old Muffin Face', and mocking his 'knickers'. None of this perturbed a temperament that took everything in its stride. He had an exceptional memory – if he went back to a club where he had played an exhibition match ten years earlier, he would remember everyone, and by name, that he had met then.

Technically, in his best years, he was totally distinctive, hooking every shot, even short pitches, and on the drive aiming off a good 50 yards then drawing the ball remorselessly back to the centre of the fairway. His ball control was exceptional, as was his judgement of distance from, say, 100 yards to the pin. But above all, Bobby Locke will be remembered as one of the greatest putters ever known in golf. Growing up on the nappy greens of Johannesburg's Rand courses, he was an impeccable judge of line and distance on the greens. He was seldom past the hole, almost never short, having his putts die as they reached the hole side. And his procedure with every putt was unchanging – a look at the line from behind the ball to the green, crouching, then

a very close inspection of the ground for 12 inches around the hole, then back to the ball, two little practice swings, and away the ball would go, from a hooded blade targeted to the hole.

He was often indicted for being a slow player. True, he did pad along rather between shots. But when he reached his ball, he had done all his thinking, was clear in his mind the shot that he wanted, and played it without the slightest delay or hesitation. And of course he played at a time when courses were not so strictly stewarded as they are now, and always had to fight his way through crowds to get to a tee or green. He once said that he could not remember when he last played golf without a gallery. Even when he played with friends at home in Johannesburg, it seemed that half a dozen people would materialise from out of the bushes and follow them along.

At the end of his active career, he was badly injured when his car was struck by a train at a level crossing near his home. He lost the sight of an eye, but shook off this and other injuries to get back into action, rather like Ben Hogan, when it was considered he would never play again. If Bobby Locke is not rated quite at the same level in the pantheon of the game as Vardon, Hagen, Jones, Hogan and Nicklaus, he is very, very close, and his career opened the way for Gary Player and a generation of South African international players to follow his path.

LONGHURST, Henry

Journalist, author and broadcaster, Henry Longhurst was awarded the CBE for his services to golf and was one of the few people to be made an honorary member of the

Royal and Ancient Golf Club of St Andrews. He played for the Cambridge University golf team in the years from 1928 to 1931, and captained a Cambridge University team which toured the United States in 1930. It was the first of many trips he was to make across the Atlantic Ocean.

After graduation he found a job writing on golf for the London *Evening Standard*, and from then on, constantly expressed his amazement that he should be paid for doing something which he loved to do. And always there would be someone to take care of the expenses – most of the time in the shape of a newspaper magnate. 'His Lordship will pay,' Longhurst would say. As a player, he was good enough to have won the German Open Amateur Championship in 1936, finish runner-up in the French Open Amateur of 1937, and hold a scratch handicap for 25 years.

Perhaps Longhurst's greatest single achievement, seldom if ever matched in the annals of sports journalism, was in writing a column for *The Sunday Times* each week for 25 years without interruption, in the post-war period. His style was discursive, seldom writing about professional events, but rather of the delights and anguishes of the game and of its personalities, of golf clubs and committees and the chores of captaincy and the like. He wrote several books – *Round in 68, Always on a Sunday, It was Good while it Lasted* among them.

He was particularly proud of, and successful in, touching on life and its many aspects whenever opportunities arose. 'A man must try everything once,' was his creed. Thus he could boast of having gone down the Cresta Run; flown in a helicopter across the Rockies when helicopters were a good deal less common than

allowing the picture to tell most of the story, astonished and intrigued the Americans, accustomed as they are to the incessant chattering of their own sports commentators. Television, as it will, made Longhurst a familiar face, and famous, but his place in the literature of the game puts him clearly beside Bernard Darwin.

LOPEZ, Nancy

Born 1957

Nationality United States

Turned Pro 1977

Majors LPGA Championship 1978, 1985, 1989

Any young American who can win a state championship at the age of 12 is surely on the way to a great career in golf. So it was with Nancy Lopez. Introduced to the game at the age of eight by her father Domingo, Nancy took to it so eagerly that she won the New Mexico Women's Amateur, against all the grown-ups, at that age, then the USGA Junior Girls' Championship twice, in 1972 and 1974. Thus in her teens, she was clearly an outstanding prospect. In 1975 she won the Mexican Women's Amateur, and entering the US Open that year, still an amateur and still a teenager, she finished second. She played in winning US Curtis Cup and World Amateur teams in 1976.

This was impressive enough, but her achievement in her first year as a professional, 1978, was quite staggering. She won no fewer than nine tournaments, five of them in succession and

Henry Longhurst who enjoyed his life and good times.

they are now; dived (in full commercial diver's equipment) into the murky waters of the Persian Gulf off Abadan; and taken a BOAC (British Overseas Airways Corporation) proving flight to Hong Kong, before that

service was inaugurated after the Second World War. Towards the end of the war, he had been a Member of Parliament for two years.

His fluency with the language took him easily into the world of television and he was effectively its first BBC commentator. In effect that meant Henry standing with a microphone and one camera behind the last green at a

tournament at Moor Park or some such London course. As television developed and extended its coverage of the game, so Longhurst became the voice of golf, erudite, discreet, selective, and matter of fact. He proved an outstanding mentor for Peter Alliss and other commentators who followed him. His philosophy of the 'inspired silence', and of

Nancy Lopez of the United States in Solheim Cup uniform, 1990.

including the first of her three LPGA Championship titles. She became an instant national figure and her effect on women's professional tournament golf was incalculable. The following year she won eight events including a successful defence of her Colgate European Open at Sunningdale, and it was clear that a player phenomenal by any standard was now gracing the game.

From 1978 to 1992, she won at least one tournament each year save in 1986, the year of the birth of her second of three daughters. She totalled wins in 46 official events, further LPGA Championships in 1985 and 1989, reached $1 million in prize money in only five years of professional play, married baseball player Ray Knight, raised three daughters and collected awards galore. She combined the sunniest of smiles and a relaxed personality with both a fierce competitive spirit and an unassailable standard of sportsmanship. She also had a very distinctive swing. Nancy's first observable action is a slight raising of the left wrist. The club is then taken away and back, noticeably outside the line, into a wide arc and a long backswing which has the club shaft, at the top of the backswing, slightly past horizontal and slightly across the line. But then it comes down very much inside the line and sends the ball very long distances indeed. Nancy has always been aggressive and positive in her shotmaking and has been a quite marvellous putter, all of which has brought her low rounds in competition, including an exceptional performance in the Henredon Classic of 1985. She scored 268, twenty under par, with a total of 25 birdies in four rounds of golf.

Yet for all that, Nancy has still to win the US Open in spite of being runner-up three times – in 1975 as an amateur, and in 1977 and 1989.

LYLE, Alexander 'Sandy'

Born	1958
Nationality	British
Turned Pro	1977
Majors	Open Championship 1985; US Masters 1988

Sandy Lyle was born to golf. He was no age at all when, shod in a pair of outsize wellies, he started swinging cut-down clubs. The game was bred in him, literally. His father Alex, a Scot, was the professional at Hawkstone Park in Shropshire, not far from Shrewsbury where Lyle was born.

He developed into a precocious talent and by the time Sandy was 15 his father realised 'he was going to be special. I could tell from the way he worked his way round the course,' Alex Lyle said.

At 16, Lyle, who had idolised Arnold Palmer and Jack Nicklaus and wanted to emulate them, said that his ambition was to win the Open within ten years – as it turned out he was a year out. At 17, he became the youngest winner of the Brabazon Trophy (the English Open Amateur Strokeplay championship) and represented England at three levels – as a boy, youth and full international. He won the Brabazon again in 1977 and played, without success, in the 1977 Walker Cup match at Shinnecock.

Undaunted, he turned professional that year, won the qualifying school, won the Nigerian Open in 1978 and was rookie of the year, succeeding Nick Faldo, perhaps his greatest and most

natural rival over the years. Faldo was to prove more prolific – although both have many competitive years left in them still – but Lyle had the satisfaction of doing several things before his rival, including declaring himself a Scot for team purposes and winning the order of merit in 1979 (and 1980 and 1985) and, of course, winning the Open in 1985 and the Masters in 1988.

The victory at Royal St George's, the first Open win by a Briton since Tony Jacklin's triumph at Royal Lytham in 1969, was described by some as lucky but Jacklin was unstinting in his praise. 'I've never seen anyone who strikes the ball better,' he said. And Henry Cotton, who won the first of his three Opens at St George's in 1934, said, 'If I'd had Lyle's power, I'd have won everything.'

The Lyle style is not all languid grace and ease, but when it is working, when the rhythm is there and the old-established tendency to swing too flat is under control (his father used to have Lyle swinging close to the wall of the garage and if he hit the wall, he knew his swing was too flat), it is awesomely effective. He has the ability to hit shots that look impossible – that probably *are* impossible for most people – without fuss or preamble. It all seems, like the man himself, deceptively simple. 'I'm a bit of a plodder,' Lyle once said with characteristic self-deprecation, but plodders do not compile his sort of record.

In 1986 he did not win in Europe but he did win the Greater Greensboro Open and in 1987 he confirmed his theory that US courses should suit him by winning the Tournament Players' Championship, the would-be fifth major. 'What's the difference between the TPC and the Open?' an

American asked him.

'About 125 years,' was the laconic Lyle riposte.

A little later that year his first marriage ended, but he went on to play his part in Europe's Ryder Cup victory at Muirfield Village, their first on American soil, and for the early part of 1988 he was simply majestic. He won at Phoenix, Greensboro and Augusta, becoming the first Briton to wear the coveted green Masters jacket. He had to birdie the last hole to win and did just that, hitting what golf historian Herb Warren Wind called the 'greatest bunker shot in the history of the game' (with a seven iron) to ten feet. He also won the Dunhill British Masters and the Suntory World Matchplay championship, beating Faldo in the final.

It was a year of years and yet it was followed by virtually a complete breakdown of his game and confidence. The man who could not stop winning the year before could not stop missing cuts, and the slump was so severe that Lyle, a member of the previous five Ryder Cup teams, asked not to be selected for the 1989 match at the Belfry. Was the child prodigy 'golfed out' at an age when he should have been in his prime?

Victory in the BMW International Open in Munich in October 1991 indicated there was competitive life in the mature Lyle (who had remarried in 1989) and he confirmed it with two victories in 1992, including the Volvo Masters at Valderrama, which he described as his most crucial win since the Masters in the heady days of 1988.

Scotland's pride and joy, Sandy Lyle, Open winner in 1985, US Masters winner in 1988, plots the route to the hole.

M

MACDONALD, Charles

The beginnings of golf as a formalised game in America came with the foundation of the United States Golf Association in 1894, and the new organisation was blessed with men of distinction and probity in such names as Havemeyer, Tallmadge, Curtis and Vanderbilt. And very prominent among them was one Charles Blair Macdonald from Chicago, who was to make a powerful contribution to American golf as a player, an administrator and above all a golf course architect. Indeed it may be true to say that he dominated the 'new' game as did no other in his generation.

Macdonald was the son of a Scottish father and Canadian mother, and was born in Niagara Falls, Ontario. His father, who had become successful in business in Chicago, sent him over to school in St Andrews in 1872 when he was 16. The boy became enchanted with the town and the game of golf, and almost certainly was able to see the Morrises, 'Old Tom' and 'Young Tom', and other worthies such as Davie Strath, play the course.

A dominant and pugnacious personality in the early days of the United States Golf Association, Charles Blair Macdonald was also a powerful player.

He became particularly friendly with Old Tom Morris and frequented his shop.

Back in Chicago in 1875, Charles had nowhere to indulge in golf, his new affectation, and in despair he knocked golf balls around an old Civil War army training ground. But five business trips to the British Isles over the next decade kept him in touch with the happenings in the game, and by 1892 he had persuaded a group of friends to pitch in enough money to allow him to design and build nine holes of golf on farmland at Belmont, 25 miles from the city centre. The Chicago Golf Club was born. The next spring he was able to add nine more holes, and in 1894 he persuaded the members to buy a 200-acre farm at Wheaton, in the same general area. So Chicago, then considered by Americans to be 'the west', had 18 holes of Macdonald-designed golf when all the people back east were stuck

with nine-hole courses.

His time in St Andrews had made Macdonald a fine player. When the Newport Club invited all the other clubs to send players to a tournament in September 1894 which would decide the country's best player, Charles was very much on hand to tackle the two rounds of medal play.

When his ball landed beside a stone wall on the course, he was penalised two shots. When he lost the 'championship' by one, Macdonald promptly protested against the penalty. He was a large, stubborn, opinionated man, a Teddy Roosevelt type, forceful in many ways. He claimed that in any case this was simply one club's competition. He said a proper championship should be match play, the St Andrews way, and this Newport thing should be declared 'no contest'.

The St Andrews Club of New York thereupon announced that it would stage a match play competition the following month which would settle things. And when Macdonald was beaten in that final, he said he had been ill, and in any case, one club could not claim to stage a 'national' championship – all the clubs must be involved. In a sense, Macdonald's outpourings over these two events may well have hastened the formation of the USGA, and when representatives from five clubs met in New York that winter to form the organisation, Charles Blair Macdonald was one of them, wearing the mantle of the Chicago Golf Club. He was able to claim that he was the first official amateur champion when he won the 1895 event, run by the USGA and at match play, of course.

Macdonald and his family moved to New York in 1900, where he became a partner in a stockbroking firm, but this left him lots of time to a) constantly harangue the leaders of the game in maintaining an almost revolutionary attitude to the playing of the game and its rules and b) work on the design of golf courses. He became obsessed with the idea that he should build a course in America which would include many of the design characteristics which he recalled from British links courses. Starting in 1902, he made annual visits to the Old Country, playing the courses and charting in detail the holes which appealed to him. He did this for five summers, at the same time searching exhaustively along the eastern seaboard of the United States to find an ideal location for his course.

He eventually chose 250 acres on Peconic Bay, near Southampton at the eastern end of Long Island. The ground was not quite linksland, the turf being of inland quality, but there was gentle movement in the ground and almost always wind off Long Island Sound on the one hand and the Atlantic Ocean on the other.

Macdonald incorporated the features of various Scottish holes, the Alps at Prestwick, the Redan at North Berwick, the Eden and Road Holes at St Andrews. Construction started in 1907 and the course was first played in 1909, at 6,100 yards following the age-old St Andrews routeing of nine out, nine back. It was the first great American golf course, attracting from all over the country groups contemplating the building of courses in their own localities but anxious to note the subtleties with which Macdonald had indulged himself at Peconic Bay. He was invited to design other courses. He did relatively few, including notably Mid Ocean in Bermuda. For Charles Blair Macdonald, the Long Island course would be his cenotaph. It was lengthened, improved, cossetted. He called it, with characteristic certainty, The National Golf Links of America.

MACKENZIE, Dr Alister

It is given to few men to make an impact on the world in three different disciplines. It was to Alister (Alexander) Mackenzie – in medicine, in the business of military camouflage, and in golf course architecture.

Born in Yorkshire of Scottish parents, he took degrees at Cambridge University in medicine, chemistry and natural science. He served at the turn of the century in the South African War, as a surgeon in The Somerset Light Infantry, and became so intrigued with the ability of the Boers to camouflage themselves on the open veld that he made a study of it. After the war, he resumed his practice in Leeds, and as a member of the greens committee at the

The Augusta National, Cypress Point and Royal Melbourne are among the achievements of architect Dr Alister Mackenzie.

local Alwoodley Golf Club, amused himself by sketching layouts for greens, tees and fairway bunkering. When Harry Colt came to Alwoodley in 1907 to revise the course, he was Mackenzie's house guest, and was so impressed with the doctor's designs that he invited him to join in the work. They subsequently collaborated on several courses in the United States.

The attractions of a life in the open air as a course designer pulled more and more strongly at Mackenzie. He held that golf, combining fresh air, exercise and excitement, could make a unique contribution to health. He allowed his medical career to run down. In 1914, he won first prize in a Charles Blair Macdonald magazine competition for the design of a two-shot hole, to be used on The Lido course in Long Island, which Macdonald was planning. The First World War took Mackenzie back into service, first as a surgeon, but very soon into developing camouflage techniques which were widely applied and highly thought of.

After the war, he made his first visit to the US and worked with other architects such as Colt and Alison on several courses in the US and Canada. By 1920, he had so codified his thinking on course design in this new profession of his that he published *Golf Architecture*, with its 13 basic principles, among which were 'a course arranged so that the high handicap player or even the beginner should enjoy his round regardless of his score' and 'an infinite variety in the strokes so that the use of every club is required'.

Mackenzie was to design dozens of courses, particularly in the North of England. He worked on the Eden course at St Andrews, on Royal Troon, and revised quite substantially Lahinch in Ireland. He vied perhaps with Charles Alison in being the first truly international golf course architect, with a litany of courses in Uruguay, Argentina and New Zealand to his credit, and several in Australia. Three courses in particular have assured his immortality, as it were. They are the West Course of the Royal Melbourne club, Cypress Point on the Monterey Peninsula in California, and the Augusta National in Georgia.

When Mackenzie arrived to tackle Royal Melbourne's new West Course, he was impressed by two things – the property was on Melbourne's 'Sand Belt', a stretch of sand dunes, heather and bracken and native oak trees; and on hand was Alex Russell. Russell was a fine amateur golfer – oddly, Mackenzie himself was one of the few course designers who were *not* particularly good players – who had won the Australian Open of 1924 and designed Royal Melbourne's East Course. Mackenzie quickly enlisted him as an ally, and they produced a gem of a course, characterised by very powerful and positive bunkering, particularly greenside bunkering, and fairways that sloped uphill in the landing area. But Mackenzie's greens, sand-based, seriously contoured and lightning fast, were to be Melbourne West's greatest defences. Royal Sydney and Royal Adelaide, in each of which Dr Mackenzie did revision work, were given the same severe bunkering treatment.

His achievements in Australia, plus the hand of fate, brought him to Cypress Point. When Seth Raynor, a 'pupil' of Charles Blair Macdonald, died suddenly, Mackenzie was asked to replace him. Raynor had been given the original Cypress Point commission. Over a magnificent terrain of pine forests, soaring sand dunes, crisp sand-based turf and three dramatic clifftop locations, Mackenzie produced what is by general acclaim a course in the top ten of the world's great golf courses, and one which led on in turn to another of matching rank, the Augusta National.

After Bobby Jones retired from championship play in 1930, he asked Mackenzie to help him design the course. It was all but completed when the Scot died in 1934. Although these matters are relative, and subjective, it may be considered his finest work.

McCORMACK, Mark

Mark Hume McCormack, born in Chicago, was educated at William and Mary College and the Yale Law School, and was a good enough golfer to qualify for four US Amateur Championships and one US Open Championship. As a young lawyer in a very conservative Cleveland practice, his interest in golf led him to start arranging, with a friend, exhibition matches and appearances by professional golfers, and by 1958 he was representing Arnold Palmer, Dow Finsterwald and several other prominent players.

Palmer had won the 1958 Masters and was approaching the height of his career. Early in 1959 he came to McCormack and said that he could no longer handle the demands being made on him and needed help, and would McCormack consider managing him exclusively. Mark agreed, they shook hands on it, and that is the basis on which their relationship, one of the most remarkable and profitable in the business and sport of

golf, has been based. In the early 1960s, with Palmer's approval, McCormack undertook to manage the affairs of Gary Player and Jack Nicklaus, and the 'Big Three' was born. Palmer, Player and Nicklaus it seemed would win all the majors that were, throughout the sixties. They were certainly the dominant force in golf in that decade, and the writers' tag of 'Big Three' seemed to McCormack too good to complain about.

In the early sixties, McCormack founded a $500 company which was to be

the basis of IMG, the International Management Group, which by the 1990s had become a multi-billion dollar business in sports management and marketing in every conceivable respect. It has 40 offices in 20 countries throughout the world, employing directly and indirectly many hundreds of people.

IMG's television arm, Trans World International (TWI), is the world's largest independent producer of filmed and televised sports events. There is an international modelling agency, another representing classical music artists and orchestras – Dame Kiri Te Kanawa, Jose Carreras, Placido Domingo, the Oslo Philarmonic Orchestra, the St Petersburgh Philarmonic Orchestra. The McCormack operation includes television fees and contract negotiations on behalf of the Royal and Ancient Golf Club of St Andrews and the All-England Club at Wimbledon. There is a successful book publishing and packaging division, and in addition to providing tax and investment advice for individual clients, IMG is now doing the same with financial advice in the corporate field.

Among golfers, IMG manages Nick Faldo, Sandy Lyle, Ian Woosnam, Greg Norman and Bernhard Langer. It has created, and manages, such events as the Toyota World Match Play Championship, the Alfred Dunhill Cup, the Dunhill British Masters, the Lancome Trophy and the Johnnie Walker World Championship. It is involved in Alpine skiing, the Rugby World Cup Sevens, representing Olympic cities,

Sports tycoon Mark McCormack, good enough in his time to play in the Amateur Championship and US Amateur.

rock concerts, tennis championships galore. IMG is unique in world sport. But then so too is Mark McCormack, workaholic, world traveller, visionary with the capability to see sooner, further and faster than anyone else in his business, the future of sport.

MERION

The Merion Golf Club in
Ardmore, Philadelphia, is a
descendant of the Merion
Cricket Club, founded during
the period of the American
Civil War. When golf started
to become popular in the US
towards the end of the 19th
century, the cricket club
members played over a
rather catch-up course on the
estate of one Clement A
Griscomb. In 1896, the club
purchased 100 acres of land
away from the cricket club
and laid out nine holes of
golf. In 1900 this was
extended to 18. But as so
many other golf clubs were
finding, the coming of the
'Haskell' rubber wound ball
was foreshortening courses.
The Merion men moved even
further out of the city and
bought an abandoned farm,
the site of the present course.
The ground did not seem
especially attractive – a layer
of clay over rock and an old
abandoned stone quarry
were its features.

The club appointed a
committee of five to arrange
for the design and
construction of the new
course, and on the
committee was Hugh Irvine
Wilson, a Princeton graduate
and a member of the golf
team there. He had settled
into marriage and the
insurance business in
Philadephia. The Merion
committee made several
visits to the National Links at
Southampton to study the
work of Charles Blair
Macdonald there, and the
other members became
impressed with the aptitude
Wilson seemed to be
showing for the subtleties of
the business. They bundled
him off to Britain, where he
spent seven months

*The Merion Golf Club
near Philadelphia –
one of the classic US
Open courses.*

checking out the championship courses of Scotland and England, mapping, charting and observing. On his return, he applied various concepts that he had picked up to the new Merion. A big depression short of the 17th green was reminiscent of the Valley of Sin at St Andrews. His short third hole (186 yards) is based on North Berwick's 'Redan' hole. These elements are now considered basic concepts in the golf course architect's vocabulary. And Wilson decided to make a virtue of the quarry. Three holes, 16, 17 and 18, play right across it and make for one of the most taxing finishes in American golf.

The Ardmore property was fairly open and has since enjoyed a good deal of tree planting. Wilson's bunkers – 128 of them with distinctive white sand – and small fast greens are the critical elements in Merion's championship reputation, plus the beautiful balance of the holes. The course is squeezed into 127 acres, and its length of 6,523 yards makes it one of the shortest championship courses in golf. Yet such is the variety of shot-making required, and the tightness of the lines the player must take, that it has become widely praised as an American classic, a brilliant example of parkland architecture, and in the opinion of wise judges quite simply the best golf course in America.

It has been the scene of dramatic happenings. In 1916, Bobby Jones appeared there in his first US Amateur Championship at the age of 14. He won the first of his five titles at Merion in 1924, and six years later the last of them, completing his historic Grand Slam. In 1950, just over a year after his appalling car accident, Ben Hogan won the US Open at Merion. In 1971, Lee Trevino beat Jack Nicklaus after a play-off to win the first of three Opens in successive appearances – US, Canadian and British, an unprecedented achievement. And when ten years later David Graham became the first Australian to win the US Open Championship, his closing 67 at Merion was one of the finest last rounds in US Open history.

MICKLEM, Gerald

The public persona of Gerald Micklem was often arrogant to the point of being abrasive and verging on rudeness. A high-pitched, often strident voice added to the impression of a highly-strung character. No doubt much of it was a mask, perhaps to hide some inherent shortcoming.

Micklem contributed massively to golf as a player, an administrator and a supporter, in every sense, of golf's most deserving causes. He was the son of a wealthy stockbroker who left a handsome inheritance and

MERION		
HOLE	YARDS	PAR
1	365	4
2	536	5
3	186	3
4	600	5
5	418	4
6	428	4
7	353	4
8	362	4
9	183	3
OUT	3,431	36
10	310	4
11	369	4
12	378	4
13	130	3
14	413	4
15	378	4
16	429	4
17	222	3
18	463	4
IN	3,092	34
TOTAL	6,523	70

Gerald Micklem, English champion, Walker Cup player and captain, and captain of the Royal and Ancient club.

Gerald too had success in the City. He had been rich enough to retire from business early in life, and lived in comfort in a house close by the lovely Sunningdale courses, which he made his base. He had been an Oxford Blue, and a Guards officer who suffered a hand injury in France in 1940, which happily did not compromise his golf. After the war, he was English Amateur Champion in 1947 and 1953, and was four times a Walker Cup player and twice non-playing captain in the late forties and fifties. He played nine times for England.

As chairman of the Championship Committee of the R & A in the sixties, he was greatly responsible for advancing the Open Championship into an era of widening television exposure and corporate hospitality, marketing the championship and in general modernising and maximising every element of proceedings. He was president of the English Golf Union, president of the European Golf Association, and captain of the R & A in 1968. Born in 1911, he died in 1988.

MIDDLECOFF, Cary

Born 1921

Nationality United States

Turned Pro 1947

Majors US Open 1949, 1956. US Master 1955

The distinctive, dipping style of Dr Cary Middlecoff, twice winner of the US Open.

Dr Cary Middlecoff was 26 years old when he turned professional, having first qualified as a dentist. During that time he won his state (Tennessee) amateur title in four successive years from 1940. After only two years in professional golf, he was US Open Champion. He won again in 1956 and in defending that title, almost made it three – he tied with Dick Mayer, but lost the play-off. In winning the Masters in 1955, he holed an eagle putt on the 13th hole in the last round which was calculated at 80 feet! A slow and deliberate player, Middlecoff nevertheless won 37 events in the 12 years before he retired in 1961, at the age of 40, and was one of the outstanding players of the fifties.

MILLER, Johnny

Born 1947

Nationality United States

Turned Pro 1969

Majors Open Championship 1976; US Open 1973

A meteor that flashed across the desert skies in the early 1970s, Johnny Miller, a tall, blond Californian, seemed certain to take on the mantle of Palmer and Nicklaus, but a decade or so later the blinding light had vanished and Miller had all but turned his back on the game – the tournament game, that is, despite having joined that small band who have won the Open Championships of both Great Britain and the United States.

Miller was a San Francisco

For Johnny Miller, the seventies formed his magic decade, with Open Championships on both sides of the ocean.

boy, born in April 1947, who became a fine player and a member of the Brigham Young University golf team. While he was there, the US Open of 1966 was scheduled for his home course, the Olympic Club of San Francisco. Miller got himself on the caddy list, but in the event found himself asked to play as a last-minute reserve. Still in his teens, he finished eighth – but he had, after all, been US Amateur Junior Champion two years earlier, in 1964.

He turned professional in 1969, won his first tournament in 1971 and each year until 1976 he repeated. His year of 1974 was one to shatter records. He won the first three tournaments of the season, which had never been done before. He won eight tournaments in all, the most since Arnold Palmer had done the same in 1960. And only two people had ever bettered that – Byron Nelson with 18 in 1945 and Sam Snead with 10 in 1950.

From 1971 to 1983, Johnny Miller won 22 events on the US Tour, and one more in 1987. Many of them were won early in the year, when the Tour was in Southern California and the American Southwest of Arizona and New Mexico, so that Miller began to be thought of as a 'desert' player. But he was one who could produce dazzling bursts of scoring at any time and on any type of course.

He set a new low closing round in the US Open of 1973 over the feared Oakmont, and held off the young Severiano Ballesteros at Royal Birkdale in 1976 with a last round 66. His Oakmont round astonished America, since the course is considered one of the US Open's stiffest tests, usually with lightning fast greens. But rains had softened the course for that last round and Miller simply peppered the

flagsticks with a brilliant display of shotmaking with his irons. He was in fact a very good 'majors' player. He was second to Tom Weiskopf in the 1973 Open at Troon (coming that close to making it a 'double' year of both Opens), and in the Masters he was second to Charles Coody in 1971, to Jack Nicklaus in 1975 and Tom Watson in 1981. Other interests – church work, golf course architecture, club design – claimed his time. He became a forthright, occasionally acerbic, television commentator.

MONTGOMERIE, Colin

Born	1963
Nationality	British
Turned Pro	1987

Colin Montgomerie, the tall, powerful Scot, is seen as a key player in future world golf, and all of his early life seems to have been a preparation for that. Born in Glasgow, he took to the game easily, particularly when his father became secretary of Royal Troon. In amateur golf, he was runner-up to Jose Maria Olazabal in the Amateur Championship of 1984. He won the Scottish Stroke Play Championship of 1985, the Scottish Amateur Championship of 1987, and played on Walker Cup teams in these same years. On a golf scholarship at Houston Baptist University in Texas, he took a degree in business management and law.

Having turned professional in 1987, Montgomerie in the next five years racked up £1.5 million in prize money. His breakthrough came in

Colin Montgomerie, the powerful Scot, in action at Tryall in the 1992 Johnnie Walker World Championship.

the Portuguese Open of 1989, when his total of 264 put him 11 shots ahead of the field. Several times he had tournament rounds of 63. His victory in the Scandinavian Masters of 1991 probably confirmed his place in the Ryder Cup match of that year at Kiawah Island, where he had a sensational and critical singles match. Mark Calcavecchia led him by four shots with four holes to play, but Montgomerie claimed all of them to give Europe an unexpected half.

The high point of 1992 for Colin was probably the US Open at Pebble Beach. When he holed out in 70 for a level par 288 total, Jack Nicklaus asked him how it felt 'to be US Open Champion'. For once, Jack got it wrong – Tom Kite and Jeff Sluman were still on the course, and Montgomerie eventually finished in third place. A big, powerful man with a full, flowing swing, Colin occasionally has been short-tempered with his game, and his temperament may prevent him reaching the very peaks of the game.

MORRIS, Young Tom 1851–1875

Majors Open Championship 1868, 1869, 1870, 1872

Young Tom Morris was born in St Andrews in 1851, the year that his father, Old Tom, moved west to the Prestwick Club. The boy learned his golf there and learned it to good effect. He could be said to be the first of golf's great champions. His first public appearance, so to speak, was in Perth, when he disposed of Master William Greig, a prominent local juvenile, in a match before 'hundreds of deeply interested spectators'. Tom was 13. At the age of 16, he won a big professional tournament at Carnoustie,

prize money £20, tying with Bob Andrew of Perth and Willie Park of Musselburgh, the first Open Champion. They scored 140 over the 30 holes and young Tom won the play-off. Famous names of the time – Bob Ferguson, Jamie Anderson, and his father Old Tom – had competed.

The Open Championship of that year, 1867, saw Old Tom's fourth and final win. Young Tom finished fourth. He then won the championship in three successive years, winning the 'Belt' outright. He did it all with remarkable scoring. In 1868 he won by three shots from his father. In 1869, he won by 11 shots from Bob Kirk, and in 1870 by no fewer than 12 strokes from his close friend Davie Strath. These early championships were

Young Tom Morris, ranked by many with Bobby Jones and Ben Hogan as one of golf's few supreme champions.

played at Prestwick, home from home for the youngster and the course where he had learned the game, but nevertheless this was astonishing scoring. There was no championship in 1871 and 'Tommy' won again in 1872. In 12 years of the Open, the Morrises, father and son, had won eight times.

In September 1875, they went to North Berwick to tackle Willie and Mungo Park for £25 a side. They won on the last green. Tom was then handed a telegram with the news that his wife was dangerously ill. A yacht was put at their disposal to cross the Firth of Forth. When they arrived in St Andrews, Young Tom's wife and newly born child were dead. He never really recovered from this and died on Christmas Day of 1875, of a broken heart, the romantics say. The likelihood is that he died of pneumonia, like typhoid, jaundice and 'consumption' often a fatal illness of the time. There had been some doubts about his health earlier, since he made little impression on the Open Championship after 1872.

It is clear that in these few seasons, through his late teens and into his early twenties, young Morris was a meteor that exploded on to golf and left a permanent mark in the records. He played with the dash of an earlier Arnold Palmer or Severiano Ballesteros, standing well back from the ball. He was an immensely confident putter, on greens that were hayfields in comparison to the immaculate surfaces modern players expect.

Such was his esteem that clubs throughout the country, including from England Westward Ho!, Blackheath, Wimbledon and Liverpool, contributed to a memorial stone at his grave in St Andrews Cathedral churchyard. It bears an image of Young Tom in golfing posture, and reads:-

'Deeply regretted by numerous friends and all golfers, he thrice in succession held the championship belt and held it without rivalry and yet without envy, his many amiable qualities being no less acknowledged than his golfing achievements.'

When his father, Old Tom, a man of probity and dignity, died 33 years later, a small memorial stone for him was laid on the grave. It remains a place of pilgrimage for golfers from every country in the world.

MORRIS, Old Tom 1821–1908

Majors Open Championship 1861, 1862, 1864, 1867

Tom Morris the father is one of the great patriarchal figures in the history of the game. He lived throughout and beyond the reign of Queen Victoria, and his life encompassed the end of the feathery ball, the life and death of the gutty ball, the first huge expansion of the game beyond Scotland, and after a fashion the evolution of golf course architecture to which he himself made a substantial contribution.

Born in North Street, St Andrews, Tom like most of his peers was playing golf before he was into his teens, left hand below right in the beginning, and he developed into a fine player. Destined, it appeared, to be a carpenter, in fact at the age of 18 he became apprenticed to Allan Robertson, the ball and clubmaker and a player of renown in challenge matches. Allan and Tom were to form a powerful playing partnership, in the main successful in grand money matches against the best of North Berwick and Musselburgh, the other centres of excellence in the mid-19th century. Some of these were for several hundreds of pounds, huge amounts at the time.

After a four-year apprenticeship, Tom worked a further five with Robertson. The latter, a very successful maker of 'feathery' balls, feared the coming of the 'gutty' ball around 1848, and rejected it out of hand. Tom Morris, on the other hand, realised that the new ball was here to stay, and there was a parting of the ways, Morris starting business on his own. In 1851, he was approached by one Colonel

Fairlie, an Ayrshire man of property, and asked to come to the Prestwick club, newly formed, as 'Custodian of the Links'. As such, Morris brought some definition to the 12 holes the Prestwick people were playing, and saw the club into the launching of the Open Championship, first played in 1860 for 'The Belt'. In that very first event, Willie Park of Musselburgh beat Tom by one stroke; over the next seven years, Tom won four times. He went on to compete in every Open until 1896, into the era of Vardon, Braid and Taylor.

With all this going on in the west, the Royal and Ancient decided that for the very first time, they should have their own professional golfer. At the General Meeting in May 1864, it was decided that:-

'Thos. Morris of Prestwick, formerly of St Andrews, be brought here as professional golfer at a salary of (£50) Fifty pounds a year, on the understanding that he shall have the entire charge of the Golf Course, and be responsible for it being kept in proper order, and that he shall be the servant of the club under the direction and control of the Committee in charge of the green.'

Clearly, the members made little distinction between 'professional' and 'greenkeeper'. In January of the following year, Tom was called in to a full meeting of members in the clubhouse, and:-

'was given a detailed account of his duties, was told that he could employ one man's labour two days a week for heavy work such as carting, and was solemnly handed the implements of his craft – a barrow, a spade and a shovel.'

Tom Morris was indeed a 'servant of the club', from then until 1904. His portrait hangs in the R & A clubhouse

to this day. In their thousands, the citizens of St Andrews attended his funeral in 1908.

MUIRFIELD

The world's greatest golf course? The Old Course at St Andrews apart (for it is a thing apart), no two golfers are likely to agree on the answer. It is a taxing, perhaps after all ridiculous question, since golf courses can scarcely be quantified; but what is certain is that in any discussion of the subject, the name Muirfield is sure to be prominent.

The course of the Honourable Company of

Edinburgh Golfers at Gullane, East Lothian, 20 miles east of Edinburgh on the south shore of the Firth of Forth, Muirfield is a classic of golf course architecture. It was the first course designed in two loops of nine holes, the first nine going round the perimeters of the property in a clockwise direction, the second nine contained inside the first and running anticlockwise. And since never more than three successive holes run in the same direction, any wind that blows at Muirfield afflicts the golfer from all points in the course of a round.

Muirfield's greatest single quality is its honesty. None of its subtleties are hidden, or even disguised. There is but one blind shot, the drive over a ridge at the 11th hole. It is all fair and open, and perfectly balanced. There are no trees or water in play. By comparison with the championship courses at Carnoustie and St Andrews, which are public, Muirfield is little played and is therefore almost always in beautiful condition. It was not, however, always so highly thought of. Indeed in its original form, it was damned by Andrew Kirkaldy, the St Andrews pro, at the end of the 1892 Open Championship as 'an auld watter meadie – I'm glad I'm gaun hame'.

The original course was designed by Old Tom Morris and 16 holes, built by hand and horse, were opened in May of 1891, and two more in December. Muirfield's first Open, played the very next year, was won by Harold Hilton of Liverpool, an amateur and an Englishman to boot, with his Hoylake clubmate John Ball in joint second place. No doubt all that coloured Kirkaldy's judgement.

That was the first championship anywhere played over 72 holes. Four more Opens were played at Muirfield before 1914, and several changes were made with the years. Indeed many were convinced that Muirfield did not become a truly great course until Harry Colt (of Sunningdale fame) and Tom Simpson were brought in to make the changes which made the present Muirfield quite magnificent. Perhaps its outstanding feature is the bunkering faced with revetted turfs, straight faces, powdery sand, and as tall as a man stands. One of these brought the great Arnold Palmer a score of ten at the 14th hole in the 1987 Open Championship.

The deceptively subtle landscape of Muirfield, East Lothian, considered by many to be the finest of the Open Championship courses.

N

NAGLE, Kelvin

Born 1920

Nationality Australian

Turned Pro 1946

Majors Open Championship 1960

Born in Sydney, Kel Nagle had one of golf's longest tournament careers, from his first Australian Professional Championship win in 1949 on into the 1970s. He won the Australian Open in 1959, then the Centenary Open at St Andrews in 1960, where he held off Arnold Palmer. He tied with Gary Player in the US Open of 1965, but lost the play-off. Kel was a quiet, unassuming, friendly man with an uncomplicated technique which brought him a score or more of wins around the world. He won World and British Senior titles in the seventies, and played nine times in Canada/World Cup matches for Australia, winning twice.

NELSON, Byron

Born 1912

Nationality United States

Turned Pro 1932

Majors US Open 1939; US Masters 1937, 1942; US PGA 1940, 1945

John Byron Nelson was born in Forth Worth, Texas on 4 February 1912, the son of a grain and feed merchant who had a house close to the city's Glen Garden golf course. By the age of ten,

Kel Nagle of Australia, Centenary Open (1960) Champion, with trophy and personal replica.

young Nelson had been well and truly introduced to the game in the caddy shed there, where a contemporary was Ben Hogan. At the age of fifteen, Byron saw Walter Hagen win his fourth successive PGA Championship, at nearby Dallas. Thus inspired, Byron went on to have a career which brought him five major championships, a total of 66 tournaments won and some quite staggering scoring achievements in 1944, 1945 and 1946. Dubbed 'Lord Byron' and 'Mr Golf' by the American sports writers, Nelson retired at the end of 1946 aged a mere 34, and strangely is often overlooked when supreme champions of the game are considered.

To some extent this may have been due to a rather self-effacing personality which covered the hard core any golfer with his successes must have had. Then again, his prime years were those of the Second World War and immediately afterwards; but even more significantly, Nelson's career was over before television came along to revolutionise the public awareness of the game.

Byron's first success was regional, in the South West Amateur Championship of 1930. He turned professional in 1932, but he earned so little money that year that he simply gave up professional golf and found a job in the oil business in Texas. Before long, his boss realised that Nelson's heart was not in the work and that in truth he still hankered after golf. He found him a job at the local Texarcana Golf Club. In 1934, second place finishes in the tournaments at San Antonio and Galveston were

encouraging and helped Nelson to a job at the Ridgewood club in New Jersey.

In the East, he found much more competition and in 1936 he broke through with a victory in the Metropolitan Open. The next year he arrived on the national scene. He won the Masters with one of the most dramatic and concentrated reverses in Augusta history. In the last round, Nelson gained six strokes in two holes over Ralph Guldhal, the leader, to win the first of his five major honours. Nelson scored the par-3 12th in 2, the par-5 13th in 3. Guldhal, in water hazards at each of these testing holes, scored them in 5 and 6. That same year, Byron Nelson was a member of the US Ryder Cup team, the first to win on British soil, and finished fifth (top American) in the Open Championship won by Henry Cotton at Carnoustie.

In 1938, he won tournaments in California, Florida and Georgia, but was becoming increasingly concerned about his swing and a habit of cocking his left wrist at the top of the backswing which he felt was making him inconsistent. The changes which Nelson made to his golf swing were to have a profound effect on all the generations which followed him. After much trial and error in the practice, Nelson found a 'new' swing which he was convinced would bring him more control, more accuracy. At the start of the swing, he took the clubhead straight back and kept it low for as long as possible, with the face of the club square to the target line as it had been at impact. This meant that his wrists did not cock, his forearms did not rotate as with current practice, and halfway up the backswing, the club was 'lifted' up in an almost vertical plane, with the right hip allowed to slide

to the right, the right elbow to drift away from the body. At the top of the swing, the left wrist would be straight in line with his forearm. In the simplest terms, it was an upright swing, severely pruned and simplified in comparison with the long, elegant swings of Bobby Jones and all the earlier hickory-shaft players.

The downswing was started with vigorous leg action and a sliding of hips to the left. There was a dip of the knees at impact, when his left wrist would still be straight, with the back of the hand square to the target. Variations of the Nelson action were copied and could be seen subsequently in the floating right elbow of Jack Nicklaus and the driving leg action of Tom Watson, one of Nelson's friends and proteges.

Having disposed of his rather flat swing in favour of this upright technique, Byron Nelson went to work. He won the US Open in 1939, after a play-off against Craig Wood and Densmore Shute. This was the championship in which Sam Snead took eight on the final hole, when a par-5 would have won it. In that same year, Byron started an exceptional run in the US PGA Championship, then a match play tournament. He lost in the final, then won in 1940, was a finalist in 1941 and 1944, and won again in 1945.

After a two year wartime hiatus, the US professional tour was able to schedule 22 tournaments in 1944. Nelson won eight of them, four in a row at one point. Indeed in 17 of these events, he finished in the first three and averaged 69.67 strokes. In 1945, he finished first or second in the year's opening tournaments. Then starting on 11 March, Nelson was touched with some strange magic. He won successively in Miami, Charlotte,

'Lord Byron' Nelson – his record of winning 19 tournaments in 1945, eleven of them in succession, will surely never be equalled.

Greensboro, Durham, Atlanta, Montreal, Philadelphia, Chicago, Dayton Ohio (the PGA Championship), Chicago again, and finally Toronto – 11 events, five months without losing, and often winning by ten clear shots. In 1945, Byron Nelson won 19 golf tournaments. He played 113 events without missing a cut. He averaged 68.33 strokes per round. There has been nothing like it in the history of the game.

In 1946 he won the first two tournaments of the year, entered 21, won six and even lost a play-off for the US Open to Lloyd Mangrum. Then he began to talk of retirement – 'I feel 100 years old,' he said at one point. At the end of that year he did retire to the cattle ranch he had bought at Roanoke, near Fort Worth. Apart from a non-playing Ryder Cup captaincy (his US team won at Royal Birkdale in 1965) and a little television commentary, Byron seemed content to be finished with the tournament game. Typically, during a European jaunt in 1955, he entered the French Open and won it with a staggering display of shotmaking. He was 43 years old.

Byron Nelson was efficient and non-demonstrative. He so seldom made mistakes that the daring elements of his play were almost always overlooked. He was, after all, the 'Mechanical Man' of golf, they said. Without the elegance of Snead or the power of Hogan, he made it look easy. He was pleasant, friendly and unassuming, but his achievement in the game was immense.

NELSON, Larry

Born 1948

Nationality United States

Turned Pro 1971

Majors US Open 1983; US PGA 1981, 1987

Apart from winning three major championships, which precious few men have done, Larry Gene Nelson has one particular claim to fame. He did not hit one single golf shot until he was 21 years old. His interest started in Vietnam, of all places. Nelson served there as an infantryman in 1968, and had a friend who never stopped talking about golf. When he was discharged, Nelson worked at a driving range, got a job at a club in Georgia, and turned professional six months later. He was 26 years old when he joined the US Tour. Nelson has been a quiet man of golf, playing and behaving conservatively in everything he does. An incomplete vertebra in his back has caused him intermittent trouble, and he largely confined his appearances to the South Eastern states of America. For all that, he played in three Ryder Cup matches and had tournament successes in Japan.

NICKLAUS, Jack

Born 1940

Nationality United States

Turned Pro 1960

Majors Open Championship 1966, 1970, 1978; US Open 1962, 1967, 1972, 1980; US Masters 1963, 1965, 1966, 1972, 1975, 1986; US PGA 1963, 1971, 1973, 1975, 1980

In terms of competitive achievement, Jack Nicklaus will be regarded as the dominant golfing figure of the 20th century who set standards that almost certainly will never be equalled. He won more major titles than any other player in the history of the game during a championship career that was one of the longest on record and spanned three decades.

During that time, he collected 18 of the acknowledged major championships of the world and in 1972 held three of the four Grand Slam titles – the US Masters, US Open and US PGA from the previous year – and was beaten by a stroke for the British Open at Muirfield. Only Ben Hogan before him had ever held three major titles at the same time.

Nicklaus was not a renowned stroke-maker nor did he bring a distinctive style or innovative technique to the game. He was, however, exhaustively thorough in his preparation for a championship. He was the first champion to produce personal yardage charts of golf courses, to take the guesswork out of club selection, particularly on seaside courses that lacked definition.

He left nothing to chance, and kept his notes from year to year so that he could even determine whether the texture of sand in bunkers had been changed. During practice for one championship, he deliberately drove into the rough to assess the kind of lie he would find for his second shot.

His thoroughness extended even to his own golf technique and every year before the start of the tournament season, he would return to his old instructor Jack Grout, who taught him from childhood, and in essence learned the game again as a beginner to eliminate any basic faults that might have crept into his golf swing during the previous season.

Such diligence earned him two US Amateur titles, six US Masters, four US Opens, three British Opens and five US PGA Championships during a career in which he amassed a total of seventy victories on the US circuit as well as winning the Australian Open six times and capturing the World Matchplay Championship once.

He was born in Columbus, Ohio, on 21 January 1940, and his father Charles, a local pharmacist, was an enthusiastic player who arranged for his only son to have lessons at the local Scioto Country Club. Nicklaus was 10 years old at the time, but even at that early age demonstrated the exhaustive thoroughness that was to become the hallmark of his golfing life. When the other children left the practice ground after the lesson, Jack worked on until dusk.

Within six years he had won the Ohio State Open and by the time he was 19 had captured his first US Amateur title. A year later, while still an amateur, he came close to winning the US Open at Cherry Hills and finished runner-up to Arnold Palmer, who was to become a lifelong friend and rival. At that time, it seemed possible that Nicklaus could have remained an amateur and still beaten the best professionals in the world, as the legendary Bobby Jones had done in the 1920s.

Jones implored him to remain an amateur but Nicklaus turned professional in 1962 and within six months had scored his first victory when he defeated Arnold Palmer after an 18-hole play-off at the US Open at Oakmont. That year he won two other tournaments, and a year later he captured the US Masters and PGA titles. By 1966, when he won the British Open at Muirfield,

The greatest collector of major golf titles in the history of the game, Jack Nicklaus, entering his fifties, was becoming one of the world's major golf course designers.

he became only the fourth player in history after Gene Sarazen, Ben Hogan and Gary Player to win all four Grand Slam major titles, and it is a measure of his consistency that although he won the British title three times, he was also runner-up on seven other occasions.

At the height of his powers, Nicklaus emerged as a statesmanlike figure in the game and is credited personally with reviving interest in what had become a US-dominated Ryder Cup match by persuading British officials to allow Continental Europeans to join their team. The result was a complete transformation of fortunes as Seve Ballesteros (Spain) and Bernhard Langer (Germany) combined with Nick Faldo, Ian Woosnam and Sandy Lyle to secure a new balance of power so that by 1985 the European team won back the trophy for the first time in 27 years and sparked off massive public interest.

By strange irony, the first ever European victory on American soil occurred on the course Nicklaus himself designed, at Muirfield Village in his native Ohio, and against a team of which he was non-playing captain. He accepted defeat gracefully at the hands of an old adversary Tony Jacklin, the European captain, whom he had faced as a player in the 1969 Ryder Cup match at Royal Birkdale. On that occasion Nicklaus conceded Jacklin's missable putt on the last green after a titanic duel and allowed the match to be tied because he thought it was an appropriate result.

When Jack turned fifty and qualified to play on the US Seniors Tour, in 1990, characteristically he won the first event he played in. Because of his many other interests, his Senior appearances were limited, but in 1991 he won the US PGA Seniors Championship, and the US Seniors Open Championship. In the main, he was devoting himself to golf course design work around the world and developed a distinctive style on dramatic and sometimes punitive landscapes. The best example of this is the St Mellion course near Plymouth, his first project in the British Isles. But even before he had finished his competitive career, Nicklaus had been voted 'Golfer of the Century' by one American magazine. It was a title to which only Jack Nicklaus could lay undisputed claim.

NORMAN, Greg

Born 1955

Nationality Australian

Turned Pro 1976

Majors Open Championship 1986, 1993

Beyond any reasonable doubt one of the world's top half-dozen golfers of the 1980s and 90s, Gregory John Norman, born 10 February 1955 in Mount Isa in the Queensland outback, might well have had half a dozen major championships by the time he was 35.

In the US Open of 1984 at Winged Foot, he lost in a play-off with Fuzzy Zoeller. When Greg holed a 40 foot putt from just off the green at the 72nd hole, Zoeller, seeing this from down the fairway, took a white towel from his bag and waved it as though in surrender – he thought wrongly that Norman had made a winning birdie instead of a par which

tied. In the 18 holes play-off the next day, Zoeller holed from 70 feet for a birdie on the second hole, where Norman dropped two strokes. Zoeller won with 67 to 75. It was a hard lesson for Norman – and there were more to come.

The fearsome finger of fate had not stopped pointing at him and the events of 1986 made the point. That year, Norman led the field going into the last round of each of the four major championships, yet won only one. In the first of the four, the Masters, he came to the last hole needing a par 4 to tie Jack Nicklaus's dazzling final round of 65 and total of 279. His shot to the green missed on the right. He scored five on the hole and took second place. At the US Open in June, at Shinnecock Hills, he had an altercation with a spectator who had cat-called him in the third round, led by one stroke going into the final round, but was overwhelmed by a stunning last round from Raymond Floyd, the winner, and took 75. In the Open Championship at Turnberry, a second round record-equalling 63 scattered the field and he won, at last, by five strokes.

At the last of the big four, the PGA Championship at the Inverness Club in Toledo, Ohio, Norman took a four shot lead into the final round, ahead of Bob Tway with rounds of 65, 68, 69. This was gradually frittered away until he and Tway were level at the last hole. Tway's second shot found a bunker. Norman's pitch spun back off the green. Tway holed from the bunker, Norman's chip missed. Last rounds, one way or the other, were a trial for Greg.

The next year at the Masters, he was beaten by another freak shot holed from off the green when Larry Mize chipped in from

30 yards at the 11th, the second extra hole of a three-way play-off, also involving Severiano Ballesteros. Then in the 1989 Open Championship at Royal Troon, Norman produced a dazzling final round 64 to tie with Wayne Grady and Mark Calcavecchia, but lost on the last hole of the four hole play-off to a brilliant birdie from Calcavecchia. So as he turned into the 1990s, Greg had won one and finished second five times.

Norman has always been an immense driver of the ball, hitting vast distances with telling accuracy, and he trained himself to be an excellent putter. He was, however a late starter. He caddied for his mother, who had a three handicap, but only started to play in earnest from the age of 16. Within a couple of years he was scratch. In his fourth tournament as a professional, the West Lakes Classic of 1976, he won after leading by a remarkable ten shots going into the last round.

In his first five years, he had won the Opens of Scandinavia, France, Europe, Hong Kong and Australia. He joined the US Tour in 1983 and in 1984 won two events, including the Canadian Open. His magical year of 1986 saw him become the first player to pass $1 million in prize money, winning among other events six consecutive tournaments – three in Europe, three in Australia. In that year he was leading money winner in the US, and again in 1990.

But 1993 was to be his annus mirabilis. In the Open Championship at Royal St George's, he became the first winner of an Open to break 70 in all four rounds, scoring 66, 68, 69 and 64. He described his golf that week by saying, 'In my entire career I have never gone round a course and not mis-hit a single shot.' He won by

Greg Norman, the great Australian, took the winner, Nick Faldo, all the way to a play-off in the Johnnie Walker World Championship at Tryall, Jamaica in 1992.

two strokes from Nick Faldo and by three from Bernhard Langer, who played with him during that staggering last round of 64. And as they came up the 18th fairway, Langer said to Greg, 'That is the greatest golf I have ever seen in my life.'

Norman's blond good looks and outgoing personality have been attractive to corporations and have enabled him to arrange hugely profitable contracts in endorsing and marketing a range of quality products. Increasingly, he has concentrated these into three or four major contracts concerning products in which he personally has an interest. As one of the outstanding personalities in golf, and a huge earner, he is a major client of his management company, IMG.

NORTH, Andy

Born	1950
Nationality	United States
Turned Pro	1972
Majors	US Open 1978, 1985

In a 20-year career, Andy North won two US Opens (one of the few men to have done so), one other professional tournament, and nothing else. Such a record, glorious and barren at the same time, is accounted for by a series of afflictions greater than anyone could be expected to bear. Nevertheless, in 1978 and 1985 he played on the US teams in the World Cup and Ryder Cup respectively.

In his school days in Madison, Wisconsin, North was a fine basketball player (he grew to be 6' 4" tall). In his early teens, it was discovered that a bone in his knee had stopped growing and was in fact disintegrating. He walked with irons for 18 months, during which time he was allowed to play golf – from an electric car. He was able to get back to basketball at a very high level, but took a golf scholarship at the University of Florida. Yet the doctors had not finished with Andrew Stewart North. In 1983, he had surgery for bone spurs in his right elbow. In 1987 and 1988 there were knee surgeries, and in 1989 operations on bone spurs in his neck! After the 1989 operations, he injured a shoulder and had to stop playing for the year. Finally in 1991, there were four separate operations to remove skin cancers on the nose and left cheek, with plastic surgery needed to 'rebuild' his face.

Andy North has but three wins in his entire career - two of them US Open Championships, in 1978 and 1985.

OAKMONT

The Oakmont course, a dozen miles north of Pittsburgh in the United States, has been described as the 'toughest course in the world'. To make it so was the clear intention of Henry Clay Fownes when he bought a 225 acre plot in the village of Oakmont in 1903. Fownes had decided that Pittsburgh should have a course to surpass any. He had qualified for the US Amateur of 1901, and his son William C Fownes Jr was brought up in the faith – he won the US Amateur Championship of 1910, qualifying for it 25 times, and was President of the United States Golf Association in 1926 and 1927.

And as far as the course was concerned, Bill was cut from the same cloth as his father. On the morning of 15 September 1903, father Fownes' workforce of 150 men and 50 mule teams broke the first sod. By the end of October twelve holes had been cleared, tees and greens laid, a watering system was in place and pre-winter seeding had been done. The following spring six more holes were completed and play began in the autumn of 1904. Henry Fownes had most of the trees taken out. He wanted the place to have a 'Scottish' look, the look of a links. Bunkering eventually totalled 350 in the early days. Oakmont was to be tough.

Bill Fownes in his time eventually devoted his entire life to the course. He lived in the clubhouse through the summer months. He would walk the course in the evenings with the greenkeeper Emil 'Dutch' Loeffler, discussing how Oakmont might be stiffened. He would observe closely good players in action, and if they were carrying fairway bunkers, or finding entrances to greens easily, Fownes would simply cut new bunkers to foil them. The Fownes philosophy was 'a shot poorly played should be a shot lost'.

The original Oakmont had eight par-5 holes, one par-6 and a card of 85. It was 6,600 yards in length at a time when the Haskell ball was only just coming into use, and steel shafts were a good 25 years away. The most penal of American courses, Oakmont has always been famous for its bunkering and above all its firm, rolling, lightning fast greens. One bunker along the 8th hole, the 'Sahara', is 75 yards long and 35 yards wide. Most famous of all is the 'Church Pews', a series of eight symmetrical, lateral traps between the 3rd and 4th fairways.

Since the course had been built on heavy clay, deep bunkering was impossible and the shallow bunkers were filled with heavy sand. From 1920, the Fownes had the bunkers furrowed with special rakes, designed with teeth two inches long and two inches apart to make the sand stand up as though it had been ploughed. The only shot playable from these traps would be a routine safety splash of a few yards.

The Fownes were men who got things done. The original property had a railway track cutting through it, in a valley. They simply bridged the railway, with seven holes designed on the far side. And later when the Pennsylvania Turnpike, one of America's first super-highways, was being routed, the Fownes arranged for it to run beside the railways, along the same valley.

The course was used for US Opens, Amateurs and PGA Championships, and until 1953 remained overpowering to the best players. That year, for its first Open after the Second World War, the club and the USGA made it less forbidding, reducing the bunkering. Ben Hogan scored a first round of 67 and overwhelmed the championship, winning by six strokes with 283. In the 1973 championship, Johnny Miller scored 63 with the lowest last round ever recorded in the US Open. Many observers claimed that it was another of those 'finest rounds every played'. Then in 1983, Larry Nelson scored the final 36 holes in 65, 67 for a record 132. But in each case, torrential rain had taken the fire out of the Oakmont greens, the 'fastest, truest, most difficult in America'.

Christy O'Connor in the long stuff at Tryall in the 1992 Johnnie Walker World Championship.

OAKMONT

HOLE	YARDS	PAR
1	467	4
2	346	4
3	425	4
4	564	5
5	382	4
6	199	3
7	435	4
8	253	3
9	478	5
OUT	3,549	36
10	462	4
11	370	4
12	602	5
13	185	3
14	360	4
15	456	4
16	232	3
17	324	4
18	456	4
IN	3,447	35
TOTAL	6,996	71

O'CONNOR, Christy

Born 1924

Nationality Irish

Turned Pro 1941

Probably the most popular and certainly the most successful of all Irish professionals, Christy O'Connor from Galway, known as 'Himself' to a legion of Irish admirers, has been a great Open Championship player without quite going the final mile to victory. He was joint third at Royal Lytham and St Annes in 1958, when Peter Thomson won from David Thomas in a play-off; fifth the next year at Muirfield when Gary Player won; third in 1961 when Arnold Palmer won at Royal Birkdale; and second again at Royal Birkdale in 1965, when Peter Thomson won his fifth title. And in 1969, Tony Jacklin's

year, Christy was fifth at the age of 45.

O'Connor was one of several fine players who were caught in the transitional decades of the 1950s and 60s, when golf professionals had to combine club responsibilities with tournament play. Tony Jacklin's example probably helped turn this around before the present extensive PGA European Tour, with its embracing Volvo sponsorship, came to fruition. Christy was a prolific tournament winner in Ireland and the UK, but seemed little interested in the Continental events. He won some 25 tournaments, excluding the Irish Professional Championship (10 times). He played in ten successive Ryder Cup matches, a record no one has equalled, and no fewer than 15 times for Ireland in the World Cup. He and Harry Bradshaw won it

for Ireland in Mexico City in 1958, when it carried its original name of the Canada Cup. In Senior golf, he won the PGA Seniors title six times, and the World Seniors title in 1976 and 1977.

His swing was long and flowing and at the top of the backswing the right hand was all over the place, but at impact and through the ball, Christy was as solid as anyone and masterly at improvising shots. In his peak years in the 1950s and 60s, whenever there was a big first prize, he was always the man to come roaring home with a low and winning last round. His career was remarkable for its longevity – in his fifth decade of competitive play, he finished second to Tommy Horton in the PGA Seniors Championship of 1992, over the Royal Dublin course, at a club he had served for 30 years.

OLAZABAL, Jose Maria

Born 1966

Nationality Spanish

Turned Pro 1985

Born to golf on 5 February 1966 at Fuenterrabia, Spain – his father was greenkeeper at the Real Golf Club de San Sebastian – Jose Maria Olazabal put together a remarkable amateur record. He actually won the Amateur Championship in 1984, beating Colin Montgomerie by 5 and 4 at Formby, before winning the British Youths Championship. His major amateur tally is: 1983 – Italian and Spanish Championships, British Boys Championship; 1984 – the Amateur Championship, Spanish Amateur Championship, Belgian International Youths Championship; 1985 – British Youths Championship.

Clearly bound for a professional career, he

entered the PGA Qualifying School at La Manga, Spain in late 1985, promptly won the competition and in his first full professional year in 1986 won no fewer than three tournaments. A star was born. In his first five years, he had won ten PGA European Tour events, others in Japan and the United States and more than £1 million in prize money. In winning the World Series of Golf at the Firestone Club in Akron, Ohio in 1990, he was 12 strokes ahead of the next player, Lanny Wadkins.

Olazabal's game is brisk, quick, and confident. His simple ambition is to be the best in the world. To that end, he has a burning desire to win major championships. To date, he has finished second in the Masters, to Ian Woosnam in 1991, when he needed four on the last hole

Jose Maria Olazabal jumping on the shoulders of fellow Spaniard Seve Ballesteros during the 1991 Ryder Cup. Their partnership appeared, at first, to be dominated by the great 'Seve'. In the early 1990s, however, Olazabal achieved better results than his out-of-form friend.

to tie. Twice bunkered, he took five on the hole. Then in 1992, he was third in the Open Championship at Muirfield behind Nick Faldo and John Cook. With Severiano Ballesteros, he was an inspired contributor to the Ryder Cup successes of the European team in the 1980s.

OPEN CHAMPIONSHIP

The Open Championship is now one of the world's great sporting events, seen by hundreds of millions on television around the world, with a budget running into millions of pounds and involving thousands of people.

The Prestwick club was responsible for its inauguration in 1860. As a new club in the West of Scotland, formed in 1851 and thus second then only to the Glasgow Club, the Prestwick members were imaginative. They had tempted Old Tom Morris from St Andrews in 1851 to be their first 'Custodian of the Links', and by 1857 were suggesting to the other clubs that a national tournament should be held. It was to be match play foursomes, with a two-man team entered from each club. Prestwick gave 15 guineas towards the purchase of a trophy. It was played at St Andrews and won by Blackheath.

At the time, there were only three clubs outside Scotland – Old Manchester, Royal Calcutta and Blackheath. Old Manchester had but a few members; Royal Calcutta was a shade far away. There was some consolation for the Scots, however, as the Blackheath team comprised John Campbell Stewart of Fasnacloich and George Glennie, both Scots who had learned their golf in Scotland. Glennie had already won medals at St Andrews, and to this day, the 'Glennie Medal' is won by the R & A member who has the lowest aggregate score in the spring Silver Cross and the Autumn Medal. Glennie was for many years secretary at Blackheath.

This 'National Amateur Competition' was repeated in 1858 and 1859, but with lessening enthusiasm from the other clubs Prestwick, in 1860, decided to go it alone. They announced that on 17 October 1860, a tournament for professionals-only would be played. They commissioned a handsome red leather belt with 'silver decoration' from James and Walter Marshall, Goldsmiths, of 41 George Street, Edinburgh at a cost of £25. Old Tom Morris had established a regular course of 12 holes and the championship was to be over three rounds. Willie Park beat Morris by a stroke, with 174 for the 36 holes. Eight players took part. For the 1861 event, it was thrown 'open to the world'. Amateurs could now join in with professionals in a truly open championship.

Then came Tom's son Young Tommy, who won in 1868–69–70, thus taking permanent possession of 'The Belt'! There was no championship in 1871, as though they were still pondering this turn of events, but in 1872, Prestwick, the R & A and the Honourable Company (still playing at Musselburgh) agreed to stage the championship in rotation, and subscribed for a cup, with the proviso that this one could never be won outright. In the event, Jamie Anderson in 1877–78–79, then Bob Ferguson in 1880–81–82, both won three successive Opens. Seventy years on, in 1954–55–56, Peter Thomson of Australia did precisely the same.

In 1872, the championship was won for a fourth time by Young Tom Morris. His prize money was £8. It was his last success. The event continued going the rounds of the three courses until 1892, when it was scheduled for Muirfield, the new home of the Honourable Company. For the first time, the event was over 72 holes. It was won by Harold Hilton, an amateur, and to the great disquiet of the Scots, an Englishman to boot. John Ball, Hilton's fellow-member at Royal Liverpool's Hoylake, had won in 1890 at Prestwick, but Hilton's win marked the end of the reign of the Scottish professional-cum-caddie-cum-greenkeeper. Now the English, or exiled Scots, would dominate the Open until the coming of the Americans after the First World War.

In the twenty years from 1894 to 1914, Harry Vardon, JH Taylor and James Braid dominated the championship; Vardon from the Channel Islands had six wins, Taylor from Westward Ho! five, and Braid, the Scot who spent most of his life at the London clubs Romford and Walton Heath, five. In the 1920s and well into the thirties, the Open was the property of the Americans. Walter Hagen (four wins) and Bobby Jones (three) were the outstanding personalities, and it was not until 1934 when Henry Cotton won at Royal St George's that the tide turned.

From then until the outbreak of the Second World War, the American interest declined. This was largely a matter of cost and time. Then, an Atlantic crossing was by steamship, with the best part of a week taken up. Then there was a week to play the championship and a week to get back home, in high summer when there were rich tournament pickings to be had in the US.

And Open week then was rigorous. Qualifying became necessary in 1914, and by the 1950s players were obliged to play qualifying rounds on Monday and Tuesday (including the defending champion!), then 36 holes on Friday. In 1963 a system of exemptions from qualifying was begun. In 1966, the third and fourth rounds were played on Friday and Saturday, and beginning in 1980, the Open was played as 18 holes each day, Thursday to Sunday inclusive.

In the 1940s and 50s, by and large, American golfers ignored the Open. One stunning exception was Ben Hogan in 1953, who completed a scarcely credible year in which he won the US Masters and the US Open, then came to Carnoustie to crown it with the Open Championship (he won five of the six events he played that year). Thus the championship fell in the main to the 'Commonwealth' players, Bobby Locke of South Africa and Peter Thomson of Australia.

But the age of Arnold Palmer was at hand. Coinciding with the advent of the jet aircraft and the development of colour television, Palmer came with a neat sense of history to the Centenary Open of 1960 and played at St Andrews, like Hogan before him, having won the US Masters and the US Open. He failed, finishing second by one stroke to a surprising winner, Kel Nagle of Australia. Palmer won in 1961 in a Royal Birkdale gale, and in 1962 with a shattering record score of 276 over a dusty Troon, still

Greg Norman with an old friend – the Open Championship Trophy, which he won at Royal St George's in 1993, with a record final round 64 in which, he said, he 'never missed a shot'.

to become Royal. Palmer showed the way to a new generation of American golfers who realised they could be over to the UK and back in a matter of days. And as progressively extensive pre-qualifying competitions disposed of the increasing number of entries, for the best of them, the championship would consist of no more than four rounds over four days.

So the best of them came, and for the next two decades after Palmer arrived the roll of honour was stiff with such names as Lema, Nicklaus, Trevino, Weiskopf, Miller and Watson, great players all. The Open Championship gradually returned to being the world's most 'open' championship. As television coverage spread to countries throughout the world, so the presentation of the event

expanded with grandstands, exhibition centres, trade fairs, corporate pavilions and a huge range of public services, so much so that the acreage required to accommodate it all was as extensive as the golf course itself. With it all came the age of Ballesteros, Lyle and Faldo, and in 1993, the 'million pound Open'.

THE OPEN CHAMPIONSHIP

Winners British, except where stated

Year	Venue	Winner	Score
1860	Prestwick	Willie Park Snr	174
1861	Prestwick	Tom Morris Snr	163
1862	Prestwick	Tom Morris Snr	163
1863	Prestwick	Willie Park Snr	168
1864	Prestwick	Tom Morris Snr	167
1865	Prestwick	Andrew Strath	162
1866	Prestwick	Willie Park Snr	169
1867	Prestwick	Tom Morris Snr	170
1868	Prestwick	Tom Morris Jnr	157
1869	Prestwick	Tom Morris Jnr	154
1870	Prestwick	Tom Morris Jnr	149
1871	No competition		
1872	Prestwick	Tom Morris Jnr	166
1873	St Andrews	Tom Kidd	179
1874	Musselburgh	Mungo Park	159
1875	Prestwick	Willie Park Snr	166
1876	St Andrews	Bob Martin	176
1877	Royal Musselburgh	Jamie Anderson	160
1878	Prestwick	Jamie Anderson	157
1879	St Andrews	Jamie Anderson	169
1880	Royal Musselburgh	Bob Ferguson	162
1881	Prestwick	Bob Ferguson	170
1882	St Andrews	Bob Ferguson	171
1883	Royal Musselburgh	Willie Fernie	159*
1884	Prestwick	Jack Simpson	160
1885	St Andrews	Bob Martin	171
1886	Royal Musselburgh	David Brown	157
1887	Prestwick	Willie Park Jnr	161
1888	St Andrews	Jack Burns	171
1889	Royal Musselburgh	Willie Park Jnr	155*
1890	Prestwick	John Ball†	164
1891	St Andrews	High Kirkaldy	166
1892	Muirfield	Harold Hilton†	305**
1893	Prestwick	William Auchterlonie	322
1894	St George's (Sandwich)	JH Taylor	326
1895	St Andrews	JH Taylor	322
1896	Muirfield	Harry Vardon	316*
1897	Royal Liverpool (Hoylake)	Harold Hilton†	314
1898	Prestwick	Harry Vardon	307
1899	St George's (Sandwich)	Harry Vardon	310
1900	St Andrews	JH Taylor	309
1901	Muirfield	James Braid	309
1902	Royal Liverpool (Hoylake)	Sandy Herd	307
1903	Prestwick	Harry Vardon	300
1904	Royal St George's (Sandwich)	Jack White	296
1905	St Andrews	James Braid	318
1906	Muirfield	James Braid	300
1907	Royal Liverpool (Hoylake)	Arnaud Massy (Fr)	312
1908	Prestwick	James Braid	291
1909	Cinque Ports (Deal)	JH Taylor	295
1910	St Andrews	James Braid	299
1911	Royal St George's (Sandwich)	Harry Vardon	303
1912	Muirfield	Ted Ray	295
1913	Royal Liverpool (Hoylake)	JHTaylor	304
1914	Prestwick	Harry Vardon	306
1920	Cinque Ports (Deal)	George Duncan	303

Year	Venue	Winner	Score
1921	St Andrews	Jock Hutchison (US)	296*
1922	Royal St George's (Sandwich)	Walter Hagen (US)	300
1923	Troon	Arthur Havers	295
1924	Royal Liverpool (Hoylake)	Walter Hagen (US)	301
1925	Prestwick	Jim Barnes† (US)	300
1926	Royal Lytham & St Annes	Bobby Jones† (US)	291
1927	St Andrews	Bobby Jones† (US)	285
1928	Royal St George's (Sandwich)	Walter Hagen (US)	292
1929	Muirfield	Walter Hagen (US)	292
1930	Royal Liverpool (Hoylake)	Bobby Jones† (US)	291
1931	Carnoustie	Tommy Armour (US)	296
1932	Prince's (Sandwich)	Gene Sarazen (US)	283
1933	St Andrews	Densmore Shute (US)	292*
1934	Royal St George's (Sandwich)	Henry Cotton	283
1935	Muirfield	Alf Perry	283
1936	Royal Liverpool (Hoylake)	Alf Padgham	287
1937	Carnoustie	Henry Cotton	290
1938	Royal St George's	Reg Whitcombe	295
1939	St Andrews	Dick Burton	290
1946	St Andrews	Sam Snead (US)	290
1947	Royal Liverpool (Hoylake)	Fred Daly	293
1948	Muirfield	Henry Cotton	284
1949	Royal St George's (Sandwich)	Bobby LockeSA)8	3*
1950	Troon	Bobby Locke (SA)	279
1951	Royal Portrush	Max Faulkner	285
1952	Royal Lytham & St Annes	Bobby Locke (SA)	287
1953	Carnoustie	Ben Hogan (US)	282
1954	Royal Birkdale	Peter Thomson (Aus)	283
1955	St Andrews	Peter Thomson (Aus)	281
1956	Royal Liverpool (Hoylake)	Peter Thomson (Aus)	286
1957	St Andrews	Bobby Locke (SA)	279
1958	Royal Lytham & St Annes	Peter Thomson (Aus)	278*
1959	Muirfield	Gary Player (SA)	284
1960	St Andrews	Kel Nagle (Aus)	278
1961	Royal Birkdale	Arnold Palmer (US)	284
1962	Troon	Arnold Palmer (US)	276
1963	Royal Lytham & St Annes	Bob Charles (NZ)	277*
1964	St Andrews	Tony Lema (US)	279
1965	Royal Birkdale	Peter Thomson (Aus)	285
1966	Muirfield	Jack Nicklaus (US)	282
1967	Royal Liverpool (Hoylake)	Roberto de Vicenzo (Arg)	278
1968	Carnoustie	Gary Player (SA)	289
1969	Royal Lytham & St Annes	Tony Jacklin	280
1970	St Andrews	Jack Nicklaus (US)	283*
1971	Royal Birkdale	Lee Trevino (US)	278
1972	Muirfield	Lee Trevino (US)	278
1973	Troon	Tom Weiskopf (US)	276
1974	Royal Lytham & St Annes	Gary Player (SA)	282
1975	Carnoustie	Tom Watson (US)	279*
1976	Royal Birkdale	Johnny Miller (US)	279
1977	Turnberry	Tom Watson (US)	268
1978	St Andrews	Jack Nicklaus (US)	281
1979	Royal Lytham & St Annes	Seve Ballesteros (Sp)	283
1980	Muirfield	Tom Watson (US)	271
1981	Royal St George's (Sandwich)	Bill Rogers (US)	276
1982	Royal Troon	Tom Watson (US)	284
1983	Royal Birkdale	Tom Watson (US)	275
1984	St Andrews	Seve Ballesteros (Sp)	276
1985	Royal St George's, (Sandwich)	Sandy Lyle	282
1986	Turnberry	Greg Norman (Aus)	280
1987	Muirfield	Nick Faldo	279
1988	Royal Lytham & St Annes	Seve Ballesteros (Sp)	273
1989	Royal Troon	Mark Calcavecchia (US)	275*
1990	St Andrews	Nick Faldo	270
1991	Royal Birkdale	Ian Baker-Finch (Aus)	272
1992	Muirfield	Nick Faldo	272
1993	Royal St George's, (Sandwich)	Greg Norman (Aus)	267

*play-off **Competition extended over 72 holes †amateur

ORDER OF MERIT

The Order of Merit is the PGA European Tour ranking system, based on one calendar year's play. Included are affiliated members of the Tour who played the necessary nine tournaments, plus those who were unable to play nine tournaments because of their lowly exemption status. The rating is based on official prize money won, and the leading official money winner leads the Order of Merit and is awarded the Harry Vardon Trophy.

OUIMET, Francis

Born 1893

Nationality United States

Majors US Open 1913

Francis Ouimet was the young American who played possibly the most significant single round of golf ever recorded when he won an 18 holes play-off against the English giants, Harry Vardon and Ted Ray, to win the US Open Championship of 1913. For just as John Ball and Harold Hilton back in the 1890s had ended the domination of Scottish professionals in the Open Championship, so Ouimet ended 25 years of supremacy by British and immigrant professionals in the US Open.

With that one victory, splashing through the rain-soaked fairways of the Country Club at Brookline, near Boston, Francis Ouimet changed the face of American golf and became an American hero. He was home-bred, a native-born American; he was an amateur; he was a former caddie who worked during his summer vacations from school. He was no socialite. He had demonstrated to the mass of Americans – his victory was reported on the front page of every newspaper in the land – that golf was no longer a society game, no longer a game for the privileged, but a game for everyone.

The Ouimet family lived across the street from the Country Club and Francis, born in 1893, was caddying as soon as it was permitted. He became a very fine player who knew the Country Club course backwards. In 1912, he had been a finalist in the Massachusetts State Amateur Championship. In 1913, he won it – in his semi-final win, he scored the six closing holes in 2,3,3,3,3,3, six under par. So when he teed up to two of the finest golfers of the time, Vardon and Ray, young Ouimet was by no means a beginner. To join them in a tie over four rounds, he had to birdie two of the last four holes. And in the play-off he beat them handsomely, scoring 72 to Vardon's 77 and Ray's 78.

Francis won the US Amateur the next year, and again in 1931. He played in every Walker Cup match from 1922 to 1934 and was non-playing captain from then until 1949. He was Captain of the Royal and Ancient Club in 1951, the first 'non-British' person to be so honoured. He was a committee member of the USGA for many years. He died in 1967 and is remembered as a gentleman of whom no evil was spoken. Ten years on from his landmark win in 1913 and America had become the dominant force in world golf.

The man who beat Vardon and Ray and put golf on the front pages of America – Francis Ouimet of Boston.

P

PALMER, Arnold

Born 1929

Nationality United States

Turned Pro 1954

Majors Open Championship 1961, 1962; US Open 1960; US Masters 1958, 1960, 1962, 1964

Above all else, Arnold Daniel Palmer was a man for his time. It was a time of the greatest significance, a watershed in the game. Arnold's prime time was essentially the 1960s, and the emergence of 'Arnie', walking stride for stride through the twilight of Ben Hogan, also saw the advent of colour television, the appearance of the jet aircraft which shrunk the world, and the making of the Masters.

Ben Hogan may well have been the most complete player that golf has known. Certainly his year of 1953 when he won the US Masters, the US Open and the British Open Championship, was unsurpassable. But Hogan was an impassive introvert who would never suffer fools gladly. Few golf fans acquired a Ben Hogan autograph. His final tournament win was in 1959, aptly enough at the Colonial Club in his home town of Fort Worth. He wore grey often on the course, but was essentially a black and white man. When he defended his US Open title in 1954, unsuccessfully against Ed Furgol at Baltusrol, the championship was televised nationally for the first time –

in black and white of course.

Arnold Palmer by contrast was all colour. He had won the Masters in 1958, and he too was to have his miracle year, in 1960. He won the Masters and the US Open, then with a nod to history, with his father, a golf pro, his mother and his wife Winnie, sped to St Andrews for the Centenary Open and a chance to match Hogan too good to miss. He failed, by one stroke, losing to Kel Nagle of Australia. He had won his US Open by scoring five birdies in an outward half of 30 on the last round, and his score of 65 was the lowest winning last round score at that time. He had made up seven strokes on the field. In the Masters that year, he had finished with two birdies to see off Ken Venturi. In his 1962 Open win at Troon, he scored a record 276, six strokes ahead of the next man, the same Kel Nagle, and 13 strokes ahead of the third-placed players, Brian Huggett and Phil Rodgers of America.

His contribution to the fame and success of the US Masters and the Augusta National Golf Club is often ignored. He was the first player to win the Masters four times (a record later passed by Jack Nicklaus with six), but the manner of Palmer at Augusta, seen by an ever-growing and increasingly international television audience, made – it is not too much to say – Augusta in particular and golf generally a spectacle such as it had never previously been. Even when he lost championships that had seemed won, Palmer was a people's man – his 'disasters' had a human element. He took six strokes on the 72nd hole at Augusta, a par four, to lose in 1961 to Gary Player. In the US Open of 1966, he squandered a six shot lead to Billy Casper. When Arnold did it, he did it with a

vengeance. He was an American original, an American folk hero.

Palmer's achievement was the sum of his victories, his technique, his personality and above all his golfing philosophy. He was born on 10 September 1929 in Latrobe, a small town near Pittsburgh. His father Deacon was greenkeeper-professional at the local 9-holes course, later extended to 18, with Deacon becoming head professional. After winning the US Amateur in 1954, Arnold turned professional and in his very first year won the Canadian Open of 1955. It was the start of a flood. On the US Tour between 1955 and 1973 he won 60 events. In the 17 years from 1955 to 1971 he won at least one tournament every year. In 1960, he won eight times. And there was a score of successes, including two Open Championships, World Match Play titles and World Cup wins, outside the US.

Success is much worshipped by Americans, and besides, Palmer on the golf course had all the qualities they identified as American – from a modest beginning reaching the top of one's trade, and doing it in a go-for-broke, over-the-top, John Wayne way. Palmer was the most swashbuckling, most thrilling golfer the game had known. He was compared with Walter Hagen, but much of Hagen's glitter was off the course. Palmer's theme was, 'If you can hit it, you can hole it.'

He would pour out long, rasping drives down the fairways of America. He peppered the flagsticks regardless of intervening sand, water or hazard. If he found the rough, he would stomp in and smash out the most improbable of recoveries. Playing out to the side or backwards from trouble was not in the Palmer

vocabulary. 'Forward' was always the cry. And during his great years, his putting was remorseless; crouching over the ball with a knock-kneed, slightly pigeon-toed stance, he would go for everything. His swing was a thrilling experience in itself. He would tee the ball, it seemed, opposite his left toes so that everything looked as though it was behind the ball, as though he were stretching to reach it. The backswing was a shade quick, then the clubhead would come pouring down and through from the inside and the ball would scream off with a slight draw in its flight. Arnold's head would be cocked, following it, as the clubhead spun high above his head with the fury of the follow through. Lightning flashed.

A glove would dangle from his hip pocket. He sniffed. He hitched his pants. Often his shirt–tail flopped out. He smoked relentlessly until forced to stop, at least in public. All of these mannerisms were common. The galleries caught them. For them, Arnie was 'one of us'. In the midst of their fantasies, they identified with him. And the television cameras caught them. Arnold, unlike Hogan, would suffer fools, and drunks and bores, and would sign autographs endlessly. For the best part of a decade, he was the idol of a nation.

Arnold Palmer was blessed with star quality. The camera was kind to him – and Arnold always knew which television camera was focussed on him.

Arnold Palmer, the great one, acknowledges yet another welcome at his most favoured course, the Augusta National, where he won the US Masters four times.

Characteristically, when he passed 50 and became a senior golfer, he won the first event he ever entered, the 1980 PGA Senior Championship. In subsequent years, he became increasingly involved in business affairs – his career-long association with Mark McCormack had made both of them wealthy – and in particular with golf design and construction. Over the years, Arnold had also become a very talented pilot, setting various flying records.

PARK, Willie Jnr.

Born 1864

Nationality British

Turned Pro 1880

Majors Open Championship 1887, 1889

The Park family of Musselburgh, like the Dunns of Musselburgh and the Morrises of St Andrews, was one of golf's earliest dynasties and contributed greatly to the advancement of the game at many levels and in many elements – as champions, ball and clubmakers, course designers, inventors, entrepreneurs, investors, authors. The head of the family, James Park, was a farmer and only incidentally a golfer, but his son Willie Park was the first Open Champion in 1860, and won again in 1863, 1866 and 1875; and Jack's second son Mungo won in 1874.

Willie Park Jr, of a famous Musselburgh golfing family, was Open Champion twice in the 1880s, and went on to become an outstanding and innovative golf course designer, both in the UK and the United States.

Willie Park in turn fathered three sons, Willie Jnr, Mungo II and John (Jack) Park. Willie Jnr was to win the Opens of 1887 and 1889, and he became something of a renaissance man in these early decades in the history of the organised game. He was to make his mark on the game as a player, of course, but even more so as an innovative thinker about the business of laying out a golf course. He wrote two books in his career, *The Game of Golf* in 1896 and *The Art of Putting* in 1920. In the former he wrote:

'The laying out of a golf course is by no means a simple task. Great skill and judgement and a thorough acquaintance with the game are absolutely necessary to determine the best position for the respective holes and teeing grounds and the situation of the hazards.'

Willie was a contemporary of Willie Dunn. As boys they had played together at Musselburgh, and 'Young Willie' Dunn too was to have success as an architect. Park, witness his second book, was persuaded that putting was the most critical part of the game, and he would practise for hours. A big man, and an imposing personality, he took this perfectionism

into all his activities.

He had spent several of his early years as a greenkeeper and professional with his Uncle Mungo at Ryton, near Newcastle upon Tyne, before returning to Musselburgh to work with his father and uncle laying out courses. In time, he struck out on his own, his brothers helping with the actual construction of his designs.

Before the turn of the century, he had spent three years in America promoting and designing courses, but it was two exceptional projects, courses opened in 1901, which confirmed his status as a great and innovative golf designer. Sunningdale and Huntercombe were links laid out on heathland, and confirmed, in the case of Sunningdale, that the abundant heathlands around London were in fact ideal for golf, and for the courses that would be needed in the new century.

So Park in a sense opened the door for other designers to enter and make use of similar stretches of heather, sand and pine territory – Harry Colt, JF Abercromby, Herbert Fowler. Huntercombe was possibly the first of the golf courses which planned for integrated housing and Park was a major promoter and shareholder in the project. But the housing plans never did materialise, and Huntercombe was something of a burden he had to bear for several years.

Willie Park Jnr designed dozens of courses the length and breadth of the British Isles. Carnoustie and Coombe Hill, Formby, Gullane, Richmond, South Herts and Worplesdon are all on his list. In Austria, there was the Vienna GC, in Belgium Royal Antwerp. In France he did Dinard, Evian, La Boulie, Monte Carlo. He went to the United States in 1916 and stayed there until 1924, when he came home to die in Scotland. He took on a prodigious amount of work in America, working on seventy courses at a time. With offices in the US and Canada, he was assisted on construction by his brothers. Willie visited each site several times as the work progressed. He had clients from Maine to Florida, all down the Eastern seaboard and west into Michigan and Arkansas, and all over Canada. He set standards that were followed by a generation and is certainly one of the finest golf course designers in the history of the game.

PAU

The Pau club is famous for being the oldest golf club in Continental Europe, founded in 1856. The course runs to just under 6000 yards and is on flat, pleasantly wooded land, bordered by the river Gave which crosses several holes. Pau is a resort town in the foothills of the 'Pyreneés Atlantiques', close to the Spanish border some 50 miles east of Biarritz.

There is evidence of golf at Pau in 1814. Scottish regiments involved in Wellington's Peninsular War had been based there, and their officers laid out a few holes of golf. As the town became more fashionable, it became an example to other French resorts, indeed to spas all over Europe, in deciding that this 'new' game would be an attraction for visitors. A club was formed, with a modest nine holes and it appears that the then Duke of Hamilton was one of its prime movers, donating a trophy. Among the other founding members were colonels with such Scottish names as Hutchinson and Anstruther. The first 18 hole course was designed by Tom Dunn of Musselburgh.

PEBBLE BEACH

The supreme course in the Western United States, one consistently in the top ten in any classification of the great American courses, Pebble Beach on the Monterey Peninsula, 120 miles south of San Francisco, is one of the world's most spectacular golf courses. It has a stretch of breathtakingly beautiful holes, from the sixth to the tenth, along the clifftops that overlook Carmel Bay, and the television broadcasts of the US Opens played there have brought its delights and its terrors to the world.

The 17th and 18th holes return to the oceanside and the 17th has produced memorable US Open shots. In 1972, a 1-iron shot into the wind from Jack Nicklaus, on the 218 yards hole, hit the flagstick and stopped six inches away, the birdie helping him to a third US Open win and a Pebble Beach double – Jack had won the US Amateur there in 1961. And in the US Open of 1982, Tom Watson holed a shot from out of the rough beside the green for a birdie at the 17th, and followed it with another on 18 for a two stroke win over the Pebble Beach specialist, Nicklaus. But on one occasion, at a Bing Crosby tournament there, that same hole was less than kind to Arnold Palmer. Too strong into the wind with his tee shot, Arnold went over the green and onto the rocks, and scored nine on the hole.

Although occasionally described as 'Pebble Beach Golf Links', it is rather a clifftop course, albeit buffeted by the Pacific winds. The fourth hole, a short par 4 of 325 yards, plays along the shore; the fifth is a par 3 of 180 yards which plays through some trees; but the sixth is a lusty par 5 which sweeps out to a dramatic headland above Stillwater Cove. Along the edge of this bluff runs the seventh, at 120 yards the shortest par 3 in American championship golf. Played downhill to a fiercely trapped green, it can be anything from a wedge to a long iron shot, depending on the wind. The eighth hole is surely one of the world's greatest two-shot holes. From a tee set on the edge of the cliff, the drive is blind and uphill. The second shot has to carry across an inlet in the cliffs, stretching a good 180 yards and leaving the player to decide how much he can cut off. The fairway skirts round it to the left, giving some kind of escape route, but one which lengthens the hole considerably.

The ninth is just as demanding, again a long par 4, all of it downhill and in view this time, but with the fairway sloping from left to right towards the ocean. The tenth follows the pattern – narrow fairway, along the shore line, small, closely trapped green. Seven, eight, nine and ten at Pebble Beach form one of the most challenging runs imaginable anywhere. The course takes an inland route back to the 17th; and the photogenic 18th, a big finish at 540 yards, skirts the bay all the way, with the Pacific Ocean now on the left.

The course, by modern American design standards, may be considered a little old-fashioned. The greens are small, contoured but not unnecessarily so, and bunkering has been left to a minimum. Pebble Beach was designed by an amateur, so to speak, as was Merion with Hugh Wilson and Pine Valley with George Crump. In the case of Pebble Beach, it was Jack Neville, many times a California state amateur champion. Neville, a native of Oakland, was working in the area as a real-estate salesman for the Pacific Improvement Company, a

The par-3 17th hole at the magnificent Pebble Beach course on California's Pacific Coast, where Tom Watson holed from off the green for a birdie in winning the 1982 US Open Championship.

property subsidiary of the Southern Pacific Railroad which owned the land. In 1914, Samuel A Morse arrived from the East charged by the railroad company to dispose of all its property interests in the area. With the idea that the Monterey Peninsula property could be developed as a resort, Morse himself bought 7,000 acres, forming the Del Monte Property Company.

Having decided that an existing and modest golf course would be quite inadequate, Morse commanded Neville, in effect his employee, to design and build a 'proper' course. Since Neville was a champion golfer, he would surely know how to do that. Neville did it with a vengeance and a little

PEBBLE BEACH		
HOLE	YARDS	PAR
1	385	4
2	507	5
3	368	4
4	325	4
5	180	3
6	515	5
7	120	3
8	425	4
9	450	4
OUT	3,275	36
10	436	4
11	380	4
12	205	3
13	400	4
14	555	5
15	406	4
16	400	4
17	218	3
18	540	5
IN	3,540	36
TOTAL	6,815	72

help from Douglas Grant, a friend and also a state champion. The result was that in 1918, a course was opened which could not long be denied. By 1929, the USGA took its amateur championship there, the first to be played west of the Mississippi. It produced one of the greatest sports stories of the year. Having made the long train journey from Atlanta, Bobby Jones lost in the first round to the 'unknown' Johnny Goodman. In the final seven years of his career, this was the one time that Jones did not reach the final of the American Amateur Championship. Johnny Goodman was not unknown for long – he won the US Open in 1933, the last amateur to do so, and the US Amateur in 1937.

PGA (The Professional Golfers' Association)

The formation of the Professional Golfers' Association in 1901 was a direct consequence of the evolution of the golf professional as club and ballmaker, teacher, retailer and tournament competitor. It was aided, even hastened by the achievements and reputations of the leading professionals at the turn of the century. JH Taylor, Harry Vardon, Jimmy Braid and Sandy Herd were champions held in high regard for their moral probity and public demeanour as much as the quality of their play. Too many of their fellows, however, were feckless and irresolute, with little thought for the future. Socially, they were close to being outcasts and were often taken advantage of by club committees in terms of work and employment.

In the final quarter of the 19th century, the number of golf clubs in the UK increased from less than 100 to more than 1000. The demand for equipment and professional services increased accordingly, and one of the first champions to make the most of this was Willie Park Jnr, Open Champion in 1887 and 1889, son of Willie, also an Open Champion. Willie Jnr became an outstanding course designer with the Old Course at Sunningdale and many fine courses in the US to his credit. He was also successful as a clubmaker and by 1897 claimed that he had sold 17,000 of his ' Patent Lofter' clubs at 7/6d (37.5p) each.

Park let it be known from time to time that the status of the professional needed much improvement. Many were part-time – slaters, joiners, plasterers who played as and when they could. Those in full-time employment with golf clubs had to be clubmakers; available to teach and play with members; available from early morning until the last member had left the club in the evening; manage caddies and caddies' shelter; conduct the draw and act as starters on Medal days; and assist in course maintenance. Often this type of contract, a form of slavery really, could be terminated on fourteen days' notice.

John Henry Taylor, Open Champion in 1894 with what was to be the first of five wins, had had the cruellest of childhoods. His father died when he was four. His education in the modest village school of his birthplace, Northam in Devon, ended when he was eleven. All of this left him with a burning desire to better himself, to raise the status of his profession and to defend the professionals against the mischief-making of some clubs, where committees would by-pass the professional and buy in goods for re-sale to members. Early in 1901, Taylor revealed his thinking on all of this to Harold Hilton, editor of *Golf Illustrated*. Hilton of Hoylake's golfing career was to notch up four Amateur Championship titles, one US Amateur, and the Open Championships of 1892 and 1897. He knew the game inside out.

In March, Hilton published a leading article demanding better treatment for club professionals. In the next issue, a letter from Taylor supporting this editorial invited other professionals to write to the magazine. Over the next few weeks came strong supporting letters from Vardon, Braid and Herd. Conspiracy from the Big Four? Surely not – but the four outstanding golfers of the day were in the ring. Letters from other professionals urged Taylor to take the initiative, one describing him as their 'ideal leader'. Taylor needed no further encouragement; he canvassed every professional he could reach and any other interested party, including Frank Johnston, a London sporting goods merchant. Following the Open Championship at Muirfield, a meeting in Paternoster Lane in London was called at which C Ralph Smith, a friend of the professionals, took the chair, and it was agreed to found the 'London and Counties Professional Golfers' Association', covering London and the South East Counties, with subscriptions of £1 for professionals, 10/- (50p) for assistants. A committee was elected, with Taylor as chairman, to draft a constitution and it was planned to hold three competitions each year. By 23 September, the first annual general meeting was held. Johnson was elected honorary secretary, and the Right Honourable Arthur James Balfour, Prime Minister to be, became President.

The first of their tournaments was played in October at the Tooting Bec Club in South London, for £15 prize money and a cup presented by the club. Taylor, perhaps fittingly, was the winner. The tournament, indeed the club, is no more, but the cup survives and is now awarded to the PGA member scoring the lowest round in the Open Championship.

Organisations had also been formed in the Midlands and the North, mainly for social reasons, but they saw the need to protect members' welfare and were keenly interested in the London constitution:

'The objects of the Association shall be to promote interest in the game of golf; to protect and advance the mutual and trade interests of all its members; to hold meetings and tournaments periodically for the encouragement of younger members; to institute a Benevolent Fund for the relief of deserving members; to act as an agency for assisting any professional or clubmaker to obtain employment; and to effect any other objects of a like nature as may be determined from time to time by the Association.'

The professionals had flexed their muscles before 1901, when the championship of 1892 was scheduled to move from Musselburgh to Muirfield, new home of the Honourable Company of Edinburgh Golfers. The championship had been on a rota, decided every third year at Musselburgh, and the local traders and professionals, among them Willie Park Jnr, were offended and concerned at the loss of trade. They decided to promote their own championship at

Musselburgh on the same dates and collected £100 for prize money. The Open in 1891 had announced only £30 in prize money. The Honourable Company quickly raised their fund to £110, whereupon Musselburgh postponed its event for a week, and played immediately after the Open!

Before the end of 1901, the name was changed to 'The Professional Golfers Association' and within a year, the Midlands and Northern people joined the fold. In time, Irish and Scottish sections made it truly national.

In 1903, Mr (later Sir) Emsley Carr of the *News of the World* newspaper offered the PGA £200 for an annual match play tournament, a sensational prize fund at the time. Emsley Carr was a keen golfer as was his associate George (later Lord) Riddell, owner of Walton Heath golf club. The newspaper was celebrating its diamond jubilee, but additionally John Henry Taylor had just started a series of weekly articles on golf, which he did for the best part of 40 years. The Match Play Championship was played at Sunningdale in October, won by James Braid and was to be sponsored for more than seventy years by the Carrs.

The idea of a trading co-operative in which the professionals would have shares and which would buy in bulk on their behalf from the manufacturers, was mooted in 1907, but did not materialise until 1921 when the Professional Golfers' Co-operative Association was formed. The first trade exhibition was held at the Muirfield Open of 1912, making a profit of £20 and becoming a regular feature of the championship. The PGA owned and managed the Ryder Cup match until 1975 when the tournament players broke away and founded the

PGA European Tour, since when the matches have been jointly owned and presented by both organisations. Now the PGA continues to watch over the welfare of its hundreds of club professionals, and from its headquarters at The Belfry near Sutton Coldfield, present a variety of competitions for its members.

PGA EUROPEAN TOUR

The existence of the PGA European Tour grew from dissatisfaction – the dissatisfaction of the young with the old, of the progressive tournament players with the conservative club professionals, and with the voting structures of the 'parent' PGA body. The scenario is not unfamiliar. In the 1940s and 50s there were perhaps no more than a dozen tournaments to play for each year and almost all the tournament players had club jobs. In those days, tournaments were played on Wednesday, Thursday, then 36 holes on Friday so that the players could get back to their clubs and tend their members at the weekend. Many attempts were made to change this. Henry Cotton in the fifties tried to get support for a move towards player independence. Later, Peter Alliss, Bernard Hunt, John Jacobs and others tried to do the same. All of these efforts, aimed at giving the players more control over the events which they were making popular, foundered on the reactionary elements in the PGA and, it should be said, on the various tournament sponsors, almost all of whom were in the golf trade one way or the other – Dunlop, Penfold, Daks, Slazenger, Saxone Shoes.

With television bringing the game to a wider public, a flame was lit in July 1969

when Tony Jacklin won the Open Championship at Royal Lytham and St Annes, the first home winner since Max Faulkner at Portrush in 1951. Seven weeks later, the Great Britain and Ireland team held the Americans to a tied Ryder Cup match at Royal Birkdale. In the following June, the same Tony Jacklin won the US Open! Jacobs, Jacklin, Hunt and Neil Coles were even more determined to win their 'independence' and they succeeded in October 1971 when John Jacobs became the first Tournament Director General of the PGA.

Jacobs was brave enough to lay down a minimum prize fund of £50,000 for any tournament. He had a trump card in Tony Jacklin, a national and international figure whom all the sponsors wanted. Jacobs saw much of the future taking place in Europe, where as a coach to national amateur teams he had built up a wide range of contacts in golf. And for the first half of the 1970s he also had Peter Oosterhuis.

The Dulwich schoolboy, a Walker Cup player as an amateur, pointed the way to a future in which British players would no longer require to be club professionals, but could be exclusively tournament players. He monopolised the Order of Merit from 1971 to 1974, winning ten tournaments in that time before going to the US Tour and eventually winning the Canadian Open. Then in the second half of the seventies came one Severiano Ballesteros. In 1975, the European Tournament Players Division of the PGA – almost immediately becoming the PGA European Tour – was formed. Jacobs, his particular work done, resigned to do other things. Ken Schofield became Secretary and eventually Executive Director. And as more and more youngsters

sought careers in competitive golf, an annual qualifying school was established in 1976.

An exciting platoon of young players, headed by Ballesteros, was on the move – Nick Faldo, Sandy Lyle, Bernhard Langer and Ian Woosnam began to appear on the leader boards. In 1979 for the first time, European players were selected for the Ryder Cup team. In 1981, headquarters was moved from the Kennington Oval in central London to the Wentworth Club in Surrey. In the 1983 Ryder Cup match, the Europeans ran the American team to one single point, and in the next match two years later at the Belfry, they won for the first time in 28 years. Two years later, at Muirfield Village in Ohio, they won again, for the first time ever in the United States. America's long golfing hegemony was over.

Ballesteros and Faldo won Open Championships and US Masters titles. Lyle, Langer and Woosnam won the Masters. Faldo and Woosnam came close to winning US Opens. By 1986, so great was the spread of tournaments and so great was the interest, as Jacobs had foreseen, that a Tour South Office was opened in Barcelona and a Satellite Tour with prize money of more than £5 million was introduced. In 1988, perhaps the single most important event in the Tour's brief history took place. Volvo, the Swedish car company, became corporate sponsor of the entire Tour. The Tour combined with TWI, the film and television division of IMG, to broadcast its events where applicable. Tour property and development companies were formed. A new charity programme with a target of $3 million was created.

Now players from more than 20 different nations compete in 14 European countries during the Volvo Tour season. The Satellite Tour was named the 'Challenge' Tour and with the Senior Tour totals more than fifty events. The regular European Tour has extended itself to Morocco, Dubai, Singapore and Thailand and has more than forty events. With a total of more than £20 million, this is big business, one of the biggest in sport.

PGA US TOUR

The US Tour evolved in much the same way and for much the same reasons as the European Tour, with its origins in the formation of a professional golfers' organisation, and an eventual breakaway by the tournament players. And the huge size and wealth of the United States saw American golf outstrip the rest of the world after the Second World War, and allowed American golfers, men and women, amateurs and professionals, to dominate the game for several decades.

The US PGA was formed in 1916 and the US PGA Championship, now considered one of the four 'major' events, was inaugurated that same year. Before then, there were precious few tournaments, prominent among them the Western Open, the North and South, the Southern and of course the US Open, but after the First World War there was an explosion in the game, with courses springing up all over the country. In the 1920s, property and hotel developments associated with golf courses were rife in all resort areas such as Miami and Miami Beach, Tampa and Sarasota in Florida. Golf tournaments and exhibition matches helped to publicise them, and so to sell them. With the northern and middle western states smothered in snow in winter,

and courses closed, club professionals would take winter jobs at Florida clubs or compete in an increasing number of winter events through the southern states. This 'Sunshine' or 'Grapefruit' circuit, as it came to be known, covered California, Texas and Florida. As early as 1919 the great Walter Hagen had quit an excellent club job in Detroit to devote himself to playing tournaments and exhibitions, which he went on to do worldwide.

Hagen's manager, Bob Harlow, had worked for many years to put some order into the professional tournaments before 1936 when a Boston Irishman, Fred Corcoran, became effectively the tournament director of the PGA. Corcoran was essentially a salesman, whether it was selling a story to the golf writers or persuading chambers of commerce, or the publicity department of resorts, that a professional tournament was a marvellous promotion which would have them mentioned in every newspaper in the country. Within a year, Corcoran found manna from heaven in Sam Snead. Fred made the most of this hillybilly slugger who could drive further than anyone, dubbing him Slammin' Sam and spinning stories of how he had whittled his own golf clubs from limbs of trees, played in bare feet in the mountains of West Virginia, and so on.

In 1936 the professionals played 22 tournaments. Ten years later, there were 45. Total prize money increased from $110,000 to $600,000. Following the Second World War there was yet another explosion of golf, like everything else in America, and that, plus the advent of television (and Palmer) in the late 1950s brought stresses between the US PGA and the

tournament players, who wanted more direct control over their affairs. In 1968, Joseph C Dey became the first commissioner of what was called the Tournament Players' Division. He was succeeded in 1974 by Deane R Beman. He very quickly deemed it the 'US Tour' and its activities have expanded hugely, incorporating a Senior Tour for professionals over 50 and a Nike Tour for 'apprentices' seeking a way into the big tour, with corporate partners such as Buick, IBM, Eastman, Kodak and Mastercard; plus golf course design and management, property investment, film and television and a host of ancillary activities. Total prize money on the US Tour is now in the region of $50 million per annum.

PINEHURST

The development of Pinehurst, in the sand and pine country of North Carolina, as a winter golf resort is linked with the

PINEHURST		
HOLE	YARDS	PAR
1	396	4
2	441	4
3	335	4
4	547	5
5	445	4
6	212	3
7	401	4
8	487	5
9	166	3
OUT	3430	36
10	578	5
11	433	4
12	415	4
13	374	4
14	436	4
15	201	3
16	531	5
17	190	3
18	432	4
IN	3590	36
TOTAL	7020	72

names of James Tufts and Donald James Ross. Tufts, of the American Soda Fountain Company of Boston, did not enjoy the best of health, and to escape the hard edge of the New England winters had bought 5000 acres of virgin timber at the village of Pinehurst in the 1890s. He paid one dollar an acre for the land and laid out a workable but rather nondescript 18 holes of golf on it. Donald Ross, from Dornoch in the north of Scotland, had arrived in the Boston area in 1898, going to work as a professional at the Oakley Club. In 1900, two events took place at Pinehurst which were to have lasting effects on the future of the village, and of American golf. Harry Vardon, the great English champion, played well-publicised exhibition matches there on his tour of America and James Tufts, who had become aware of Ross in Massachusetts golfing circles, invited the young Scot to become winter professional at Pinehurst.

Ross had trained as a carpenter, then become a professional at Dornoch, and had spent two years working with Old Tom Morris as a clubmaker at St Andrews before returning to his native village.

With the Dornoch course and the Old Course very much in his mind, he had very clear ideas as to what a golf course should look like. Ross arrived at Pinehurst in December 1900, and got to work first tidying up and improving the existing course and then building second and third 18s as Pinehurst became progressively more popular and profitable as a winter golfing resort, under the benign management of the Tufts family. Today Pinehurst boasts seven golf courses despite a resident population of just a few thousand.

Ross made of the No. 2 course a masterpiece, a classic of design that is virtually a 'links in a forest'. In its original form, finished in 1907, it ran to less than 6000 yards, but he tinkered and improved and polished his creation for the rest of his life.

The Pinehurst courses had been built originally with sand greens, the summer climate being unfriendly to grass, and the sand greens had reached high standards of design, appearance and playability. But by 1936, the greens had been converted to Bermuda grass, the No. 2 course was touching 7000 yards and it was considered good enough to stage the 1936 US PGA Championship, won by Densmore Shute.

Ross's Pinehurst No. 2 combined in a most intriguing way the 'underfoot' conditions of a Scottish links course and the 'overhead' conditions of a great American parkland course. The holes march comfortably through the pine forest, each screened from the other by stands of mature pines. The drive at the par-5 fifth hole is possibly the only blind shot on the course. The only water is a modest lake in front of the 16th tee. Ross did not much care for water as a defence against the golfer, holding it to be too penal. Any shot off the fairway, however, would find a lie among pine needles, or tufts of wiry grass in the sand. Recoveries from off the fairway are seldom very successful. But the course's greatest defences are the greens.

They are small, raised slightly, sloped, and inclined so as to throw off the less than perfect shot into swales and little valleys just off the greens, demanding those chip shots or running pitches so commonly encountered around the greens of links courses. Pinehurst No. 2 is

accepted as an American classic. Only the remoteness of the village and the absence of a large supporting population has prevented it from being widely used as a championship and tournament venue. It did stage the Ryder Cup matches in 1951.

PINE VALLEY

In February 1913, George Crump started to chop his way through a pine forest in southern New Jersey. Ten years and 22,000 tree stumps later, the Pine Valley course was opened. Donald Ross, one of golf's finest architects said, 'This is the finest golf course in America.' His judgement is such that Pine Valley is considered one of the two or three finest courses in the world.

Pine Valley is a beautiful monster. It has been described as the most difficult course in the world, but is a masterpiece of design, with classic golf holes which incorporate all the wiles of golf course architecture in spite of having being built essentially by the amateur Crump. The basic principle of its design makes it unlike any other in the world. It is an 'island' course, a course without fairways as such, with the exception of the formidable par-5 15th of 584 yards, one of the few straightaway holes on the course and the only one with a continuous fairway.

From the tees, the target landing areas are islands of grass, surrounded by sandy wastes and forests. The approach shots must then carry further deserts of sand to island greens. There are no bunkers as such at Pine Valley, merely sandy wastes. In them grow shrubs and dwarf pine trees and so extensive are they that it would be impossible to keep

them raked. So in addition to everything else, they are pitted with the footprints of half a century of benighted golfers. When a ball is in the sand at Pine Valley, the player can forget about advancing the ball with a polished, copybook recovery shot – what is needed is a heave to get it back onto the nearest island.

Through the dense forest, each hole is isolated from the next, so that a man can feel abandoned by the entire world. Roger Wethered, in his day an Amateur Champion, Walker Cup player and a man who played off for the Open Championship of 1921, was once playing the 8th hole, a drive and a pitch to a minuscule green, which he missed. He then went to and fro from sand to sand and holed out in 11. Bernard Darwin, the golf writer and Walker Cup player, was level par after seven holes, and drove nicely up the 8th. When he holed out, he was 12 over par.

The course makes all of this clear immediately, at the very first hole. The drive is played over a spread of sand to a fairly reasonable fairway. But the angle of its dog-leg to the right is sharp, and the ball needs to be out better than 200 yards for a sight of the green. Then a long second – the hole is 427 yards – must fly all the way to the green. There is no possibility of running shots into these Pine Valley greens.

The par-3 holes are beautiful, two of them over water. The 5th, stretched by Harry Colt to 232 yards, is world renowned, a full shot over water, over a swathe of sand to a two-tiered green, raised and mounded. The 14th at 184 yards has fifty yards of water, then bunkers guarding the front of the green, and with more water at the back left demands a precision strike.

The par-5 holes, the 7th at 567 yards and the 15th at 591 yards, are unreachable in two in any conditions by your average, mortal golfer. The 7th epitomises Pine Valley. The drive is to an island in the sand. The second has to cross 'Hell's Half Acre' of scrub to another island in the sand and the third shot is to a green surrounded by sand! And the 15th demands a drive over water.

Pine Valley is a masterpiece. The club is also, simply, a golf club and the members take a patriarchal attitude to the game and to maintaining the dignity of the course. They have never sought a major championship of any kind, not even the US Amateur. But Pine Valley has staged two Walker Cup matches, in 1936 and 1985.

PINE VALLEY		
HOLE	YARDS	PAR
1	427	4
2	367	4
3	181	3
4	444	4
5	232	3
6	388	4
7	567	5
8	318	4
9	427	4
OUT	3351	35
10	146	3
11	392	4
12	344	4
13	448	4
14	184	3
15	591	5
16	433	4
17	338	4
18	428	4
IN	3304	35
TOTAL	6655	70

The 9th hole at the Pine Valley club in New Jersey, considered by many to be the world's most difficult golf course. ➤

PLAYER, Gary

Born 1935

Nationality South African

Turned Pro 1953

Majors Open Championship 1959, 1968, 1974; US Open 1965; US Masters 1961, 1974, 1978; US PGA 1962, 1972

The career of Gary James Player has been unique. His story has been essentially that of the little fellow from the distant, foreign country who went to the big country and tackled all the big fellows there and beat them, over and over. It has been a career which has brought him nine major championships, the 'Grand Slam' of golf, 21 wins on the regular US Tour, 13 South African Open titles, seven Australian Opens, five World Match Play Championships, two Brazilian Opens, in one of which he had a round of 59; individual and team victories in the World Cup, the Senior Opens of both Britain and America, and a total of at least 30 golf tournament wins worldwide.

The achievement is virtually incomparable, yet Player, born in Johannesburg on 1 November 1935, had nothing in his background to suggest such a life. For one thing, he did not play golf until he was 15. He had no successes in Johannesburg amateur golf. But within a few weeks of first playing the game, he knew that he would become a golfer. At 17, he became an assistant professional at the Virginia Park club, and got some local competitive experience which produced one solitary victory, in the East Rand Open. In the 1955 South African Open, he failed to qualify, but nevertheless went ahead with a trip to England. His father Harry organised an overdraft. His club members raised a

collection. George Blumberg, who was to be a lifelong friend, gave him £50. So he left home with £200 and an air ticket, a very limited wardrobe, and an atrocious golf grip and swing. En route, he won the Egyptian Match Play Championship and £300 – a fortune at the time.

In England, his grip was an immediate target of attention and criticism. Gary had his right hand under the shaft, showed four knuckles on his left hand, and hit huge storming hooks. More than a few people in the game told him he would never be a player with such a grip. He went home chastened, but unbowed, believing then, as for the rest of his life, in a creed that holds that 'nothing is impossible if you go at it long enough, persistently enough'.

He made some changes in his grip, removed some of the violence from his swing and went back to England in 1956, this time as the reigning South African Open Champion. He promptly won a Dunlop Tournament over five rounds at Sunningdale in a fine battle with Arthur Lees, for many years the club professional there.

He was fortunate that Bobby Locke, the first of South Africa's great international champions, had gone before him to Britain to win four Open Championships within a decade, and to play with outstanding financial success in America. Gary Player followed the trail. In 1958, he finished second to Tommy Bolt in the US Open. In 1959, he won the British Open at Muirfield, scoring 70 and 68 on the final day's 36 holes. In May 1960, he agreed to be

Gary Player above them all at Augusta. The South African has won the Masters there three times.

represented by Mark McCormack and the next year, 1961, was successful beyond his wildest dreams. Concentrating mainly on the US Tour, he was leading money winner for the year there and won three tournaments, including the Masters. His win was dubbed 'the Masters that Palmer lost'. Arnold walked onto the 72nd tee needing a par 4 to win the tournament. He took six on the hole. Player had 'backed in' to the title, but he was the champion – it made him a national figure in America.

When he won the US PGA Championship in 1962, Player within five years had seen five of his dreams, his fantasies, come true – he had won the British Open Championship, the US Masters, the US PGA, had been leading money winner in the US, and top of the averages there. All that remained was the Open Championship of the United States. It came in 1965, when he beat Kel Nagle of Australia in a play-off. So a remarkable career was complete. He had won the Grand Slam of the four major championships in world golf. Only Gene Sarazen and Ben Hogan before him had done it. Jack Nicklaus was to do it later.

Gary's career had been punctuated with preposterous shots and bursts of scoring; by outrageous statements and opinions held from time to time; and some bizarre suggestions as to what is needed to be a champion. In winning his Open at Carnoustie, on the 14th hole par 5 he hit a 3-wood second shot blind, over 'The Spectacles' (a pair of bunkers set in a ridge) to within three feet of the hole for an eagle which held off Jack Nicklaus and brought Player the second of his three wins.

On the 16th hole of the last round of the US PGA Championship at Oakland Hills, Detroit in 1972, his tee

shot went 20 yards into the right rough on a hole that is a par-4 of 400 yards, dog-legged to the right. Between his ball and the green was a stand of willow trees. Between these and the putting surface was a wide lake. There were three bunkers beyond the flagstick, in line with his shot. He was 150 yards from the flag. His 9–iron shot finished four feet from the hole. The birdie helped him win the championship by two strokes. For his third Masters success in 1978, at the age of 42, he produced a last round 64, with an inward half of 30 and with seven birdies in the last ten holes. In the semi-final of the Piccadilly World Match Play Championship in 1965, he was seven down to Tony Lema with 17 holes to play – and won on the 37th green. After that Masters win in 1978 incidentally, he was so supercharged that he won the next tournament, in California, then the next, in Texas, to make it three in succession, the last man to do such a thing on the US Tour.

No one, not even Ben Hogan, practised more than Gary Player. He made himself an outstanding bunker player, wearing out the flanges on several sand wedges. He studied dieting and became a food faddist, spurning alcohol, tobacco, tea, coffee and sugar. He exercised endlessly, weight-training to put a couple of inches on his thighs when he wanted more power in his legs. He studied the power of positive thinking and ran through a variety of putting strokes.

His has been a lengthy career, spanning forty years of competitive play and made all the more astonishing by the fact that he has remained a resident of Johannesburg, travelling 12,000 miles to compete on the US Tour. It has been a career founded on determination, a dogged

dedication to winning and to proving that he can take on the world and beat it. Gary Player's achievement is one of the most remarkable of any champion in any sport.

PORTMARNOCK

In a country bursting with magnificent golf courses, Portmarnock is generally considered to be the finest course in the Republic of Ireland. It is a majestic links, laid out on a peninsula some 10 miles north of Dublin, and thus, in the classic links tradition, its playing is affected constantly by wind and weather. In its championship setting, it plays to more than 7000 yards, laid out in two loops of nine which march through the duneland, and mean that in any one round, the wind will challenge the player from every direction.

The club celebrates its centenary in 1994, and it all began when two hardy souls, George Ross and JW Pickeman, rowed over to the peninsula from Sutton and found something of a

PORTMARNOCK		
HOLE	YARDS	PAR
1	388	4
2	368	4
3	388	4
4	460	4
5	407	4
6	586	5
7	180	3
8	370	4
9	444	4
OUT	3591	36
10	380	4
11	445	4
12	144	3
13	565	5
14	385	4
15	192	3
16	527	5
17	466	4
18	408	4
IN	3512	36
TOTAL	7103	72

wasteland. They decided it had golf potential, however, and soon had nine holes going. Four years later, Pickeman had designed a further nine and by 1899, they had their first professional tournament, won by – Harry Vardon! There had already been golf of a kind on the peninsula, on land owned by the Jameson whiskey family and indeed John Jameson became the first president of the club.

The course has matured and been modified or extended over the years to designs by the famous Hawtree architects, father and son, and there are now 27 holes available to the members. The championship course boasts many magnificent holes, none more striking or demanding than the 15th, a beautiful par-3 of 192 yards running along the shoreline. Major national and international events, such as the Dunlop Masters, the Canada (now World) Cup and Irish Opens have been played at Portmarnock. In 1949, the only Amateur Championship to be played outside the UK was played there, provoking the late Henry Longhurst, the golf writer and broadcaster, to complain about playing the championship 'in a foreign country'. That championship was won by Sam McCready, an Ulsterman.

PRESTWICK

In July 1851, a group of golfers who played intermittently over sandy ground at Prestwick, gathered in the Red Lion Inn, which happily still stands at Prestwick Cross. They formed Prestwick Golf Club, which was to have a singular place in golfing history. The Earl of Eglinton, the local lord of the manor, became President and among the original members, 57 in

number, was one Colonel James Ogilvie Fairlie of Coodham, a friend of Eglinton. The Coodham property was but five miles from Prestwick, and the Colonel was a golfer, described as a 'handsome gentleman, skillful at all manly exercises'. In a sense, he was the founder of the club. With John Cuthbert, a friend who was to become secretary and treasurer, he arranged a mailing to potential members, calling the meeting.

Later that year, Fairlie persuaded 'Old' Tom Morris of St Andrews to come to the west with his family ('Young' Tom was an infant then) to become the Prestwick club professional, at a salary of £50 per annum. Being the professional meant in effect that Morris would serve the club as a ball and club maker and would lay out a definitive course for them, and maintain it in good condition. Old Tom's days as a busy golf architect lay ahead of him – he was only 30 years old – but he set out 12 holes on a stretch of ground bounded by the railway, the Pow Burn, and the water of the Firth of Clyde. It was classic linksland with sandy subsoil, bent grasses, heather, large and deep bunkers, fast undulating greens and constant movement in the fairways. The Morris course lasted for 30 years, then was extended to 18 holes by taking in land beyond the Pow Burn. That was a decision not hailed rapturously by the more conservative members.

The club and its 12 holes course was host to the first Open Championship in 1860 and indeed created it by inviting the other clubs to send professional players for an event which would be 'open to the world'. The prize was to be The Belt, of red Morocco leather with silver clasps. It cost £25. The

PRESTWICK

HOLE	NAME	YARDS	PAR
1	Railway	346	4
2	Tunnel	167	3
3	Cardinal	482	5
4	Bridge	382	4
5	Himalayas	206	3
6	Elysian Fields	362	4
7	Monkton Miln	430	4
8	End	431	4
9	Eglinton	444	4
OUT		3250	35
10	Arran	454	4
11	Carrick	195	3
12	Wall	513	5
13	Sea Headrig	460	4
14	Goosedubs	362	4
15	Narrows	347	4
16	Cardinals Black	288	4
17	Alps	391	4
18	Clock	284	4
IN		3294	36
TOTAL		6544	71

championship was won by Willie Park of Musselburgh with a score of 174 for 36 holes, three rounds of Prestwick's 12, by two strokes from Tom Morris.

There were eight players in the field. The Open was sponsored by the Prestwick club until 1872, when the Royal and Ancient and the Honourable Company of

Trying to carry this ridge on the 5th can provide all sorts of problems for the golfers of Prestwick.

become 'Royal' and all in all, it can be said that as Muirfield is to Edinburgh and the East of Scotland, so Prestwick is to Glasgow and the West of Scotland.

PRICE, Nick

Born 1957

Nationality Zimbabwean

Turned Pro 1977

Majors US PGA 1992

Probably the only contemporary golfer who has seen war service, Nick Price has yet another distinction. He holds passports of three countries – South Africa (he was born in Durban on 28 January 1957), Great Britain (his parents are British born) and Zimbabwe, to which country the Price family moved when he was a child. Nick, now resident in the US, is thus the most international of golfers.

He served in the Rhodesian Air Force in the war which ultimately brought Zimbabwe into being, but he had already made a mark in golf. Starting the game at eight, he was invited to play in the Junior World Cup in California at the age of 17, and promptly won it. He had played the South African and European tours as an amateur in 1975 before war service took the next two years out of his life. After it

For many years one of world golf's top ten, Nick Price of Zimbabwe acknowledges his sucess in the 1992 US PGA Championship at the Bellerive club in St Louis.

he turned professional and within two years had won the first of several South African events. He won the Swiss Open of 1980, the Italian Open of 1981, and in 1982 had the first of two near misses in the British Open Championship.

Nick Price stood on the 13th tee at Royal Troon leading the field by three strokes, but over the closing holes he dropped four shots and lost the championship to Tom Watson. In his first year on the US Tour, 1983, he qualified for the World Series of Golf as leader of the South African Order of Merit, played brilliantly and won the tournament by four strokes from Jack Nicklaus. His second disappointment in the British Open was less harrowing than the first. Going into the last round at Royal Lytham in 1988 leading by two strokes, Price scored a perfectly fashioned final round of 69 only to be beaten by a brilliant closing 65 by

Severiano Ballesteros.

At the presentation Ballesteros forecast that Price would certainly win a major championship before long, a fact confirmed in 1992 when Nick took the US PGA Championship at the Bellerive Club in St Louis. It was a carry over from his 1991 season when he won the Byron Nelson tournament and the Canadian Open, and the quality of Price's play was confirmed by the fact that before the end of 1992 he had won three more events and had passed $3 million in tournament earnings.

The Nick Price technique and swing is all brisk and businesslike. He is a crisp mover, with a swing that is both fast and compact and controlled, the whole thing rather in the Tom Watson manner. Serious critics of the game are convinced that more major championships will fall to the highly popular Zimbabwean.

Edinburgh joined them and it was played in rotation at Prestwick, St Andrews and Musselburgh.

Progressively into the 20th century, with the coming of the Haskell ball and steel shafts and an increasing interest in the game reflected in ever-increasing crowds at major events, Prestwick could no longer cope. Open Championships continued to be played there up to 1926, with a total of 24 since 1860, and Amateur Championships were held up to 1987, a total of 10 in all.

Narrow fairways and blind shots make Prestwick somewhat old-fashioned. It has been called an 'ancient monument', but as such, in the view of its members, it must be preserved. The club is inordinately proud of having been the birthplace of the Open. Like the Honourable Company of Edinburgh Golfers, it has never seen the need to

R

RAY, Ted

Born 1877

Nationality British

Turned Pro 1894

Majors Open Championship 1912; US Open 1920

Harry Vardon and Edward Ray, close friends all their lives, were both born in Jersey, in the Channel Islands, and there the similarity ends. In contrast to the quiet, self-effacing, almost introverted Vardon, Ted Ray was an outgoing, ebullient type, given to vigorous outspoken expression in a relaxed attitude to life. He was a huge, lumbering figure of a man, who gave the ball a fearful smash with a swing that was described as 'a rhythmic lurch'. Most of the time, the ball went far and sure and when it didn't, Ted was a master at recovery shots and at niblick play in general. One of the classic golfing photographs is of Ted Ray following through, both feet pointed to the hole, pipe clenched in his teeth, Trilby hat firmly on his head and the buttoned jacket, like the moustache, the fashion of the time.

Ted is almost certainly the originator of the well-worn phrase, in response to being asked how to get more distance, 'Hit it a bloody sight harder, mate.' Yet his game was not simply power. He was an excellent putter and had a delicate touch at, of all things, lawn bowls. And he was a fine player long before he won his Open in 1912. He was runner-up to James Braid in the very first News of the World Match Play Championship in 1903, the first of a series that ran until 1969. He was runner-up to Braid again in 1911, and to Vardon in 1912. His 295 in winning the Muirfield Open of 1912 equalled the championship record set by JH Taylor in 1909. In defending his title at Hoylake the following year, he finished second to JH Taylor – but by eight strokes!

With Vardon, Ray of course suffered at the hands of the 19-year-old Francis Ouimet in the US Open of 1913 at Boston, when the youngster beat them in a three-way playoff. And only an inexplicable collapse by Vardon over the last nine holes allowed Ray, at the age of 42, to win his US Open in 1920 in a raging storm. He was the oldest winner until Ray Floyd, at the age of 43, won in 1986. Ray, Vardon and Tony Jacklin are the only British golfers to have won the Open Championships of both Britain and America.

From left to right, Ted Ray, Harry Vardon and George Duncan, all Open Champions. Like Vardon, the pipe-smoking Ray also won the US Open.

Ted was active off the course, in professional golfing matters. He helped keep the impoverished PGA afloat after 1918 by arranging a gift of £500 from the Earl of Winton and he was a founder member of and investor in the Professional Golfers Co-operative Association. He played in the first Ryder Cup match against the United States, finished second to Jim Barnes in the 1925 Open, the last played at Prestwick, by a single stroke, and played in his last championship in 1932, at the age of 55.

REES, Dai

Born 1913

Nationality British

Turned Pro 1930

David James Rees had one distinction above all in British golf – he captained a winning Great Britain & Ireland Ryder Cup team. At Lindrick in 1957, it was a famous victory. Dai was an ebullient

Welshman who played nine times against the Americans. He was runner-up three times in the Open Championship. He won the PGA Match Play Championship at the age of 23, and finished second in a major tournament at the age of 60. In his time, he won tournaments in Britain, Continental Europe and Australia, and his endless enthusiasm for the game, not to mention his two-fisted baseball grip and flashing swing, typified the man. He was made an honorary member of the Royal and Ancient club in 1976, and died in 1983 at the age of 70.

ROBERTSON, Allan

Born 1815

Nationality British

Turned Pro 1830

Golf historians have been prone to describe Allan Robertson as 'the first professional golfer'. In terms

of the modern game, there is little evidence to sustain this, but what is certain is that Robertson was a powerful personality in all aspects of the game in St Andrews at a time when it was becoming less and less localised. He was born in the year of Waterloo so that by the middle of the century, at the time of the coming of the railway to St Andrews, for example (1852), Allan was in his prime. He was a short, thick-set fellow with a smooth, elegant swing, with perhaps not quite the length of the bigger men. But he was an outstanding short game player, and probably the first golfer to use the 'cleek' as an approach club, often from 100 yards out. Golf clubs of the time were still almost made of wood, but the iron-headed cleek (from the Scottish word 'cleik' meaning hook) had been developed principally for extracting balls from ruts in the ground. Golf courses of the time were rather less well manicured

than they are today.

As a boy, Allan was seldom away from the links, and he made himself the outstanding golfer of his time. He was the son of Davie Robertson and grandson of Peter Robertson, ball and clubmakers both, and he followed these trades.

'Professionals' then were apt to be ball and clubmakers, and rather more than caddies in that they would caddy, but also make up foursomes with 'the gentry', Royal and Ancient club members. Golf remained largely match play and the Dunns, Parks and Andersons would caddy, play and clash in challenge matches for substantial amounts.

It was said of Robertson that he never lost a match, which seems hardly likely. Certainly he was never beaten when partnered by Tom Morris, his apprentice. It

Young Dai Rees in the Match Play final of 1936, his first breakthrough.

The smaller of these two figures, Allan Robertson (1815-1858) is generally considered to be the first 'professional golfer'. With him is the revered Old Tom Morris (1821-1908).

was also said that in later years he avoided challenges, or ignored them, from other prominent players.

The most famous of the challenges involved the Musselburgh Dunn twins, Willie and Jamie, in 1849 over three courses. In the first meeting at Musselburgh, the Dunns won handily on their own ground. In the second at St Andrews, Robertson and Morris won. The decider would be at North Berwick and produce one of the greatest recoveries in golf. The Dunns were four up with eight of the 36 holes to play. A tremendous finish by the St Andrews men saw them square the match with two holes to play then win them both to take the £400 stake, a vast amount at that time.

Robertson and Morris disagreed over the merits of the newly-arrived gutta percha ball in 1848. Allan, after all, had a thriving business as a maker of feathery balls. A man could make only two or three featheries in one day, so that they were labour intensive and expensive. In one year, Robertson's workshop had produced some 2500. He resisted the advent of the new, cheap 'gutty' so much that Morris left him and set up in business on his own. Robertson eventually had to come to terms with the new ball, and when in 1858 he became the first man to break 80 over the Old Course, with a remarkable 79, he did it with a gutty.

Allan Robertson was never employed by the R & A, but his love of the links, and of

the town in which Robertsons had lived for generations, contributed greatly to the development of St Andrews golf. He never did play in the Open Championship, dying in 1859 following an attack of jaundice. On his death, a member of the R & A said, 'They may toll their bells and shut up their shops, for the greatest among them is gone.' The club minuted a resolution that they 'desired to record…the opinion, universally entertained, of the almost unrivalled skill with which he played the game of golf, combining a ready and correct judgement with most accurate execution. They desire also to express the sense of propriety of his whole conduct, and unvarying civility'.

ROSS, Donald

When, in the last decade of the last century, Robert Wilson, professor of astronomy at Harvard University, went to the village of Dornoch in the north of Scotland to play golf, he took lessons from and played with Donald James Ross. Their meeting was to have a profound and lasting effect on the pattern of golf and of golf courses throughout North America and indeed the world.

Golf had been played freely on the Dornoch links for 300 years. In 1877 the Dornoch Golf Club was formed. In 1886, one John Sutherland, a remarkable man who among other things was to be secretary of the club for more than 50 years, invited Old Tom Morris to come from St Andrews and redefine the existing course into a proper championship 18 holes. To this day, Morris's work is little changed. At the same time Donald Ross was growing up in Dornoch,

where his father Murdo was a stone mason, and growing into a fine golfer. He was apprenticed to Peter Murray of Dornoch as a carpenter, but John Sutherland, seeing his potential in golf, arranged for him to go to St Andrews. There, aged 20, he spent two years learning clubmaking in Forgan's shop and played golf with, and talked to, Old Tom Morris.

When Ross returned to Dornoch, Sutherland made him club professional and greenkeeper, with a small shop and workshop and his younger brother Alec as assistant. Sutherland also instilled in the young man an abiding interest in grasses and greenkeeping and the basic qualities of a good golf hole. The Harvard professor Wilson was impressed in turn with Ross and excited him about the booming potential of the game in the United States. Ross was persuaded to emigrate. In 1898 he set out for Boston by way of Glasgow and New York, and arrived at the Wilson house in Cambridge, having walked the last few miles, with two dollars in his pocket. The very next day, he started a job at the Oakley Golf Club at Watertown in suburban Boston, which Wilson had arranged.

At Oakley, Ross ran across the Tufts family, grown wealthy in the soft drinks business, and one of whom knew Dornoch. James Tufts became impressed with Ross's history, his traditional view of the game, and his thoughts on golf course design. Not blessed with robust health, Tufts had taken to spending his winters in North Carolina where the climate was more agreeable and where at Pinehurst he had bought some 5000 acres of land at giveaway prices. With the notion that Pinehurst could develop into a successful winter resort, he had a golf course

of sorts laid out on it.

Tufts invited Ross to be his winter professional at Pinehurst and the Dornoch man arrived there in 1900, the year that Harry Vardon made his first American tour, playing exhibitions at Pinehurst. In his early years there, Donald Ross spruced up the existing course and in 1912 began work on 'Pinehurst No. 2'. It was to become a gem, now acclaimed as one of the great American golf courses.

The Pinehurst land bought by James Tufts in the sandhills country of North Carolina was desolate – pine forests, scrubland, but with a quick-draining sandy soil oddly reminiscent of Ross's familiar sandy linksland back in Scotland. And much of his original design work at Pinehurst was an adaptation of Scottish links terrain. He wanted his fairways to flow naturally into his greens. Ross greens might be raised slightly to allow for little run-off slopes and swales that would direct the errant shot into his artfully placed and attractive (in appearance) greenside bunkers. He never did use water, thinking it altogether too punitive. In the beginning, Pinehurst greens were of sand, but when grass strains were developed, Ross moulded greens that had all the subtleties of those at St Andrews – or Dornoch.

Ross advocated that there should be more than one route in the playing of a golf hole, that it should not be one way only. His creed was: 'The championship course should call for long and accurate tee shots, accurate iron play, precise handling of the short game, and finally consistent putting. These abilities should be called for in a proportion that will not permit excellence in one department of the game to affect too large deficiencies in another.'

As the Pinehurst resort grew in popularity – it came to be a Mecca of winter golf with seven courses – so Ross's services were in greater demand, and he was said to have been involved directly or indirectly with the design and construction of as many as 600 courses in North America. Oddly, apart from a few suggestions for his native Dornoch course, he did no work elsewhere. He remained at Pinehurst for the rest of his life as golf professional, course architect and builder, manager and finally a director of the Tufts company, until his death in 1948. And of Donald Ross, truly it could be said that 'if you want his monument, look around you', to Pinehurst No. 2, and to such magnificent courses, US Open venues among them, as Oakland Hills, Inverness, Interlachen, Aronimink, Scioto and Seminole, the finest course in Florida.

ROYAL AND ANCIENT GOLF CLUB

The fact that the governing body of golf in Britain, indeed of the entire world with the exception of the United States and Mexico, is a private club, is no more than yet another British idiosyncrasy. The Royal and Ancient Golf Club of St Andrews, rather like the Marylebone Cricket Club for cricket and the Jockey Club until 1993 in racing, is a prime example of how institutions in Britain have come to pass from evolution and not from decree.

The R & A in its governance of the game is responsible for the Rules of Golf; the Rules of Amateur Status; the organisation of the Open and other Championships; the selection of teams to represent Great Britain and Ireland in international competition, and the organisation of these competitions when they are played in Great Britain or Ireland. With regard to the Rules of Golf, the R & A acts in harmony with the USGA through a joint standing committee. Quite separately, it is a golf club of 1800 members of whom 750 are overseas members. It is a membership as democratic as could be, embracing all classes and all professions. The result is that it provides a vast compendium of human experience, knowledge and, it chooses to think, wisdom, so that in almost every matter arising which requires the club's attention, the best possible advice is available from its own members. And with 240 years of activity behind it, one would expect it to have a library of experience to hand.

The club was formed on 14 May 1754 when 'twenty-two noblemen and gentlemen' formed the Society of St Andrews Golfers, and drafted 13 rules for the playing of the game. Ten years earlier, 'The Company of Gentlemen Golfers', now known as 'The Honourable Company of Edinburgh Golfers', had been formed by the Edinburgh men who played their golf over Leith Links. They drafted golf's very first rules, 13 of them. Not surprisingly, the St Andrews rules were almost identical, since many of the Edinburgh golfers had taken to escaping from the crowded public links at Leith and playing in greater comfort at the much better St Andrews ground. The 22 St Andrews men embraced distinguished soldiers, Fife lairds, Members of Parliament, Edinburgh solicitors and professors at St Andrews University.

The St Andrews golfers flourished and prospered, probably because of the ever-improving quality of the links. In 1834, King William IV granted the club the title 'Royal' and the Society became 'The Royal and Ancient Golf Club of St Andrews'. The present clubhouse, massive, strong and square, was built in 1857, and during the second half of the 19th century when the game exploded dramatically at home and to a healthy extent throughout the Empire and elsewhere, more and more of the new clubs looked to the R & A for guidance. The Prestwick Club (1851) laid the foundations of the Open Championship, organising it themselves from 1860 to 1870. Then the R & A and the Honourable Company joined them and the championship rotated around the three courses, Prestwick, St Andrews and Musselburgh, until the Honourable Company moved to Muirfield in 1892 and it in turn became a venue.

The Royal Liverpool Club (1869) had instituted the Amateur Championship at Hoylake in 1885, and by 1897 the leading UK clubs suggested that the R & A should become the governing authority of golf. Since then more than 60 countries plus various unions and federations have become affiliated to it. Until the First World War, individual clubs had been responsible for organising the Open and Amateur Championships as they hosted them. In 1919, they confirmed that the R & A, as the governing body of the game, should run both championships and become responsible for the Rules of Amateur Status. All of this was confirmed in 1924 at a meeting with the Golf Unions to direct a system of Standard Scratch Scores and Handicaps. In 1948, the R & A took on the Boys, in 1963 the Youths, in 1969 the Senior Amateur and in 1991, in co-operation with the PGA Senior Tour, the British Seniors' Open Championship.

The presentation of these events involved capital expenditure and staffing. The financial affairs of the R & A as a golf club on the one hand and as a 'tournament promoter' on the other, are kept rigidly separate. Such is the organisational demand of the Open Championship that there is a specific championship staff employed and such is the enormous success of the Open now, that these other events can be financed comfortably from the 'profit' of the Open. This is better expressed as a surplus which allows the R & A to make grants and donations to such organisations as the Golf Foundation and support greenkeeping research, university scholarships and in general promote the advancement of the game.

The affairs of the club are conducted in the usual way through committees, which include Rules of Golf, General, Financial, Selection, Rules of Amateur Status, Championship, and Implements and Balls. This latter keeps an eye on the more outrageous products of technology. But perhaps the most remarkable fact about this massively important club is that it does not own a golf course. The St Andrews courses are controlled by the St Andrews Links Trust and managed by the Links Management Committee, to which the R & A has a substantial input. Three trustees and four members of the management committee are appointed by the club, and equal numbers by the local authority, the North East Fife District Council. One trustee is the current Member of Parliament for the constituency. The R & A contributes an annual agreed fee for the Trust for its members' playing privileges.

ROYAL BIRKDALE

All of the courses on the roster of Open Championship venues, it goes almost without saying, are great golf courses by any definition. Royal Birkdale is certainly that, and in many ways it is the most dramatic. The course is laid out on and through a wasteland of sand dunes – perfect country for links golf. At Birkdale, the dunes are huge. The course runs along valleys between

Tom Weiskopf driving at Royal Birkdale in the Open Championship of 1971, watched by Bert Yancey and Tony Jacklin.

them, giving shelter and a tranquil sense of isolation to the golfer, though not of course during a championship. Then, these great terraces of sand dunes lining the fairways become natural grandstands and vantage points for thousands.

The course is open, fair, and immense. There are no blind shots. There is no excessive movement in the fairways. But the greens in many cases are pushed firmly into the dunes, often with a screen of willow scrub on either side, making them, depending on the wind, challenging targets.

The club and the original course date from 1889, the design generally credited to George Lowe, who had come from Hoylake to

Lytham St Annes to be the first professional there. In 1897 the club moved to its present site on the southern fringe of Southport and in 1931 Southport Corporation, as was, bought the land and leased it to the club for 100 years. At the same time, a new clubhouse was built in controversial contemporary style and the course was modernised by Fred Hawtree and JH Taylor to accommodate steel-shaft golf.

Following the Second World War, Birkdale quickly came to be seen as a major test and Open Championships, Amateur Championships, Walker, Ryder and Curtis Cup matches and many professional tournaments testified to that. Its

ROYAL BIRKDALE		
HOLE	YARDS	PAR
1	448	4
2	417	4
3	409	4
4	203	3
5	346	4
6	490	4
7	154	3
8	458	4
9	414	4
OUT	3,339	35
10	395	4
11	409	4
12	184	3
13	506	5
14	199	3
15	543	5
16	414	4
17	525	5
18	472	4
IN	3,647	37
TOTAL	6,986	72

champions have been distinguished golfers, none more so than the finalists in the Amateur Championship of 1946 – Jimmy Bruen of Ireland winning 4 and 3 over Robert Sweeney of the United States.

Royal Birkdale's Open Champions have been Peter Thomson of Australia (twice), Arnold Palmer of the United States, Lee Trevino, Johnny Miller and Tom Watson, all three also Americans, and finally Ian Baker-Finch of Australia. Inevitably, they have produced memorable moments. In winning in 1965 against one of the most powerful fields the championship has known, Peter Thomson hit a 2-iron shot on the 18th (the 72nd) which threaded perfectly between the two front bunkers into the flat of the green. Tom Watson did exactly the same in 1983, each of these shots in the last round, each to secure the championship. Arnold Palmer in 1961, when a gale raged over Birkdale shredding exhibition tents and leaving many fairways partly waterlogged, gave a masterly exhibition of foul weather golf and long iron play, holding 1-iron shots under the tempest. They never seemed to rise more than six feet in height.

And at the 15th hole (now 16th) on the final round, Palmer hit a shot from the right rough so stunning that the club later marked the spot with a plaque. The hole was 414 yards, and from dense rough, Palmer smashed a 6-iron shot which soared out, carried a ring of bunkers onto the raised plateau of the green and finished 15 feet from the hole. Johnny Miller in 1976 played a near-flawless final round of 66. Ian Baker-Finch in 1991 did the same, scoring the outward half in a trance-like 29.

ROYAL CALCUTTA

The most obvious claim to fame that Royal Calcutta, the patriarch of Indian golf clubs, can make is that it is the oldest club in the world outside the British Isles. But more important has been the achievement of Royal Calcutta in demonstrating that grass, in its case dhoob grass, a form of broad-leafed Bermuda, could be grown and maintained in India. This simple fact contributed a great deal to the development and spread of golf in the East.

There is some evidence that officers of Scottish regiments were concerned in its foundation in 1829, but the prosperity of the club has been carried along through the years by the merchants of the city. Its original home was at Dum Dum – indeed it started life as the Dum Dum Golf Club – on land now used for Calcutta's international airport, and after several moves, it was established at Tollygunge in the southern suburbs of that vast city. After Indian Independence, some of its land was sold to the Government of Bengal, leaving it with 7,177 formidable yards of par 73 championship golf. The course has since been revised and modernised by the design partnership of Peter Thomson and Mike Wolveridge.

The land is flat, like the entire area of the Hooghly river and the delta of the Ganges, and Royal Calcutta is only a few feet above river level. Its tees and greens are the highest points on the course. Its most striking feature is its 'tanks', which are ponds used for water storage and also part of a systematic run-off to cope with monsoon rains. The soil extracted from these tanks was used to build Royal Calcutta's greens and tees

ROYAL CALCUTTA		
HOLE	YARDS	PAR
1	366	4
2	156	3
3	436	4
4	525	5
5	415	4
6	418	4
7	455	4
8	401	4
9	404	4
OUT	3,576	36
10	448	4
11	508	5
12	359	4
13	187	3
14	431	4
15	493	5
16	364	4
17	374	4
18	437	4
IN	3,601	37
TOTAL	7,177	73

and they are the dominant architectural feature of the course. In the course of a round, they have to be carried no fewer than 11 times. And when they are not in direct play, the tanks are always in distracting view. On the very first hole for example, one huge tank fills the entire fairway on the shot to the green. And the 7th, a par 4 of 455 yards, calls for a long second shot which must carry a good 100 yards across one, protecting the green. The extent of these tanks has diminished the need for bunkers – there are a mere 30 at Royal Calcutta.

ROYAL COUNTY DOWN

Royal County Down at Newcastle, on the Irish Sea coast 30 miles from Belfast, must surely vie with Pebble Beach and Cypress Point as one of the world's greatest and most beautiful ocean-side courses. It was laid out on The Warren, a patch of ground tumbling with sand dunes, a place of gorse-strewn ridges and shallow

valleys, rising and flowing, perfect linksland. The course is in an area of exceptional natural beauty, the massive Slieve Donard dominating to the south, the Mountains of Mourne sweeping around to the west, the Irish Sea, beyond a stretch of five miles of dazzling beach, to the east.

If County Down does not have the enormous sandhills of Lahinch or Ballybunion, or the fearfulness of a Portmarnock or Royal Portrush, it has its own characteristics. Rather like Birkdale, its holes run along secluded valleys, flanked by masses of flaming gorse, whins, bracken, heather. It has five blind shots. Three of its four par 3 holes are 200 yards or more. After a run of three opening holes along the shore of Dundrum Bay, it turns inland into marvellously isolated golf.

The club was formed in 1889, one of the earliest in Ulster. Newcastle had become a summer resort for Belfast businessmen with the establishment of the Belfast and County Down Railway Company, and in March of that year a meeting was called 'in the hall of Mr Lawrence's Dining Rooms, Lord Annersley (landowner) presiding, and over 70 ladies and gentlemen were present'. Golf had been played over the ground on a casual basis, but at the first meeting of their newly-formed committee in June, it was decided to ask Old Tom Morris to lay out a course 'at an expense not exceeding £4'. Morris spent two days there in July, making 'valuable suggestions'. A professional, Alex Day, was appointed.

Initially, accommodation was provided by the railway company on the platform, but by 1895, a clubhouse costing £2,200 was in place, with 'dining room…dressing rooms…lavatories and

ROYAL COUNTY DOWN		
HOLE	YARDS	PAR
1	506	5
2	424	4
3	473	4
4	217	3
5	440	4
6	396	4
7	145	3
8	427	4
9	486	5
OUT	3,514	36
10	200	3
11	440	4
12	501	5
13	445	4
14	213	3
15	445	4
16	265	4
17	400	4
18	545	5
IN	3,454	36
TOTAL	6,968	72

baths…ample accommodation is provided for bicycles'.

One of the founder members, George Combe, an early captain, was for many years chairman of the Greens Committee and was responsible for changing the routeing of the course to two loops of nine holes, the ninth returning to the clubhouse in the manner of the new Muirfield. County Down from the beginning was to be a proud club. In 1898, it put up 199 guineas for a professional tournament, attracting the best of the day. Harry Vardon beat JH Taylor by 12 and 11 in the final, a result which left John Henry less than pleased. By 1902, the Irishmen were sending a delegation to the Amateur Championship Committee, pointing out that their course was entirely fit for the championship. Request denied – they had to wait for 68 years, until 1970 when Michael Bonallack won.

In 1904, Seymour Dunn, then club professional, suggested changes in the course. In 1908, Harry Vardon returned and suggested others. Not until Harry Colt, one of the most talented of all course designers, visited in 1926 did the course take its present form. Since then, in addition to that elusive Amateur Championship, County Down, or Newcastle as it is often called, has staged the Irish Open Amateur, the Irish Close Amateur (both men and women), the British Ladies Championship – several times – a Curtis Cup match, and the Home Internationals.

The par 3 holes are outstanding at Newcastle, just one of the elements that make golf at Royal County Down a privileged and memorable experience.

ROYAL DORNOCH

Royal Dornoch might well be called the Shinnecock Hills of Scotland. Like that splendid course at the far end of Long Island, Royal Dornoch, in the far north of Scotland, is probably the least known and least played of the world's exceptional golf courses.

Dornoch is a village with a population of 1000 on the east coast of Sutherland, some 60 miles north of Inverness. Thus its links as a championship venue has been dismissed as 'too far from anywhere' by the sophists of golf, save for an enlightened few who have taken the trouble to see the course for themselves and rejoice in the splendour of a wonderful links course set in magnificent scenery. But its distance from population centres and possibly a lack of sufficient accommodation has seen it very much under-used for major events and championships. Exceptions have been the Scottish Ladies Championship in 1971 and 1984, and a year later when the Amateur Championship

was taken there experimentally and was a complete success.

Golf has been played at Dornoch for at least three centuries, the game there pre-dated only by St Andrews and Leith. A golf club was formed in 1877 and significant dates in its early history were 1883, when John Sutherland was appointed secretary, and 1903, when the railway and an overnight sleeper service from London reached Dornoch. Sutherland, an estate agent and the town factor, remained secretary for 50 years. He was an exceptional man and a fine player, an administrator, a designer of courses in the north and an amateur agronomist of sorts. And incidentally, he wrote a weekly article on golf for a London paper for more than 20 years. He added nine holes to the original nine designed by Old Tom Morris and he and JH Taylor, a Dornoch fan, made revisions. Years later, George Duncan was invited to make some improvements and the course stretched to 6,500 yards.

In 1909, the Amateur Championship, held at Muirfield, saw the 'Dornoch Invasion', when Sutherland and TE Grant, a baker's apprentice who was to become a professional, went down and disposed of the two leading amateurs of the day. Sutherland beat Harold Hilton, and Grant beat the famous John Ball. The two Englishmen made a special trip to Dornoch later to play an exhibition and see what this great course was like.

The publicity and the train service brought Dornoch to life as a summer resort and soon wealthy southerners there were building houses, or renting for the summer. Prominent among them were the Wethered and Holderness families. Ernest Holderness was Amateur Champion in 1922 and 1924, Roger Wethered in 1923, and Joyce Wethered, his sister, English and British Ladies champion over and over, dominated women's golf throughout the 1920s. Dornoch had taught them well.

The course is probably more like the Old Course at St Andrews than any other of

ROYAL DORNOCH			
HOLE	NAME	YARDS	PAR
1	First	336	4
2	Ord	179	3
3	Earls Cross	414	4
4	Achinchanter	418	4
5	Hilton	361	4
6	Whinny Brae	165	3
7	Pier	465	4
8	Dunrobin	437	4
9	Craiglaith	499	5
OUT		3,274	35
10	Fuaran	148	3
11	A'chlach	445	4
12	Sutherland	504	5
13	Bents	168	3
14	Foxy	448	4
15	Stulaig	322	4
16	High Hole	405	4
17	Valley	406	4
18	Home	457	4
IN		3,303	35
TOTAL		6,577	70

the great links courses. The movement in its fairways, the deep bunkers, the raised greens, all smack of St Andrews. There are no double greens of course, and the Dornoch greens by comparison are rather small. But their plateau effect allows little banks to carry the ball off into swales and hollows – and bunkers – garlanding them. And the contours of these greens are very demanding.

The links run eight holes out, ten back along the shore. The outward holes play along a raised shelf, the inward holes hard by the beach. Probably the most notable hole is 'Foxy', the 14th, an intriguing par 4 for 448 yards. The fairway runs out straight for about 240 yards, then takes a quick dog-leg squiggle to the line from the tee, so the temptation is to play straight across the dog-leg carry, a spread of dunes and gorse! What a shame that Dornoch is so remote. What a delight for the local citizenry to have the place to themselves for most of the year, for Royal Dornoch beyond any doubt is one of the hidden gems of Scottish golf.

ROYAL LYTHAM AND ST ANNES

If first impressions can be deceptive in golf as in other affairs, Royal Lytham and St Annes is a prime example. One comes upon the clubhouse at the end, to all intents and purposes, of a residential suburban street. But beyond the clubhouse, deceptively spacious in its turn, lies one of the world's great golf courses. Lytham, as it is generally known, is not

The spacious Victorian clubhouse of the Royal Lytham and St Annes club.

arrestingly beautiful. The club's compact property is bounded on three sides by housing and on the fourth, the seaward side, by the Lytham-Blackpool railway line. But the more one plays Lytham, walks it and studies it, the more its greatness is apparent in its shot-values and the demands it will make on the championship player.

Lytham's fairways are slender ribbons of pure linksland turf. Its greens are small, many of them raised above the level of the fairway but almost all of them leaving entrance enough to take a running approach shot. The design has holes running in every direction so that in the course of a round, the wind will apply from every direction in turn, triangles being formed at holes 4, 5

ROYAL LYTHAM AND ST ANNES		
HOLE	YARDS	PAR
1	206	3
2	437	4
3	457	4
4	383	4
5	212	3
6	490	5
7	549	5
8	394	4
9	164	3
OUT	3,302	35
10	334	4
11	542	5
12	198	3
13	342	4
14	445	4
15	463	4
16	357	4
17	462	4
18	412	4
IN	3,555	36
TOTAL	6,857	71

and 6, and more or less at 15, 16 and 17. Lytham is severely bunkered, with close on 200 traps, and as much as any Open Championship course it demands long, accurate careful striking, and calculated putting on delicately contoured greens. It is altogether a splendid golf course.

The club history begins in 1886 and as in the case of so many other British clubs, to a large extent it was a consequence of the expansion of the railway system, in this case by the Lancashire and Yorkshire Railway Company, which linked Lytham and Blackpool to the busy industrial and cotton towns of the interior of Lancashire. At that time, the ground between Lytham and Blackpool was a wasteland of sandhills and scrub, but a group of hard-nosed businessmen later saw some merit in 'the establishment of a new watering place' at St Annes. In 1874 a square mile of land was leased by the St Annes-on-Sea Land and Building Company. The railway company built a splendid new station, a pier and promenade were built, and after various financial hiccups, St Annes-on-Sea was alive and well.

A prime mover in the formation of the golf club was Alexander Doleman of Musselburgh, a teacher who had opened a school in Blackpool. He had been good enough to play in the 1870 Open at Prestwick and the first Amateur Championship at Hoylake in 1885. In 1888, George Lowe came from the Liverpool club to be Lytham's first professional, and he is generally credited with designing a course on new ground, the present site, in 1897. Over the years, Herbert Fowler, Harry Colt and CK Cotton have kept the links up to date.

Lytham records a distinguished list of Open Champions in Bobby Jones (1926), Bobby Locke (1952), Peter Thompson (1958, after a tie with David Thomas), Bob Charles (1963, after a tie with Phil Rodgers), Gary Player (1974) and Severiano Ballesteros (1979 and 1988).

ROYAL MELBOURNE

Golf in Australia was a fits and starts business in its earliest days. The occasional gold rush in the middle of the 19th century was a distraction. Immigrants from Fife had started to play on the outskirts of the Port Phillip settlement, the origin of Melbourne, and had formed a club of sorts in 1847. It was short lived. Sir James Fergusson, the Scottish governor of South Australia, introduced golf to Adelaide in 1869, but that club too did not last. The Melbourne club regrouped in 1891 when some determined Scots rounded up 100 foundation members to get the Melbourne Golf Club started. Only four years later Queen Victoria made it 'Royal', and Royal Melbourne is the oldest Australian club continuously in existence.

The spread of the city saw

Action in one of Dr Alister Mackenzie's sizeable bunkers at the Royal Melbourne club during the Johnnie Walker Australian Classic. ➤

ROYAL MELBOURNE		
HOLE	YARDS	PAR
1	424	4
2	480	4
3	333	4
4	440	4
5	176	4
6	428	4
7	148	3
8	305	4
9	440	4
OUT	3,174	36
10	460	4
11	455	4
12	433	4
13	354	4
14	470	4
15	383	4
16	210	3
17	575	5
18	432	4
IN	3,772	36
TOTAL	6,946	72

the club move twice, outwards, but it eventually settled in what has become famous in international golf as 'The Sand Belt' of Melbourne. This is a long ridge of rolling, sandy duneland, with heather and whin and healthy stands of native trees, which now contains a score or more of fine golf courses. Royal Melbourne's 'composite' course is the greatest of them. Its East and West courses are separated and bounded by busy public roads, and for the Canada Cup matches of 1959 a composite course was put into effect to eliminate traffic and movement problems.

With new land secured in 1924, the club went for the best advice in design for their West course. They chose Alister Mackenzie, the Scottish doctor fresh from designing Cypress Point in California, who after Melbourne also helped create the Augusta National course in Georgia. Mackenzie wisely enlisted a club member and fine golfer in Alex Russell – he had been Australian Open Champion

in 1924 – as his man 'in situ'. Mackenzie's West Course was opened for play in 1931. The design of the East was substantially Russell's work and it was ready in 1932.

The composite course, used frequently for Australian Open Championships, is magnificent and is considered by many eminent judges as quite simply the finest golf course in the world. By happy chance, one Claude Crockford joined the club staff in 1934, became a quite brilliant head greenkeeper and over the years made the Royal Melbourne greens – dry and firm, true and fast – one of the most frightening features of the course. Mackenzie and Russell seemed to be of one mind when it came to designing golf courses. Almost every one at Royal Melbourne is a dog-leg. Vast splashes of bunkering cover the angles. Greenside bunkers are huge, often deep, but almost every green has an entrance open at least in part to receive a running approach shot, links style.

ROYAL ST GEORGE'S

Through an immense spread of sand dunes, marching in file along the North Sea coast of Kent are three magnificent golf courses, Royal Cinque Ports, Royal St George's and Princes Golf Club. The greatest and most senior of these is Royal St George's, followed by Royal Cinque Ports, commonly known as Deal and founded in 1920; in 1932 came a Princes course that was destroyed in the Second World War, but happily rebuilt.

Royal St George's, usually

A prime example of the cavernous Royal St George's bunkers, this one on the 9th hole.

called simply 'Sandwich' from the neighbouring small town, is a massive links course, threading its undulating fairways through 300 acres of isolating duneland so that the golfer may sometimes feel abandoned in the midst of a wilderness. It is a classic links

course which in fine summer weather can be a place of beauty and tranquility, and in winter storms, simply unplayable.

The origins of the club and course are in part romantic and connect with the Wimbledon club, formed in 1865, which in turn grew out

of the London Scottish club. In the 1880s, in the midst of the first great English golf boom, play over the common at Wimbledon was becoming more and more tedious, as other users of the common took a poor view of golfers disturbing them. Dr Laidlaw Purves, an Edinburgh man who was an eye specialist at Guy's Hospital and who had been a rather truculent Wimbledon captain in his time, and Henry Lamb, the club secretary, were briefed to find another site, out of the city and far from Wimbledon's madding crowd. The story goes that they spotted the huge expanse of duneland from the tower of St Clements, the Norman church in Sandwich. The truth may have been that they spotted it from the train to Deal. And some 20 years earlier, a local schoolmaster, another Scot named Ogilvie, had played golf over the ground.

Purves and his group leased the land from the Earl of Guildford and formed the new club in 1887. Purves was its first captain. He laid out the course, and his basic routeing remains, although in later years Dr Alister

ROYAL ST GEORGE'S		
HOLE	YARDS	PAR
1	445	4
2	376	4
3	214	3
4	470	4
5	422	4
6	156	3
7	529	5
8	415	4
9	387	4
OUT	3,414	35
10	399	4
11	216	3
12	362	4
13	443	4
14	508	5
15	467	4
16	165	3
17	425	4
18	458	4
IN	3,443	35
TOTAL	6,857	70

Mackenzie and then Frank Pennink modified and modernised it. Five years on, John Ball won an Amateur Championship at Sandwich, and only seven years after its formation it was good enough to stage an Open and a historic one it was – the first played in England and won by JH Taylor.

In 1899, Harry Vardon won his third Open there. In 1904, the Open was back again and 'Sandwich' was clearly established. Jack White won then, Vardon came again in 1911 and Walter Hagen for America won twice in the 1920s. Until 1993, Sandwich's greatest Open may have been that of 1934, when Henry Cotton became the first home winner in eleven years, his second round record 65 bringing golf the famous 'Dunlop 65' ball.

When Bobby Locke beat Harry Bradshaw of Ireland in a play-off in 1949, it was clear that the Open was becoming so big in terms of galleries and traffic that the cramped, medieval town with its single lane toll bridge over the river, was no longer capable of absorbing the championship. Sandwich was ignored for 32 years until improved roads and access brought the R & A back in 1981, when Bill Rogers won. In 1985, Sandy Lyle was the first, and immensely popular, home winner since Tony Jacklin in 1969; and in 1993, Greg Norman produced the most sustained and brilliant scoring that anyone could imagine in winning his second title.

The course, if not its fairways, is spacious. Its 100 bunkers are deep and archly placed in prime positions. There remain one or two blind shots, at the fourth and seventh, perhaps, but the inward half is a real champion's test. The triangle of holes 13, 14 and 15 means coping with three different wind directions. The 14th is one of Sandwich's few straight holes, with Princes Golf Club over the fence and out of bounds along the right side, and a broad stream, the Suez Canal, crossing the fairway at 320 yards. Holes 15, 17 and 18 are all demanding par-4s of more than 400 yards each, making for dramatic finishes. There is no more testing championship course than Royal St George's.

ROYAL TROON

Royal Troon, known intimately to a passing generation of Scottish golfers as 'Old Troon', is one of the greatest of Scotland's many great championship courses, and is probably dominant in that string of excellent courses that run through the coastal dunes of Ayrshire, overlooking the lower

The stately home of Royal Troon golf club on the west coast of Scotland.

reaches of the Firth of Clyde.

It owes its existence in large part to the example of its close neighbour the Prestwick Golf Club, and to the coming of the railway system to that part of the world. One of the earliest of Scotland's railways, Kilmarnock to Troon Harbour, dates from 1811

and the important Glasgow to Ayr line running through both Troon and Prestwick was opened in 1840, bringing the fine beaches of Troon within comfortable reach of the growing populations of Glasgow and Paisley. A station was opened at Prestwick largely for the benefit of the golfers

– the Prestwick club was founded in 1851 – and no doubt many from Ayr and Troon in those days played over the Prestwick 'green'.

Inevitably, as interest in the game grew, the Troon men wanted their own course and by the spring of 1878, one James Dickie of Paisley, who had a summer house on Troon's South Beach, had negotiated with the factor of the landowning Dukes of Portland for the use of a piece of ground at Craigend Farm. Dr John Highet, a local GP, wrote to a score or more of interested parties. They included local bankers, teachers, one man of the cloth and one doctor, drawn from Troon, Kilmarnock and Glasgow. Dr Highet became the club's first secretary (he remained so for 15 years) and James Dickie was the first captain. Charles Hunter, 'Keeper of the Green' at Prestwick, laid out Troon's initial six holes. In time, more and more land was acquired, running along the shore line, until Troon reached out to Prestwick and the two courses were now separated only by the Pow Burn. In time too, various famous names in the world of course design have made their marks on Old Troon – Willie Fernie, James Braid, Dr Alister Mackenzie, Frank Pennink and Charles Lawrie

ROYAL TROON			
HOLE	NAME	YARDS	PAR
1	Seal	364	4
2	Black Rock	391	4
3	Gyaws	379	4
4	Dunure	557	4
5	Greenan	210	3
6	Turnberry	577	5
7	Tel-el-Kebir	402	4
8	Postage Stamp	126	3
9	The Monk	423	4
OUT		3,429	36
10	Sandhills	438	4
11	The Railway	481	4
12	The Fox	431	4
13	Burmah	465	4
14	Alton	179	3
15	Crosbie	457	4
16	Well	542	5
17	Rabbit	223	3
18	Craigend	452	4
IN		3,668	36
TOTAL		7,097	72

– so that now, at its championship length of just over 7000 yards, it is one of the most forbidding of courses.

It is a test of long carries to narrow fairways, with fearsome rough, a couple of blind shots, high sand dunes and rather flat greens. Perhaps only at Royal St George's do the fairways toss and tumble as they do at Troon, especially through the middle of the course. The route is St Andrews-style, straight out and back, running to the south with wind almost always coming in from the Firth and a ridge of dunes separating the course from the beach. It enjoys dramatic seascapes and views of the islands of Arran and Ailsa Craig.

Incidentally, Royal Troon (it received the accolade in its centenary year, 1978) features both the longest and the shortest hole on the Championship rota of courses. The eighth hole, the 'Postage Stamp', at 126 yards and fiercely trapped at the front and on both sides, is one of the most famous short holes in golf, played from a high tee atop one sand dune

across a small valley to a narrow green set in another dune. In championship play, a score of 15, with one putt, was made by a German amateur, who kept blasting from one bunker to another in 1950. Then in 1973 came the much-told tale of Gene Sarazen, making a nostalgic return after 50 years to a course on which he failed to qualify. This time, at the age of 71, he swung a five iron and made a hole in one.

The sixth hole at 577 yards is a strip of fairway running southwards parallel with the shore, with the wind invariably across the line from the right. The tee shot demands a carry of close on 200 yards, and 230 yards out, one bunker on the right and two on the left narrow the landing zone. There is a further bunker forward on the left, 50 yards short of the green, with another on the right 30 yards short. They have a narrowing effect on the second shot. Two very deep bunkers close out the left side of the green.

Royal Troon has staged half a dozen Open Championships, each of them producing a fine

champion – Arthur Havers in 1923, Bobby Locke in 1950, Arnold Palmer in 1962, Tom Weiskopf in 1973, Tom Watson in 1982 and Mark Calcavecchia in 1989. One of the great championship-winning shots was played by Calcavecchia at the 18th (452 yards), the fourth extra hole in his play-off with the Australians Greg Norman and Wayne Grady, when he hit a 5-iron second from the rough to within seven feet of the flagstick, for a birdie.

THE RULES OF GOLF

The Rules of Golf number 34 and cover 100 pages of a closely printed handbook. There are appendices covering designs of clubs and balls, and other subjects, and separately a book of Decisions on the Rules. The entire code runs into thousands of words and has evolved over 250 years of the game's development, as all legal systems should.

The Rules, their extent and their interpretation, have provided a rich seam of disputation for golfers on the course and in the clubhouse alike, and indeed this represents one of the game's most distinctive sources of pleasure. Not all golfers approve. Henry Longhurst, the golf writer and broadcaster, no doubt tongue in cheek and with impish intent, used to claim and write that the rules 'should be written on the back of a postcard'. Peter Thomson, the great Australian champion, claimed that it should be quite enough to 'play the ball as it lies and do not touch it between tee and green'. Thomson was a keen, incisive student of every aspect of the game and no doubt was in one of his arch moods when he said this. Jack Nicklaus, on the other hand, had a clear

understanding of what the Rules of Golf should mean to the player – 'A Bill of Rights, and not a penal code'. The Rules, according to Jack, were to protect the player from himself as much as anything.

The game had been played after a fashion for a good three centuries without any formal body of rules. In the beginning, of course, the game was one of individual matches over some very rough ground and no doubt the players made up rules as they went along, or came to some rough agreement before they teed off. It was only when clubs or societies were formed that general, if not quite universal rules were laid down, the first of them by the Company of Gentlemen Golfers. On 7 March 1744, Edinburgh Town Council, responding to direct approaches that had been made from time to time by 'several Gentlemen of Honour skilful in the ancient and healthful exercise of Golf', recognised the existence of the Gentlemen Golfers and presented to them a Silver Club, to be played for annually according to the 'proper regulations' drawn up by these Gentlemen Golfers.

This was minuted by the Town Council and from it sprang the birth of the world's oldest golf club, subsequently named 'The Honourable Company of Edinburgh Golfers' and their famous '13 Articles', the first code of rules in golf. These applied in the first playing for the Silver Club, on 2 April 1744. The 13 Articles were influenced by the fact that Leith Links, where the golfers played, was a public place, open to the populace – and to cattle and horses – for all manner of activities and more often than not was quite crowded.

The Edinburgh articles remain strangely relevant to

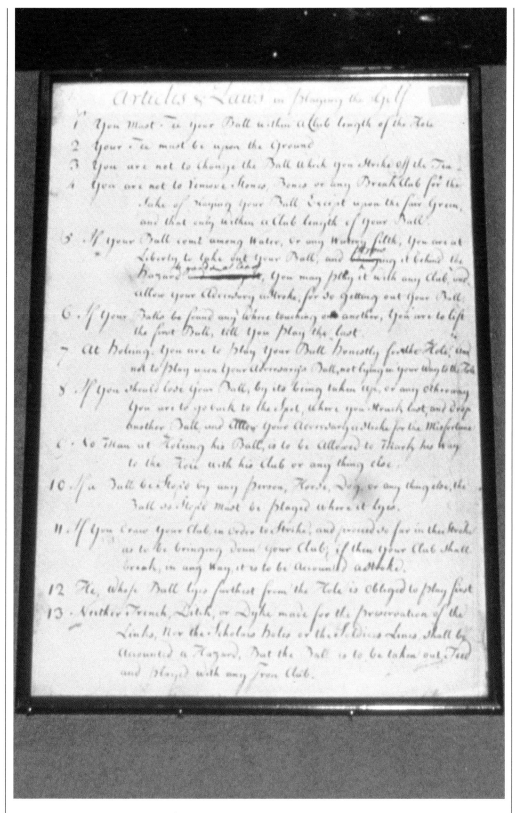

the first ball, till you play the last.

7. At holing, you are to play your ball honestly for the hole, and not to play on your adversary's ball, not lying in your way to the hole.

8. If you should lose your ball by its being taken up, or any other way, you are to go back to the spot where you struck last and drop another ball and allow your adversary a stroke for the misfortune.

9. No man at holing his ball is to be allowed to mark his way to the hole with his club or anything else.

10. If a ball be stop'd by any person, horse, dog or anything else, the ball so stop'd must be played where it lyes.

11. If you draw your club in order to strike, and proceed so far in the stroke as to be bringing down your club – if then your club shall break in any way, it is to be accounted a stroke.

12. He whose ball lyes farthest from the hole is obliged to play first.

13. Neither trench, ditch or dyke made for the preservation of the links, nor the Scholars' holes, or the Soldiers' lines, shall be accounted a hazard, but the ball is to be taken out, teed and played with any iron club.

These 13 might just have been squeezed onto Henry Longhurst's postcard. In those earliest of days, there was no out of bounds to contend with, nor yet railway lines rubbing shoulders with fairways, for example. And

the contemporary game. They were:-

1. You must tee your ball within a club's length of the hole.
2. Your tee must be upon the ground.
3. You are not to change the ball you strike off the tee.
4. You are not to remove stones, bones or any breakclub for the sake of playing your ball except upon the fair green, and that only within a club's length of your ball.
5. If your ball come among water, or any watery filth, you are at liberty to take out your ball and bringing it behind the hazard, and teeing it, you may play it with any club and allow your adversary a stroke for so getting out your ball.
6. If your balls be found anywhere touching one another, you are to lift

oddly enough, these original rules made no point about playing the ball as it lies. Peter Thomson would have put that right.

When the St Andrews golfers, ten years later, formed the society which was to become the Royal and Ancient Golf Club of St Andrews, they adopted the 13 articles with one slight difference – under Rule 5, 'if your ball come among water or any watery filth', at Leith you had to lift and tee it up. The St Andrews idea was that the ball should be dropped, not teed. Methods of dropping the ball were to stay in the rules up to the present day. Before the end of the 18th century, other clubs had been formed – Edinburgh Burgess, which claims to be the oldest of all golf clubs but unlike the Honourable Company has no written evidence to sustain that, Montrose, Aberdeen, Musselburgh, Crail, the Glasgow club and several in England. All had their codes of rules.

The Leith rules, revised in 1775 and in 1809, were broadly accepted for the best part of a century. But early in the 19th century, the Honourable Company had fallen into decline for a spell. Their lease of the course on Leith Links lapsed, and for five years they were homeless; then in 1836, they shared a course with Royal Musselburgh. On the other hand, the R & A went from strength to strength. In 1834, it became 'Royal'. When the Prestwick club was created in 1851, it adopted the St Andrews rules. The other clubs were inclined to do the same. In 1889 the minutes of the Royal Blackheath recorded that the club's rules would be those promulgated by the R & A, and at the same time, the Honourable Company accepted St Andrews rules.

From 1848, a major change

had come over golf. The feathery ball was replaced by the gutty, which flew further, lasted longer, was much cheaper, and brought changes in clubmaking and indeed in the pattern of the golf swing and stroke making. With it came the need for more sophistication, more centralisation in the rules. Towards the end of the century, with the Open Championship and the Amateur Championship established and golf enjoying immense popularity, the clubs began to feel that the game's legislation was adrift. A number of clubs, led by Royal Wimbledon, encouraged the R & A to take the initiative in instituting a uniform code of rules. After some huffing and puffing, it was agreed that the R & A rules should be accepted by all, and that the R & A should appoint from its members a Rules of Golf Committee. This committee came into being in 1897 and remains in place to this day.

The original 13 articles had been left far behind. They had expanded by 1829 to a score of simple regulations, but by 1893 the R & A code ran to 40 rules, quite detailed, with 14 special rules for medal play and ten additional paragraphs dealing with the etiquette of the game. It detailed the round and the match, the tee and the hole. It should be remembered that 150 years earlier there had been no 'greens' as we know them now, but in 1893 there were specific regulations about play on the greens. Sections dealt with 'the honour', order of play, rules for disputes, markers, and instructions yet again on how to drop the ball. In 1774 at St Andrews, the player could lift his ball out of water 'or any watery filth and throw it behind the hazard six yards at least'. The

Burgess Society in 1773 said the opponent should drop it! In 1776 it was to be thrown over his head by the player, in 1807 over his shoulder, in 1839 over the right shoulder. In 1809, the Honourable Company said the player should face the hole when dropping. In 1829 and 1934 Musselburgh said the caddie should drop it!

In 1902, golf suffered another sea change with the coming of the wound ball, the Haskell ball. In time, with the huge advance in the technology of manufacture of golf balls and clubs, a complete appendix to the Rules of Golf regarding the dimensions, form and qualities of clubs and balls was required.

The whole subject of penalties for balls being dropped – for lost ball, out of bounds and the like – differed widely. The stymie was another contentious subject – back in the mid-18th century, the Edinburgh Burgess rules allowed a player to 'play on' the other ball, i.e. to have his ball strike his opponent's ball.

The creation of the United States Golf Association in 1894 brought American golf and golfers to the forefront. Walter Travis, an Australian-born American and a tough, self-taught player, came to Sandwich in 1904 and swept off with the Amateur Championship. He was amongst other things a deadly putter, using a centre-shafted club, the so-called 'Schenectady Putter'. So miffed were the British at losing their championship to an American that they promptly banned such putters, deeming them illegal. So started a period of aloof, if not strained, relationships between the R & A and USGA, at least as far as the rules and equipment were concerned.

The Americans went their own way. They abolished

the stymie. In the 1920s they legalised steel shafts some years before the R & A. They preferred a bigger ball, 1.68 inches in diameter against the British 1.62, claiming it sat up better on their more lush fairways and was more pleasant for their average player. Not until the 1960s in fact did the British PGA change to the larger ball. It is now in common use. It was clear that these continuing differences were not in the best interests of the game. Representatives from both sides conferred in London and St Andrews in 1951, and through a joint committee which was set up, agreed upon a unified Code of Rules which would apply to golf throughout the world. This was subsequently ratified by all of golf's governing bodies. The chief changes were the abolition of the stymie; the legalisation of the centre-shafted putter; and the uniformity of the penalty (stroke and distance) for lost ball, out of bounds, unplayable and the like.

The Joint Committee meets every four years to review the rules and propose any changes which seem necessary. These are now on the whole minor, and it has all become an exercise in fine-tuning. The executive staffs of each body are in constant touch regarding definitions and the solving of freak incidents which still arise in the game. The Joint Committee has been a complete success.

THE RYDER CUP

The first Ryder Cup presentation was to Walter Hagen, captain of the United States team, at Worcester, Massachusetts in 1927 after a match in which the Americans gained a convincing 9½ – 2½ win. The magnificent solid gold trophy was put up for a biennial competition between Great Britain and United States professionals

The Ryder Cup – the figure on top was modelled on Abe Mitchell, for many years private professional to the donor, Samuel Ryder

by Samuel Ryder, a wealthy Englishman who had made his fortune from flower seeds.

The previous year, in an unofficial match at Wentworth, Surrey, Great Britain trounced the American team 13½ – 1½. Such a resounding victory was never achieved in Ryder Cup competition; in fact after sharing the honours over the first four meetings, Great Britain lost the next seven and in 1947 they just avoided the humiliation of a whitewash by winning the last singles, to finish the match 11 – 1 down.

We had to wait until 1957 for the first British post-war victory, but what a magnificent triumph by

The 9th hole at the Brabazon course of The Belfry – 400 yards, par 4, dog-leg to the left, the green tucked to the right, carry the approach shot over water!

Great Britain. After losing the foursomes 3 – 1 they won six singles, halved one and lost only one to run out winners by 7½ – 4½. Dai Rees, captain of the British side, won both his matches. He probably enjoyed a longer association with the Ryder Cup than anybody, having first taken part in it in 1937, and even after his last appearance in 1961 he came back as a non-playing captain in 1967. As his career was interrupted by the war, he made only nine playing appearances; Christy O'Connor Sr leads at present with 10; Nick Faldo has so far played in nine and looks set to pass O'Connor's total.

Faldo was the youngest-ever competitor when he first played in the competition in 1977 at the age of 20, and his achievement on his debut was truly outstanding as he was undefeated in foursomes, fourballs and singles.

Over the years the format of the match has changed from time to time. In 1961 the four foursomes and eight singles, which were all 36-hole matches, were changed to two series of 18-hole matches in order to create more interest. It only served to make the American dominance more apparent as they gained more of the extra points which were at stake.

A further change in 1963 saw the introduction of fourball matches and the fixture extended from two to three days. Once more the United States continued to

Celebrations by American wives in uniform after the narrow US victory at Kiawah Island in 1991.

The critical putt, last green, last hole of the match, by Bernhard Langer. Had it gone in, the 1991 match would have been tied and Europe would have retained the Cup.

pile up the additional points and apart from a tie at Royal Birkdale in 1969 their run of success lasted from 1959 to 1983. Their superiority from the time fourball matches were introduced is reflected in the size of their victories; 23 – 9 in 1963 and 23½ – 8½ in 1967.

A notable feature of the tie in 1969 was the sporting gesture by Jack Nicklaus, the American team captain. The teams were level and Nicklaus was playing against Tony Jacklin, the British team captain, in the last singles match. They were all square with one to play. On the 18th green Nicklaus sunk a difficult putt, then conceded by picking up Jacklin's ball from where it lay, about two feet from the hole; thus the hole was halved and the match tied 16 – 16.

From 1979 it was decided that a European team would oppose the United States in the Ryder Cup. This soon brought a real improvement and 1983 saw the closest match since the tie in 1969. The European team actually led 4½ – 3½ after the first

THE RYDER CUP

Year	Venue	Winning Captain	Margin
1927	Worcester (Mass)	Walter Hagen (US)	9½ - 2½
1929	Moortown	George Duncan (GB)	7 - 5
1931	Scioto	Walter Hagen (US)	9 - 3
1933	Southport & Ainsdale	JH Taylor (GB)*	6½ - 5½
1935	Ridgewood	Walter Hagen (US)	9 - 3
1937	Southport & Ainsdale	Walter Hagen (US)*	8 - 4
1947	Portland	Ben Hogan (US)	11 - 1
1949	Ganton	Ben Hogan (US)*	7 - 5
1951	Pinehurst	Sam Snead (US)	9½ - 2½
1953	Wentworth	Lloyd Mangrum (US)	6½ - 5½
1955	Thunderbird (Palm Springs)	Chick Harbert (US)	8 - 4
1957	Lindrick	Dai Rees (GB)	7½ - 4½
1959	Eldorado (Palm Desert)	Sam Snead (US)	8½ - 3½
1961	Royal Lytham & St Annes	Jerry Barber (US)	14½ - 9½
1963	East Lake (Atlanta)	Arnold Palmer (US)	23 - 9
1965	Royal Birkdale	Byron Nelson (US)*	19½ - 12½
1967	Champions (Houston)	Ben Hogan (US)*	23½ - 8½
1969	Royal Birkdale	Sam Snead (US)* tied Eric Brown (GB)	16 - 16
1971	Old Warson (St Louis)	Jay Hebert (US)*	18½ - 13½
1973	Muirfield (Scotland)	Jack Burke (US)*	19 - 13
1975	Laurel Valley	Arnold Palmer (US)*	21 - 11
1977	Royal Lytham & St Annes	Dow Finsterwald (US)*	12½ - 7½
1979	Greenbrier	Billy Casper (US)*	17 - 11
1981	Walton Heath	Dave Marr (US)*	18½ - 9½
1983	PGA National (Palm Beach)	Jack Nicklaus (US)*	14½ - 13½
1985	The Belfry	Tony Jacklin (Eur)*	16½ - 11½
1987	Muirfield Village	Tony Jacklin (Eur)*	15 - 13
1989	The Belfry	Tony Jacklin (Eur)* tied Ray Floyd (US)*	14 - 14
1991	Kiawah Island	Dave Stockton (US)*	14½ - 13½
1993	The Belfry	Tom Watson (US)*	15 - 13

non-playing captain

half hour of the very last day, when the US team eventually prevailed by 15 – 13. The last six meetings have produced one tie and four winning margins of two points or less, a wonderful advertisement for a truly thrilling event.

day but the United States drew level 8 – 8 at the end of the second day. Of the twelve singles on the final day only one was decided before the 17th and the final score was 14½ – 13½ to the Americans.

Eventually in 1985, at the Belfry, the headquarters of the European PGA, the European side triumphed 16½ – 11½. Then in 1987 there followed a further significant victory, this being the first on American soil by either a British or European side, and it took place at Muirfield Village, Ohio.

Once again in 1989 the venue was the Belfry and Europe kept one hand on the Cup with a 14 – 14 tie.

In 1991 at Kiawah Island, South Carolina, the Americans regained the trophy by the narrowest of margins, winning 14½ – 13½. The match was finally decided on the last hole of the last singles match, between Hale Irwin and Bernhard Langer.

In the 1993 event at The Belfry, the match hung in the balance until the very last

The official insignia of the 1993 Johnnie Walker Ryder Cup.

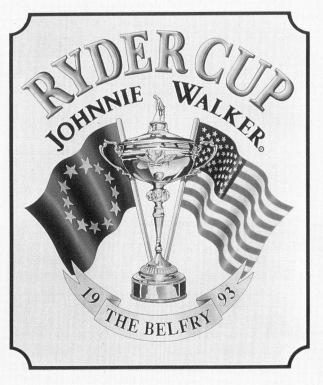

S

SARAZEN, Gene

Born 1902

Nationality United States

Turned Pro 1919

Majors Open Championship 1932; US Open 1922, 1932; US Masters 1935; US PGA 1922, 1923, 1933

On the grounds of longevity alone, Gene Sarazen, born in Harrison, New York on 27 February 1902, would be one of the most remarkable figures in American golf. But he is more than that – he is an American institution. Into his nineties, he was still able to inaugurate Masters championships by making a token drive from the first tee at Augusta, before retiring to a shaded chair to reminisce, receive his friends and gossip with the world.

Sarazen's fame survives to an extent because by winning the Masters of 1935 he became the first golfer to complete the 'Grand Slam' of the four major championships. Only Ben Hogan, Gary Player and Jack Nicklaus have achieved this since. But Sarazen was an outstanding champion long before that Masters victory. When he won the Open Championship at Princes in 1932, by a five stroke margin and with a record total of 283, he joined an exclusive club of golfers who have won both British and US Open Championships in the same year. The other members are Bobby Jones, Ben Hogan, Lee Trevino and

Tom Watson.

Gene's start in life was by no means privileged. He left school at 15, had a factory job, caddied and eventually found a place as a general dogsbody in the professional's shop at the nearby Brooklawn Country Club. The son of Italian immigrants, he learned something of clubmaking

and found time to play the game. Soon he was good enough to tackle the winter tournaments in Florida and his breakthrough came in winning the Southern Open at New Orleans in 1922, by five shots from Leo Diegel. He was 20 years old. Sarazen, at 5' 6", stocky, olive-skinned, his trade mark increasingly plus fours or

Gene Sarazen aged 91, who won the Open of 1932 on the adjoining Princes course, addresses the galleries at Royal St George's, in 1993!

'knickers' as the Americans call them, had become a ferocious competitor and a determined shotmaker with his interlocking grip and punchy, low-flighted ball. He seldom seemed to need a practice swing and in the US Open of the same year, he finished with a blazing round of 68 and a birdie on the last hole to record a 288. He was champion by one shot from – Mr Robert T Jones.

In winning his Open Championship in 1932, Sarazen scored 283 without a single six on his cards. It was a record that stood until 1950. He won by five strokes. And a few weeks later in the US Open, he finished with a 66 and victory by three strokes – that meant the last 28 holes of the championship in 100 strokes, averaging 3.57. That was Gene Sarazen; when the magic struck him nothing, it seemed, could stop him. He was cocky, occasionally bumptious, but always likeable. And he was not yet finished with dramas at the highest level of the game.

In 1935, at the second playing of the Augusta Masters, Gene Sarazen hit one of the most preposterous shots in the history of the game. After playing his tee shot at the 15th hole, a straight par-5 of 485 yards then, but with its big lake screening the entire front of the green, he learned that Craig Wood had finished with a 282 total. Sarazen, not really in contention in the tournament, would need four birdies over the four closing holes to win the Masters. Sarazen let fly with a 4-wood second, carried the pond – and holed the shot! With that one stroke, he had made up three shots. Playing carefully, he tied Craig Wood, then beat him by five strokes in the play-off.

Sarazen had yet more to contribute. His first crack at the Open Championship had been at Troon in 1923 when, swept away by a storm, he failed to qualify. When the championship of 1973 was

played at Troon, Gene returned on a nostalgic final visit. He broke 80 both rounds with his punchy swing quite unchanged, but did not make the 36-hole cut in rainy, sometimes windy conditions. But on the 8th hole of his first round, at the famous 126 yards 'Postage Stamp' hole, he holed his tee shot, with a five iron. On the second round, at the same hole, he drove into a greenside bunker, and promptly holed his recovery shot. Thus in two rounds, he had scored one, then two, on the hole. The man was 71 years old.

SCHOFIELD, Ken

Born and raised in Perthshire, Scotland, Ken Schofield, 47, left an early career in banking and entered golf administration in 1971 as a Press and Public Relations assistant to John Jacobs, the PGA's first Tournament Director. When this became the PGA European Tour in 1975, and Jacobs stood down, Schofield succeeded him as Executive Director. Since then Schofield has presided over an ever-growing organisation which brought European players into Ryder Cup teams with great success; embraced Safari Tour (Africa) events; introduced the Satellite Tour, Challenge Tour, Senior Tour; involved itself in golf course and property development, and above all expanded into 40 tournaments and £20 million of prize money each year.

Ken Schofield, executive director of the PGA European Tour.

SHINNECOCK HILLS

As one of America's 'Founding Father' clubs, Shinnecock Hills commands the same reverence there as do the Royal and Ancient and Prestwick in Scotland. With the Country Club of Brookline, Boston, the St Andrews Club of New York, the Newport Club in Rhode Island and the Chicago Golf Club, Shinnecock in December 1894 formed the Amateur Golf Association of America, which quickly became the American Golf Association and equally quickly the United States Golf Association

The new organisation staged Open and Amateur Championships in 1895, at Newport, and the following year it was the turn of Shinnecock Hills, at Southampton on the far end of Long Island. The club had a romantic, even patrician origin. Three Americans of substantial means, William K Vanderbilt, Duncan Cryder and Edward S Mead, were wintering in Biarritz in 1890–91 when they came across Young Willie Dunn of the famous Musselburgh family working on the design of an 18-hole course and hitting some impressive ranging shots in the process. Intrigued, the visitors suggested that when he had finished in France, Dunn had better get over to Long Island and do the same for them.

He was there in March 1891 and eventually, after some searching, decided on an area of scrubland close by the resort town of Southampton, only a couple of miles from the ocean. With a crew of 150 Indians from the nearby Shinnecock reservation, from which the new club was to take its name, Dunn had cleared 12 holes by mid-summer. In September, the golf club was incorporated. A short 9 hole course was added for ladies,

SHINNECOCK HILLS		
HOLE	**YARDS**	**PAR**
1	399	4
2	221	3
3	454	4
4	379	4
5	498	5
6	450	4
7	185	3
8	336	4
9	418	4
OUT	**3,340**	**35**
10	412	4
11	159	3
12	470	4
13	367	4
14	445	4
15	399	4
16	513	5
17	167	3
18	425	4
IN	**3,357**	**35**
TOTAL	**6,697**	**70**

but shortly both courses were amalgamated to a full 18. A grand custom-built clubhouse, the first in America, was soon in place and the club was established completely. The course itself is a gem. Dunn's original was no more than 5000 yards long, and in 1931, Dick Wilson was invited to modernise it when new land was acquired to replace some lost to a new highway. Wilson created a course of rolling movement, heavy rough, ridged fairways, greens guarded by swales and dips at the front and sharply bunkered. The sandy soil gives Shinnecock crisp, Scottish links-type turf, and the area is seldom without wind from Long Island sound or the Atlantic Ocean.

When Ben Hogan played the course in the 1960s, he described it as 'one of the finest I have played'. Its remoteness from the city and from population areas, plus general access and a certain degree of quaintness in the minds of some legislators, kept Shinnecock off the championship rota for many years. But it was not without success. In 1977, a successful Walker Cup match was held there, bringing it back to the attention of legislators and public, and in 1986 the USGA, it seemed bravely at the time, took the National Open there after all those years. The championship was won by Raymond Floyd, one of the most mature of modern professionals, with a score of 279. He was the only player to beat Shinnecock's par of 280, and the championship was an outstanding success.

SMITH, Macdonald

Born 1890

Nationality United States

Turned Pro 1905

'Swing – don't hit!'

That was the credo of Macdonald Smith of Carnoustie and no golfer was ever more steadfast in living his philosophy. Hailed by all his contemporaries as having the most beautiful of golf swings (Tommy Armour described him as the 'master artist of golf'), Smith was also considered to be the finest golfer never to have won a major championship. He was the youngest of a remarkable Carnoustie family of five sons, all professional golfers, all of whom descended on America. Alex crossed first in 1898 (he was to win US Opens in 1906 and 1910). The following year Willie arrived, followed by George and Jimmy and eventually came Mr and Mrs John Smith and the youngest boy, Macdonald.

In terms of swinging a golf club, he was the greatest of them. Harry Vardon in 1913 said that he was the best golfer he had seen in America. But Smith is remembered in the history of the game for failures at great and critical times. In that 1910 US Open, aged just 20, he tied with brother Alex and Johnny McDermott when a par at either the 71st or 72nd hole would have won him the title. He lost the play-off by six to Alex, two behind McDermott. From then on, he finished within three strokes of the winning total in British and US Opens a total of eight more times and never did win.

In the 1925 Open at Prestwick, a 79 in the final round would have made him champion. He had an outward half of 42, a round of 82 and someone else, this time Jim Barnes, was champion. Maybe it was the

Macdonald Smith, driving in the 1925 Open at Prestwick, where he was 'swept away' from his chance to win by vast unruly crowds. Jim Barnes took the title.

vast crowd swarming over an unfenced course which unnerved him But Mac Smith was famous for his temperament, never ruffled in winning 50 routine tournaments. Then in the 1931 Open at Carnoustie, a par finish of 3,4,5 would have caught Tommy Armour. Smith scored 6,5,5. He was a

heavy drinker and at times left the golfing scene. But Macdonald Smith never complained, never sought excuses and it is clear that throughout the reigns of Vardon, Jones and Hagen, no one ever swung a golf club more perfectly than Macdonald Smith of Carnoustie.

One of the greatest swings in the history of the game – full, flowing and graceful, an entity, without parts. Macdonald Smith won four tournaments in 1926, but couldn't quite win the Open. He finished second twice, third twice, fourth twice, and fifth.

SNEAD, Sam

Born 1912

Nationality United States

Turned Pro 1934

Majors Open Championship 1946; US Masters 1949, 1952, 1954; US PGA 1942, 1949, 1951

Samuel Jackson Snead won his first national tournament in 1936 at the age of 24. He won the last of his 84 official PGA events in 1965 at the age of 53 (his total career victories in all events, official and unofficial, may be as many as 162). In August 1974 at the age of 62, he finished third in the US PGA Championship behind Lee Trevino and Jack Nicklaus. It was a championship which he had won three times, the first of these 32 years earlier. And late in his seventies, Sam Snead was playing golf most days.

The man is a marvel. This immense career, in which he won seven major championships, was the product of one of the most beautiful swings that golf has known. Gene Sarazen called it 'perhaps the finest natural swing of all time'. It featured a slow, almost languid backswing, a lightning strike at impact and a full, high, perfectly balanced finish – a thing of beauty and of power and grace.

Snead was born in Ashwood in May 1912, neatly as it happened between

Byron Nelson and Ben Hogan, with whom he was to form an outstanding American 'triumvirate' in the 1940s. Ashwood is a village near Hot Springs, Virginia, close to the West Virginia line and very much mountain country. Snead was a hillybilly, an image he was happy to promote through his career. He was the fifth son of Harry Snead and Laura, who was 47 when Sam was born. Harry worked in a local hotel, but also had a small holding, so that for the boy Snead, childhood was rural, a world of woods and streams and 'critters'.

At school, his sporting interests were American – football, baseball, basketball. He was also a pretty good sprinter. Having broken a hand at football, he took to golf hoping to strengthen it. An older brother encouraged him and school was soon abandoned for a job at the nearby Hot Springs course, caddying in the manner of Nelson and Hogan. He moved to the bigger Cascades course and was soon scoring under par over its 6800 yards.

Fred Martin, manager of the Greenbrier Hotel in neighbouring White Sulphur Springs, was impressed and gave Snead a job. He was soon competing in state and regional events and more than held his own against quality players who came to the Greenbrier. By January 1937 he was ready for the regular PGA tour. Snead won the third event he played in, at Oakland, and there and then a star was born: 'Slammin Sam' was a national figure. No one on the tour could knock out drives of 300 yards the way Sam could. He was Virginia's gift to the sporting press, the 'good ol' boy' from the backwoods, and Fred Corcoran, the tournament Director of the US tour, soon to become Snead's manager, was quick to capitalise on that aspect of Snead's history. Fred splashed out unashamedly stories of how Sam used to play barefoot and could still shoot par without any shoes, and how he fashioned his first clubs from branches of hickory trees and the like.

From 1937 to 1965, with the exception of 1947 and 1963, Sam Snead won at least one tournament in the US

Sam Snead at his peak - owner of one of golf's finest and most abiding swings.

every single year. In 1950, he won ten of them. And he went on to win six US PGA Senior Championships and five World Senior Championships. But the fickle finger of fate touched him in the US Open of 1937, and no doubt affected his whole future attitude to that championship. A birdie at the par-5 72nd hole at the Spring Mill Club in Philadelphia would have won it. In a series of disasters, Snead took eight and Nelson eventually won the championship. In 1947 Snead

was beaten in a play-off with Lou Worsham. In 1949 he was second to Dr Cary Middlecoff and in 1953 he was second to Ben Hogan by six shots.

He won his British Open, the first post-war event in 1946, almost by default. On the final round he went to the turn in 40 and had almost given up the fight when he realised that the rest of the field was making a poor fist of it. Snead came back in 35 for a 75 and 290, to win with one of the highest final rounds in recent times.

In his later years, Snead, like everyone else, had putting problems. He sought to resolve them by putting between his legs, croquet fashion. The USGA put a stop to that, re-writing the rule book to require both feet to be at the side of the line to the hole. Snead simply changed to 'side-saddle', standing facing the hole, feet together and putting from the side. It looked slightly bizarre and one could scarcely imagine either of his old adversaries, Nelson or Hogan, putting that way.

THE SOLHEIM CUP

Donated by Karsten Solheim, the creator of Ping golf clubs, the Solheim Cup is a handsome piece of Waterford Glass for biennial competition between the American Ladies Professional Golf Association and the Women's Professional Golfers European Tour. The first match was held at the Lake Nona club at Orlando, Florida in 1990, which the American team won by $11\frac{1}{2}$ to $6\frac{1}{2}$ points. In 1992, at the Dalmahoy Club near Edinburgh, the Europe team won $11\frac{1}{2}$-$6\frac{1}{2}$.

SONY RANKING

The Sony Ranking is a computerised method of evaluating the relative performances of the world's leading players. It was devised by the International Management Group and was launched by the Sony Corporation during the week of the Masters Tournament in 1986. It is sanctioned by the Royal and Ancient Golf Club, and is endorsed by the various professional tours of golf. A Sony Ranking Advisory Committee, composed of senior administrators and personalities in golf from Britain, the USA, Japan, Australia and South Africa, and of course the European Tour, meets at St Andrews each October. Its recommendations are passed to the R & A for approval.

All the tournaments in the tours are considered, and points are awarded according to the quality of the players participating in each event. Each player receives points depending on his finishing position. The four major championships, and the major event of each tour, are weighted particularly. The system is based on a three-year rolling average, more weight given to the more recent results, and a divisor is applied to take into account the number of events played by each golfer.

The Sony Ranking is published each Monday, the events of the previous week applying.

ST ANDREWS

'Would you like to see a city given over,
  Soul and body, to a tyrannising game?'

These words were written in 1885 by RF Murray, the American poet who studied at St Andrews. The 'auld grey toon', perched out on a promontory on the coast of Fife, has been famed as the

The joyous Solheim Cup team, winners for Europe at Dalmahoy in 1992 against the powerful US women professionals.

traditional home of golf. There is much more to it than that. There is some reason to believe that there was a pre-historic settlement on the site. The city reached a pinnacle of prominence in medieval times, being made a free and Royal Burgh in the middle of the 12th century. The cathedral was founded in about 1160 and took 159 years to complete as the greatest church in Catholic Scotland, with St Andrews the ecclesiastical capital of the nation. In 1411 was established St Andrews University, Scotland's oldest and preceded in the British Isles only by Oxford and Cambridge. The Protestant Reformation in the 16th century inevitably brought bloody times and bloody deeds to the town, and neglect and ruin came to the Cathedral and the Priory.

Indeed by the 18th century, St Andrews was at its lowest ebb, the university sharing in the general

OLD COURSE ST ANDREWS			
HOLE	**NAME**	**YARDS**	**PAR**
1	Burn	370	4
2	Dyke	411	4
3	Cartgate out	352	4
4	Ginger Beer	419	4
5	Hole o' Cross out	514	5
6	Heathery	374	4
7	High out	359	4
8	Short	178	3
9	End	307	4
OUT		**3,284**	**36**
10	Bobby Jones	318	4
11	High coming home	172	3
12	Heathery, home	316	4
13	Hole o' Cross, in	398	4
14	Long	523	5
15	Cartgate in	401	4
16	Corner of the Dyke	351	4
17	Road	461	4
18	Tom Morris	354	4
IN		**3,294**	**36**
TOTAL		**6,678**	**72**

The rolling, sweeping Old Course at St Andrews – the second green and third fairway.

decline. Now, a modern city embraces the remains of the medieval town, one of the best preserved in Britain.

Golf had its part to play in the St Andrews recovery. The game was certainly played there in the 16th century, over the ground of the Old Course which was naturally formed and evolved so that no one can really put a date to its beginning. Some say it was being played over as early as 1400. The Royal and Ancient Golf Club, formed in 1754, has been a major influence on the development of golf at St Andrews and its courses, traditionally laid out over common or public land. Often it had to defend the courses, and the citizen's rights on them, from St Andrews Town Council, throughout the 19th century. In 1894, at which time the R & A actually owned the Old Course, it was returned to the ownership of the town and a Joint Links Committee of Town and Club formed to manage it. In 1895 the New Course was laid out and in 1897 the Jubilee followed, celebrating Queen Victoria's Diamond Jubilee. Initially it was of 12 holes. The Eden was opened in 1914 and in 1971 came the 9-holes Balgrove. Anticipating a local government reorganisation in 1975 and the disappearance of the Town Council, an Act of Parliament set up the St Andrews Links Trust in 1974, to ensure continuity in the management of the courses through the Links Management Committee. The ground is now owned by North East Fife District Council, who, with the R & A and the local member of Parliament for the moment, comprise the Links Trust.

Intense and increasing traffic on the courses in the 1970s and 80s produced a major expansion of the golf facilities of St Andrews. Donald Steel extended and modernised the Jubilee Course. A completely new 18, the Strathtyrum, was also built. Together with a re-designed Balgrove, it was opened in 1993. In addition, a private course designed by Peter Thomson was announced for the Craigton District Park which overlooks the town, and scheduled to open in late 1995. It was a project of the Old Course Hotel. The Links Trust has five 18 hole courses, one of nine holes, an extensive practice area and all the complementary clubhouse and parking facilities which all of that demands. The St Andrews links remain a national treasure, to be protected at all costs.

STEWART, William Payne

Born 1957

Nationality United States

Turned Pro 1979

Majors US PGA 1989; US Open 1991

One of the great 'majors' players, in addition to his two championship wins to date Payne Stewart has finished second in the British Opens of 1985 and 1990, and the US Open of 1993. At 6' 1", Stewart has a distinctive flowing swing, with a spinning body turn. He has consistently been in the top ten of American players, save in 1991 when he missed ten weeks of competition including withdrawing from the Masters field just before the tournament began. A herniated disc in his neck and degenerative discs in his lower back constituted the problem, putting him into a collar and brace for a time. In the PGA Championship of 1989, his closing round made up seven shots on Mike Reid, the third round leader. He had four birdies in the last five holes for his 67. As much as his golfing style, Payne Stewart's wardrobe makes him unmissable. Wearing plus fours, or 'knickers' as the Americans call them, he dresses in the vivid colours of American football teams, members of the National Football League.

STRANGE, Curtis

Born 1955

Nationality United States

Turned Pro 1976

Majors US Open 1988, 1989

Curtis Strange is a member of one of golf's most distinguished companies, those who have successfully defended their US Open Championship titles and won

in successive years. In the first decade of the 20th century, Willie Anderson did so in 1903-5 (he won three in a row). In the second decade, Johnny McDermott, the first native-born American winner, won in 1911 and 1912. Then came Bobby Jones in 1929, 1930; Ralph Guldahl in 1937, 1938; and Ben Hogan in 1950, 1951. Anderson, Jones and Hogan

indeed were all four-times winners. Finally Strange, in the 1989 championship at Oak Hill in Rochester, New York, after a tie with Nick Faldo, retained the title he had won the previous year at The Country Club in Brookline, near Boston.

Born on 30 January 1955, the son of a Virginia golf professional, Curtis had an outstanding amateur career,

winning all the major national events with the exception of the US Amateur, and playing on the 1975 Walker Cup team. He turned professional at the age of 21, and had his first win in 1979 with the Pensacola Open. From then on, he had outstanding tournament success through the 1980s, winning 15 Tour events, two

Given to colourful matching plus-fours ensembles, the flamboyant Payne Stewart nevertheless has the US Open and US PGA titles to his credit.

Canadian Opens among them, but leaving his supporters wondering if the great championships of the world would somehow remain beyond him. This fear was heightened by his performance in the 1985 Masters. With a two-stroke lead, and only six holes left to play, he hit second shots into Augusta's water hazards on the 13th and 15th holes to finish two strokes behind Bernhard Langer.

Curtis was something of a mechanical player. He'd say, 'My strengths are that I have no weaknesses.' There was nothing extraordinary about the swing – sound, solid, unsurprising, consistent

might be said of it – but he could produce bursts of dazzling scoring, as with his record 62 over the Old Course at St Andrews in Dunhill Cup matches in 1987. He played four times in Ryder Cup matches in the 1980s. And at last, when his Open win of 1988 did come, and he repeated in·1989 and finished second in the PGA of that year, the American media was persuaded that he was the finest golfer since Tom Watson.

Had he not been leading money winner three times? Had he not been the first golfer to amass more than $1 million in one year (1988), when he won three

Curtis Strange splashes out at the 72nd hole of the 1988 US Open at The Country Club, near Boston. He won the championship by beating Nick Faldo in a play-off.

tournaments in addition to the Open? And he had reached third in the overall earnings list, behind Tom Kite and Tom Watson. But in 1992, he played in only 17 tournaments, managing to finish in the top ten only twice, his immediate future in the game apparently compromised by an undetermined malady.

SUNNINGDALE

One of the most important discoveries in the evolution of golf and golf courses, and their design, was that of a stretch of land running through Surrey and Berkshire to the south west of London that was something of an inland linksland. Heather, pine and whin, and a sandy subsoil that permitted the growth of fine fescue and bent grasses, was ideal for the Scottish game. Its merits were discovered towards the end of the 19th century and led in time to such excellent courses as Walton Heath, Wentworth, The Berkshire, Woking and above all Sunningdale. Indeed when the R & A asked the Sunningdale club to stage the 1987 Walker Cup matches, it was the first time the event had been played on an inland course and not on links by the sea. It was an acknowledgement of the course's qualities of beauty, subtlety and frank and sympathetic challenges to the golfer.

When the course was built in 1900, the ground was little more than a heath. The founding father of the club, TA Roberts, had built himself a house on what is now Ridgemount Road, running parallel to the first fairway. He was appointed agent to St John's College, Cambridge, landowners since 1524, acquired the land for golf purposes and retained Willie Park Jr to design the course. Park was a fine player, Open Champion in 1887 and 1889, but more important, was also the first modern golf architect and one of the finest thinkers on all aspects of golf that the game has known. The course was opened to the Park plan which had been based on the gutty ball. A general redesign some years later, to accommodate the wound ball, was done by Harry Colt, the club secretary for several years. He left to practise golf architecture and he in turn became an outstanding and successful designer, doing the New Course at Sunningdale in 1922. The club then had two of the most beautiful courses to be found anywhere in world golf.

Sunningdale and the 12th green, well protected by any standards.

Possibly the most famous single round every played over the Old Course was that of Bobby Jones, who scored 66 in a qualifying round for the 1926 Open Championship which he went on to win. It may be considered as close to perfection as any round could be. He had 33 shots, 33 putts. All the holes were scored in threes and fours. He missed only one green, the short 13th, by a few feet, chipped up close and made his par. In his second qualifying round he scored 68, this time with one five and one two, and then declared, 'I wish I could take this course home with me.'

Of its four par 5 holes, only one, the 14th, is over 500 yards, and at that only 509 yards long. That seems to indicate the subtlety of the course. Length is not an obsession with the club. One extraordinary feature of Sunningdale's history, giving a clue to its management, has been the longevity of service of many employees. Hugh McLean and his son Jimmy were head greenkeepers through the first 73 years of Sunningdale's history. Arthur Wigmore was the dressing-room guv'nor for 50 years, whilst the most famous of all was Jimmy Sheridan, a kenspeckle Scottish caddiemaster, who after his 56 years service was made an honorary member of the club and had his portrait painted. It was shown at the Royal Academy, and now hangs proudly in the clubhouse.

SUNNINGDALE		
HOLE	YARDS	PAR
1	494	5
2	484	5
3	296	4
4	161	3
5	410	4
6	415	4
7	402	4
8	172	3
9	267	4
OUT	3,101	36
10	478	5
11	325	4
12	451	4
13	185	3
14	509	5
15	226	3
16	438	4
17	421	4
18	432	4
IN	3,465	36
TOTAL	6,566	72

T

TAIT, Freddie

'I never heard a word said against him except a solitary complaint that, in the lightness of his heart, he had played pibrochs around the drowsy town at midnight. What would we not give to hear his pipes again?'

These pensive words were written by Andrew Lang, Scottish man of letters, about Freddie Tait, one of the most romantic figures in golf, who was killed in the Boer War. Freddie was a cavalier spirit, idolised in his native Scotland, a dashing golfer who could lace out huge drives despite an easy, controlled swing, and a match player supreme who dismissed medal play golf as 'rifle shooting'.

He was born in Edinburgh in 1870, the son of a professor of mathematics and philosophy at Edinburgh University. Professor Peter Guthrie Tait spent more than 30 summers at St Andrews – he was a member of the R & A for 36 years – and was obsessed with golf, playing several rounds each day and theorising and

Freddie Tait, one of the great amateurs of his day, in action at North Berwick. He once beat Ben Sayers, the top golfer there, by eight holes, with Sayers producing the comment that has persisted in golfing lore – 'It's not possible, but it's a fact.'

experimenting on the capabilities of the golf ball in flight. He eventually declared that 190 yards was the maximum distance a ball could travel. In 1892, not long after he propounded that, his son Freddie belted out a drive at the 13th hole of the Old Course a distance of 341 yards. It was reckoned to have carried 250 yards, exceptional hitting with the gutty ball.

Shortly after becoming an R & A member in 1890, Freddie had lowered the Old Course record to 77. Again, in 1894, he brought it down to 72. He won the Amateur Championship in 1896 at Sandwich, beating Harold Hilton in the final by 8 and 7, then won again at Hoylake in 1898. In 1899 at Prestwick, he and John Ball, the pride of Hoylake, played one of the greatest finals the championship had known, when Ball, after being five down with 14 holes played, won at the 37th. Both of these players went to South Africa to fight in the Boer War, Ball with the Cheshire Yeomanry, Tait with the Black Watch. Ball survived, to win three more Amateur Championships. Freddie Tait did not. He was killed in action at Koodoosberg Drift on 7 February 1900.

TAYLOR, John Henry

Born 1871

Nationality British

Turned Pro 1888

Majors Open Championship 1894, 1895, 1900, 1909, 1913

In the two decades before the First World War, three men changed the face of golf. They were to dominate the Open Championship by winning a total of 16 events in 21 years. They became the first super-champions and household names. Collectively they helped the game make the transition

from gutty ball to wound ball, gave golf in America an impetus which led to the US dominating the world game at all levels for most of next half-century, and they contributed hugely to the creation of the Professional Golfers' Association. They were James Braid, Harry Vardon, and John Henry Taylor, the latter known throughout his long life as 'JH'.

Taylor, the youngest of the three by a matter of months, was born on 19 March 1871, at Northam in North Devon. All three of these men came from modest beginnings, but none more stark than those

of JH. His father died when he was four years old. He had a basic education in the village school, which he left at the age of 11 to find whatever work he could. That included caddying at the nearby North Devon Golf Club at Westward Ho! He became a talented player over the course as a member of the Northam Working Men's Golf Club, and automatically became a professional when he accepted a job on the greenkeeping staff. In 1892, he went to Burnham as greenkeeper-professional, and in 1893 played in the Open Championship for the first time. After a record 75 in his first round at Prestwick, he was swept away by a storm, scoring 89 in the second round. The following year, the championship was played in England for the first time, at Royal St George's, Sandwich. Taylor won, with the highest score, 326, up to that time. Thus he became the first non-Scottish professional to win the Open (Harold Hilton, the English amateur, had won at Muirfield in 1892).

JH won again in 1895 at St Andrews, always a profitable place for him. Touring the US with Vardon in 1900, he finished second to him in the US Open, by two shots, but he took the British Open that same year, yet again at St Andrews. His career encompassed five British Open wins, French Opens in 1908 and 1909, and the German Open of 1912.

Taylor was 5' 8" tall, the shortest of the three great contemporaries. His swing was rather punchy, with a short follow through. He stood solidly to the ball, with little body movement, and the ball would go off with a low trajectory, no doubt since he had learned the game in the winds of Westward Ho! and Burnham. The swing was powerful and

Taylor an aggressive player who would attack the flag at every opportunity. He was pugnacious and could be testy, on and off the course. And he had a real awareness of the value of being a champion. He moved to Winchester, then to Royal Mid Surrey, the busy metropolitan club, where he reigned until his retirement in 1947. In partnership with George Cann, a friend from Devon, he went into a successful clubmaking business. With golf courses galore being built, JH became a designer, working on Mid Surrey and Royal Birkdale among others.

He was also very much aware of his social shortcomings and by practice and study taught himself to be a capable public speaker. JH was always concerned about standards, on the one hand among his fellow professionals, and on the other about their often haphazard arrangements

JH Taylor, one of the great Triumvirate, gets down to it.

with their employers, the clubs, whose standards of employment often fell short of being acceptable. In 1901, he was very much one of the leaders in what was to become the forerunner of the Professional Golfers' Association, the 'London and Counties PGA'.

John Henry Taylor, like Old Tom Morris in the preceding century, became something of a Grand Old Man of golf. He was non-playing captain of the British Ryder Cup team of 1933, which beat the Americans at Southport and Ainsdale. He was made an honorary member of the R & A in 1947, and finally, back where it all started, President of the Royal North Devon Golf Club. When he died in February 1963, JH Taylor was a month short of his 92nd birthday.

THOMAS, David

Born 1934

Nationality British

Turned Pro 1949

David Thomas, born at Newcastle-upon-Tyne on 16 August 1934, with a Welsh background, turned professional at 15 and was immediately seen as a young man of immense talent. His physique if nothing else justified the judgement. He grew to be six feet tall and powerfully built – he was able to drive the ball vast distances with a swing that had the minimum of foot and body action, and was beautifully crisp and controlled. When he won the Assistants' Championship and the Belgian Open in the same year, 1955, the length and accuracy of his driving and long iron play, plus a positive attitude on the greens, suggested that he might reach the very heights of the game. One weakness that did emerge was his uncertainty in playing pitch shots into the greens.

Wins in the Dutch and French Opens and a dozen PGA tournaments followed, as did four Ryder Cup appearances and 11 selections for Wales in the World Cup, but the high points of his career, and the greatest disappointments, came in the Open Championships of 1958 and 1966. In the first of these, he tied with Peter Thomson, dropping the stroke on Lytham's treacherous 71st hole that would have given him victory. At that time, all the entrants for the championship had to play two qualifying rounds over the Monday and Tuesday of championship week, then the Open proper – 18 holes on Wednesday, 18 on Thursday, and 36 on Friday. And play-offs were decided over 36 holes on Saturday.

Over the first 18 of the play-off, Thomson took 68, Thomas 69; still all to play for. Peter Thomson wrote subsequently that in the early holes of the second 18, he was desperately tired and didn't think he could go on. But when he looked across at David Thomas, he looked even more tired, so Thomson soldiered on. He scored 71 against David's 74 and took the fourth of his five Open titles.

Then in 1966 at Muirfield, one errant shot by Thomas cost him his chance of holding off Jack Nicklaus. It was at Muirfield's long par five 17, a prime birdie hole for players of Dave's power. His 6-iron second shot pitched into the bank above the hole and stayed there. He chopped it down, but failed with the putt. Nicklaus, playing behind, did birdie the 17th and won the championship by one shot

from Thomas and Doug Sanders.

Since his playing career ended, David has had an outstanding career as a golf course designer, his body of work ranging from the delightful Newmachar course in Aberdeenshire, through very extensive commissions in Andalucia, Spain, where he is now resident, and in Japan.

THOMSON, Peter

Born 1929

Nationality Australian

Turned Pro 1949

Majors Open Championship 1954, 1955, 1956, 1958, 1965

Peter Thomson of Melbourne, Australia, is one of golf's greatest champions and one of only two living members of golf's most

exclusive society. He is one of five men who have won the Open Championship five times. The others are Harry Vardon, who in fact won six times, James Braid and JH Taylor, all three of whom won their titles before the First World War and are long gone, and finally Tom Watson of the United States who is still very much active in tournament play.

Thomson was the most pragmatic of champions, an apparently completely self-

contained person. Like Jack Nicklaus, he would never suffer fools gladly. If he didn't want to accept an invitation, he would say quite simply, 'No, thank you', and that would be the end of the matter. He seldom waited around the clubhouse when the round was over, he was off. He was inclined to be patriarchal, with a sardonic sense of humour. He had decided that the world was an imperfect place and he accepted that, but he kept the world at arm's length. He never did write, as almost all the great champions did, a golf instructional book, believing that the game was essentially too simple to justify such an impertinence. His walk along the fairways of the world was brisk and jaunty, giving the impression that he was a man who knew exactly where he was going.

His entire technique was rooted in the premise that the ball must be kept in play. That was always his advice to young Australians pondering their first trip to the Old Country – he knew well how gorse and heather could destroy a score. Technically, Thomson was not impeccably correct. He had a very strong left hand grip, which meant that the right hand had to go under, with the effect of giving him a 'high left shoulder'. There was the slightest suggestion of a sway as he took the ball away, but the backswing was compact, the entire movement simple – and repeating.

On the greens, he stood rather upright and with a long backswing popped the ball away with very little follow through. There was no single factor in his game which was outstanding, save his thinking. The quality of his mind was exceptional, described by one observer as 'the greatest club in his bag'. He often said that the tighter the situation, the more clearly he saw the challenge, and he wrote of how when the leader of the championship came to the drive on the 72nd hole, his mind should focus down to 'a patch of fairway 20 feet square' which would be his target. Thomson was not a slavish practiser. When his game went wrong, he would simply sit in a corner and think about what he was doing until he had solved the puzzle. He believed very much in the set-up, holding that a wrong set-up was responsible for most of the ills in a swing. He once made a special journey to Sandy Lodge in Hertfordshire to see John Jacobs, the eminent coach, and asked him to 'check the set-up'. He did not hit one ball, but was content that Jacobs had put him back in the correct set-up position. Thomson dressed conservatively in blues or greys and wore white shoes – always the white shoes.

Peter Thomson was born in Melbourne on 23 August 1929, and does not seem to have had a noteworthy career in amateur golf. However, after he finished as leading amateur in the Australian Open of 1948, he turned professional the following year, finished second to Norman von Nida in 1950, and in 1951 won the first of his three Australian Opens. That year of 1950 had brought the first of no fewer than nine New Zealand Open Championships over 21 years, and the future was to bring, in Europe, the championships of Italy, Spain and Germany, and elsewhere those of India, Hong Kong and the Philippines. His massive achievement in the British Open Championship, dominating the event in the 1950s with three successive wins and four in all, in hindsight seems to have followed an inevitable progression. On his first appearance, at Max Faulkner's Open at Royal Portrush in 1951, he had finished sixth. In 1952 he was second, only one stroke behind Ben Hogan at Carnoustie, and in 1954 he won at Royal Birkdale. He was 25 years of age.

Peter Thomson, smooth and simple, and five times an Open Champion.

No one has played links courses better than Peter Thomson, with the judgement of distance, wind effect and the behaviour of the running ball that is required. Throughout the 1950s and most of the 60s, he was a world master of the small (1.62 inch) ball. He enjoyed the first of his British tour successes in the PGA Match Play of 1954, making a neat double with the Open. The last of them came in 1971, making his total 22 in 18 years. He played eleven times for Australia in the World (Canada) Cup, winning in 1954 and 1959, each time with Kel Nagle. After his win in the Victorian Open of 1973 and approaching 45 years of age, he turned his mind to other things. He stood for Parliament in a Melbourne constituency, losing by a mere 4% of the vote. He did much to promote tournament golf in India and the Far East and showed a lively interest in golf course architecture with 25 designs, many of them in Japan.

The rise of senior tournament golf, particularly in the United States, brought a fantastic climax to his playing career in the 1980s. He had played the regular US Tour in the fifties, making several visits and always making a profit. He won the Texas Open of 1956 and finished fourth in the US Open of 1956. In 1982, he joined the US Senior Tour and in 1984 he won two events including the PGA Seniors Championship, but 1985 became an enchanted year for the Australian. He set a record of nine victories to be leading money winner with more than $380,000 and all told, his Senior Tour earnings passed $1 million. He won the 1988 British Seniors Open, was awarded the CBE, and was made an honorary member of the R & A.

THOMPSON, Stanley

One of five brothers in a Scottish family which emigrated to Toronto before the First World War, Stanley Thompson became a first-class golfer, as did all of his brothers. He left his studies at the Ontario Agricultural College in 1915 to join the Canadian Expeditionary Force in France. Surviving the war, he set up a modest design practice with early commissions in Toronto and Winnipeg, where he built his first 18-holes course.

His greatest triumphs came quickly, both in the Rockies: Banff, commissioned by the Canadian Pacific Railway and opened by the Prince of Wales in the late 1920s, and Jasper Park, ordered by the 'other' railway, the Canadian National, and opened in the same year by Field Marshal Earl Haig, were immediately hailed as masterpieces. The huge Banff Springs Hotel, the flagship resort of the CPR, had already built nine holes on its magnificent mountain site in 1911, and a further nine had been built by German prisoners of war. In 1927, Thompson was invited to rebuild the course. He ran it along the banks of the Bow River and beneath the massive Mount Rumble. Thompson cut down hundreds of pine trees and blasted tons of rock out of the mountain. Vast quantities of top soil were imported from the East, transported no doubt by the wagons of Thompson's client, and 144 bunkers were scattered across the course. Clumps of them, sited at critical areas, became a Thompson feature and indeed he was one of the earliest architects who took a strategic view of his work, seeking always to give the player an alternative route.

His most famous hole is the par-three 8th on the championship course, 171 yards and forbiddingly

named 'Devil's Cauldron'. It is played from an elevated tee, over a small lake to a green planted deep into the forest, severely bunkered, with a massive wall of mountain behind it. Robert Trent Jones joined Thompson as an 'apprentice' in the reconditioning of the course, and in 1930 they became partners. In Banff, they created perhaps the most spectacular course in the world. Bobby Locke described it as 'out of this world'.

Further west is another Thompson course which comes close to matching it. Capilano was designed and constructed by Thompson in 1937 and remains little altered to this day. On the lower slopes of British Columbia's Coast Mountains, it overlooks the city of Vancouver to the south, the Strait of Georgia and Vancouver island to the west. It was part of a grandiose project by Guinness Estates for a quality property development with golf course in West Vancouver in the early 1930s, and as he had to at Banff, Thompson had to cut and blast through virgin forests and outcrops of rock.

The course runs across a slope, the first six holes dropping by as much as 300 feet from first tee to sixth green. The view from this hole of the Lion's Gate Bridge, crossing Burrard Inlet to Vancouver city, is delightful. The next six holes in general are on the flat, and the final six uphill. The last hole is a monster of 575 yards, with three diagonal bunkers screening the green. The Thompson achievement with fascinating short holes is evident again, as at Banff and Jasper. The 'Lilly Pond', the fourth, is 168 yards over a lake to a small two-tiered green behind three huge bunkers. The 11th, the 'Wishing Well', is also across

water, but at only 155 yards its challenge lies in an undulating green, closely trapped all round.

Thompson worked through Canada, in New York State and Florida, and reached as far south as Jamaica, Colombia and Brazil. He made and spent several fortunes, was known as 'The Toronto Terror', but beneath his flamboyant lifestyle was a deep concern for the landscape. He died in 1952 at the age of 58.

TILLINGHAST, Albert

'A controlled shot to a closely guarded green is the surest test of a man's golf'.

The Winged Foot Golf Club in Westchester County, in the outer suburbs of New York City, is one of the finest in America. It is an extension of the New York Athletic Club in Manhattan, whose symbol is a winged foot, hence the golf club's name. It was organised in the summer of 1921, when a group of NYAC members set out to find a suitable site for golf within reasonable reach of the city. They found it in affluent Mamaroneck, and a splendid site it was, of rolling meadowland peopled with mature oak, birch, beech, ash, spruce and all kinds of flowering shrubs. Of equal importance to the project was the fact that the New Yorkers decided that the man to design their courses should be 'Tillie the Terror'.

Albert Warren Tillinghast would surely rank in the top half-dozen golf course architects in American golf history. He was certainly one of the most colourful. Tillie was a big man of striking appearance. His huge moustache had spiky, waxed ends. He wore knee boots and riding breeches with matching jacket while at work, striding through virgin ground, but always wore a

'Tilly', Albert Tillinghast, a man of many parts and designer of many of America's finest courses.

collar and tie – a man not easily forgettable. He was born in Philadelphia in 1874, the indulged son of a rich manufacturer, and made an extended trip to St Andrews in his twenties, when he became very friendly with Old Tom Morris. No doubt they talked of golf and golfers and courses. In the early years of the new century, Albert was good enough to play in the US Amateur several times. In 1906, with the blessing of the owner, he laid out a course on private land. It was to become the well-known Shawnee-on-Delaware. He was soon busy with other courses. When the founders of Winged Foot reached agreement with Tillie, they said, simply, 'Build us a man-sized course.' He did exactly that. By 1923, Winged Foot had not one but two, East and West, man-sized courses.

The man's talents were impressive. He edited *Golf Illustrated*, an important golf magazine of the time, and wrote a good deal of golf humour and fiction. He was a big drinker. He invested in Broadway shows in the 1920s. He was one of the first golf architects to combine design with construction by his own company – he offered clients the complete package. In the Depression he lost his fortune and, it seemed, his interest in golf course design. He went west to California and had an antique shop in Beverley Hills for a time.

Of Winged Foot, and his work there, he wrote that the contouring of its greens placed great premium on the drives, explaining this by claiming that 'only the knowledge that the next shot must be played with rifle accuracy brings the realisation that drives must be placed'. Tillinghast's greatest contribution to the science may have come with his attitude towards greens, many of them raised, mounded, pear-shaped with narrow entrances and bunkers right front and left front, the wider back part giving a variety of pin positions. 'If the shots home are wide of the green centres, the boys will be using niblicks rather than putters,' he wrote. And his philosophy was summed up with 'the controlled shot to a closely guarded green is the surest test of any man's golf'.

'Tillie the Terror' died in 1942. In 1974, no fewer than four USGA championships were played on Tillinghast courses – Winged Foot, San Francisco Golf Club, the Brooklawn Country Club (Connecticut) and Ridgewood Country Club (New Jersey). His courses at Baltusrol, Winged Foot and Fresh Meadow have been US Open courses. Five Farms in Baltimore has had a PGA Championship and a Walker Cup match; Ridgewood has also had a Ryder Cup match. It is an exceptional legacy from an exceptional man.

TOLLEY, Cyril

A larger-than-life character, Cyril James Hastings Tolley was a dominant figure in amateur golf between the wars. In the First World War, he served in the Tank Corps, was wounded, won the Military Cross and was a prisoner of war. As a post-war student at Oxford, he won the first of his two Amateur Championships in 1920 at Muirfield, beating Robert Gardner of the United States at the 37th hole. The other was at Royal St George's in 1929, which made him favourite for the 1930 championship at St Andrews. Against Bobby Jones, in the fourth round and before a huge crowd, Tolley went down at the 19th hole – to a stymie. He took part in all the early Walker Cup matches and played international golf until 1938. Tolley was an immense driver of the ball, hitting huge distances, but with a delicate touch in the short game. In later life, he became a croquet buff. He was Captain of the R & A in 1948 and died in 1978 at the age of 82.

TRAVIS, Walter

A champion golfer who began to play the game at the age of 35, and won the last championship he played in at the age of 54, is someone special. So in truth was Walter J Travis, the first 'Grand Old Man' of American golf. Travis was born in Australia but moved to the United States with his family when still a boy. In his youth he played tennis, and had no interest in golf. He saw it played on a visit to England in 1896, and at the request of some Long Island friends who were planning to start, and lay out a course, he brought back with him some clubs and balls. He thought he should help out further, and that winter he read all the golf books and instructional manuals he could find. It was quickly clear to him that putting would be critical in this game, and he devoted many hours to working out a method that would satisfy him. The next spring he was ready to try a few shots, play a few rounds, with a swing that, above all else, was completely controlled and which allowed him to hit the ball unerringly straight. He was quickly too good for his friends on Long Island. The following year, he entered the US Amateur Championship and reached the semi-final. Two years later, less than four years after he had started playing golf, he was the National Amateur Champion. He was champion in 1900, 1901 and 1903; and in 1901, he also finished third in the US Open.

Walter Travis was as icy as a Ben Hogan. He was perfectly polite, but said little to a partner or opponent on the course. He smoked long, black cigars and burned up opponents with the relentless repetition of his down-the-fairway golf. In the winter of 1901, he spent some time in Scotland and got the flavour of links play against some good Scottish golfers. The top British amateurs were still considered the best in the world, but by 1904, Travis was ready to cross the ocean again and tangle with them. He entered the Amateur Championship, to be played at Royal St George's, Sandwich. He spent three weeks in preparation, ten days at St Andrews and North Berwick, and ten days at Sandwich. When he arrived there, concerned about his form, he borrowed from an American friend the so-called 'Schenectady' putter, one with the shaft inserted into the centre of the head. With that putter, Walter Travis won the Amateur Championship and invoked a sensation that had British

and American golf officialdom estranged for years.

Much of it stemmed in fact from the aloofness of the reception he got at Royal St George's – he was not to be the last golfer to experience that. He was thought to be impolite and unfriendly. Travis, intent on winning the championship, had refused all social invitations. On the other hand, when he had asked to play practice rounds with leading British players, somehow that was not possible. He was not given a locker. He was given a caddie whom Travis was convinced was an idiot, and between the first and second rounds, when a rain-soaked Travis asked for time to dry out, it was refused. So this abrasiveness from both sides went on.

With a little luck here and there, Travis marched through the rounds, wielding his odd putter. He beat Harold Hilton in the fifth round, 5 and 4. Hilton had won the championship twice and the Open twice. In the semi-final, Travis beat Horace Hutchinson, another former champion twice over, and in the final he met Ted Blackwell, a huge, rather fiery man and an immense hitter who was said to have driven a gutty onto the last green at St Andrews, a swipe of at least 300 yards. There was little conversation in the match. Blackwell was often 40 yards in front, but Travis won 4 and 3, with steadfast shotmaking and what seemed a magic putter. His victory was received in silence. Aged 44, he was the first 'foreigner' to win the Amateur Championship, an achievement which might well be considered the greatest feat in the history of the game. Some years later, the Royal and Ancient banned 'Schenectady-type' putters.

Walter was the first great

international champion to come from the United States. Not until Jess Sweetser in 1926 did another American win the Amateur Championship. Travis won the Metropolitan Amateur in 1915 at the age of 54. He took to golf course architecture and re-modelling. He founded *The American Golfer* in 1908. It lasted until the mid 1930s and he edited it with distinction.

TREVINO, Lee

Born 1939

Nationality United States

Turned Pro 1957

Majors Open Championship 1971, 1972; US Open 1968, 1971; US PGA 1974, 1984

'A lot of guys on the Tour gripe about the travel and the food and the laundry. Well, no matter how bad the food may be, I've eaten worse. And I couldn't care less about the laundry, because I can remember when I had only one shirt.'

Thus Lee Buck Trevino, twice winner of the British Open Championship, twice winner of the US Open, twice winner of the US PGA, and a man who, in the space of four weeks, won the US, Canadian and British Open Championships.

Over the past two decades or more, the US Tour has been nourished by 'college boys', almost all of them from middle-class backgrounds, who are the products of the American university system of sports scholarships whereby talent in golf provides subsidised places in universities, and courses of study guaranteeing tuition, accommodation, practice and competitive experience in golf, as much as the study of Assyrian pottery. This was not the Trevino experience.

On the contrary, home for the young Trevino at one time was a wooden shack without power or plumbing. He was born on 1 December 1939 in Dallas, Texas. His father, of the same name, vanished early from the scene and the boy never knew him. He was brought up by his mother Juanita and his grandfather, neither of whom could read or write. He left school at the age of 14 and worked at a driving range, where he evolved a golf swing of such distinction, not to mention contradiction, that years later when he first appeared in public, so to speak, there were experienced observers prepared to say that he could not hope to win anything, much less six major championships.

At the age of 17 he enlisted in the US Marine Corps, and served in Okinawa where he spent a good deal of time playing golf with officers. On his return he found a job as an assistant professional at a course in El Paso, on the Mexican border, where he took on all comers, often for a dollar – a dollar was that important to Trevino. He'd tackle any bet – 'down in two from a bunker, chip and one-putt from 50 yards', giving a man strokes and a start of 100 yards down the fairway.

In 1965 he won the Texas State Open and finished second in the Mexican Open. In 1966 he qualified for the US Open. In 1967, he finished sixth and took a cheque for $6000 at Baltusrol. For Lee Trevino, the earth moved.

He was only now beginning to hear about

An ebullient extrovert, Lee Trevino is one of golf's finest shotmakers and competitors, with six major championships to his name.

Bobby Jones and Ben Hogan. This vast new world opening up was going to be too good to miss. The very next year, he won the US Open at Oak Hill. And he did it by tying the Open record of 275, becoming the first man to play four consecutive rounds under par in the US Open. On the 72nd hole, under burning pressure from Bert Yancey and Jack Nicklaus, he made a winning par without touching the fairway – drive into left rough, advance the ball further along the rough, pitch to the green, and hole the putt from four feet.

That seemed to typify a certain outrageous element in Trevino's game. He could make the most preposterous recoveries. In the third round of the 1971 Open at Muirfield at the short 16th , he hit a bunker shot that came sizzling out of the sand, cracked the flagstick and fell into the hole. At the last hole, he knocked in a chip shot from over the green. And in the last round, he holed another chip shot from off the 17th green. His playing partner was Tony Jacklin, making a superb assault on the championship, but those killing strokes broke him. He was never quite the same player again.

This is not to say that these capers personify Trevino's game. Considering his early life experiences, he had a marvellous sense of humour. Although he was a compulsive talker and joker – his form of release from the tensions of major championship golf – and has been a gambler, he was ice cool in a finish, and a conservative tactician who drove almost monotonously into the fairways and hit the middle of the green relentlessly with a swing that seldom failed him. He worked from a very open stance, the ball opposite his left foot, his grip strong. He

took the club straight back, sometimes outside the line, with his hips sliding to the right. With his left wrist arched back and a powerful leg and hip action, he hit late, drove through the ball with a long extension of his right arm through it, maintaining contact with the ball much longer, it seemed, than the more upright, elegant swings.

Lee Trevino has been a very considerable champion, and an irresistible public entertainer. He has lasted the course well, in spite of some back trouble. His PGA Championships were ten years apart, the second when he was 44 years old. Characteristically in 1990, his first Senior year, he won seven events, including the US Seniors Open.

TUFTS, Richard

For more than thirty years, Dick Tufts was director of Pinehurst Inc., and in his lifetime was involved in every aspect of golf administration. At one time or another, he served on every committee of the USGA and was president in 1956–57. He was taught to play to a high standard by Donald Ross and later dabbled in course design after the great Pinehurst architect died.

His grandfather, James Walker Tufts, was the originator of the Pinehurst resort and created something of a Tufts dynasty there. James was a phenomenal success in business. A druggist by profession, he owned three shops by the

time he was 21, and foresaw the expansion of the 'soda fountain' in American drug stores. He developed equipment and materials which eventually sold nationwide and by 1891 had formed the American Soda Fountain Company. In 1895, when he was sixty, he turned the business over to his son Leonard, Richard's father, and retired to Pinehurst. There he developed the resort, bringing in Donald Ross in the first place as the professional. Leonard in turn was more interested in Pinehurst than in the business, and by 1906 was devoting all his time to it. His

Richard S Tufts, scion of the famous Pinehurst family.

son Richard succeeded him in 1930. Richard laid out a Pinehurst No. 4 course to a Donald Ross design, revised the famous No. 2 for the 1962 US Amateur Championship and worked with architect Ellis Maples on Pinehurst No. 5 in the 1960s.

His son Peter followed him as director until 1971, when the rest of the family, owning a majority of the shareholding, elected to sell Pinehurst. Richard Sise Tufts was clearly the doyen of a family which, directly and indirectly, contributed greatly to American golf and American golf architecture.

TURNBERRY

In that long necklace of fine courses that decorates the Ayrshire coastline in the West of Scotland, there is no more brilliant jewel than the Ailsa course of the Turnberry Hotel. Indeed it is one of the most spectacular, most dramatic seaside courses in the world, rivalling Pebble Beach and Cypress Point in California in beauty and quality. Its early holes run to and fro through vintage linksland. The short 4th plays from beach level across a little inlet to a green cut into the high end of a long sand-ridge that overlooks the mile-long golden sands of Turnberry beach, and on the landward side, falls into a valley that contains holes five to eight. The course bursts out to the 8th green, and from there runs along clifftop and shore to the 11th tee. The views of the Island of Arran, and of Ailsa Craig, are magnificent.

The Turnberry courses have had a chequered history. The Ailsa, and its neighbour the Arran on the landward side, equal in quality if less famous, date from the turn of the century when the local third Marquis of Ailsa commissioned Willie Fernie to design a private course for him, originally of 13 holes. By 1905, Fernie had designed a second 13. The Marquis, from whose family title the 'big' course takes its name, had leased adjoining land to the Glasgow and South Western Railway Company. By 1907 it had built its planned hotel, and also took over all of the golf facility to create one of the earliest hotel/golf resorts in the world. With Fernie's son Tom as the first professional, Turnberry was only just settling down when the First World War meant the coming of the Royal Flying Corps and an airfield of sorts built on the courses. After the war, the courses were restored, Major CK Hutchinson being retained to put things right, with the emphasis on the Ailsa. Yet again, war plagued Turnberry – in the Second World War, the Royal Air Force this time devastated the place by laying down concrete runways and building an extensive airfield across the courses.

After that war, the four major rail networks were nationalised into British Rail, and with that the railway hotel and golf courses at Turnberry became part of British Transport Hotels, a BR subsidiary. The courses seemed gone beyond recall, but an exceptional man, Frank Hole, managing director of BTH, conducted an inspired and stubborn campaign for compensation from the RAF and the government and eventually succeeded. He selected Philip Mackenzie Ross, a Musselburgh man and an experienced international golf architect, to redesign the courses, and Ross, in the Ailsa course, produced a masterpiece.

The work was completed by 1951 and progressively the Ailsa was host to the Amateur Championship, the Walker Cup match and

TURNBERRY AILSA			
HOLE	NAME	YARDS	PAR
1	Ailsa Craig	362	4
2	Mak Siccar	428	4
3	Blaw Wearie	462	4
4	Woe-be-tide	167	3
5	Fin' me oot	477	5
6	Tappie Tourie	222	3
7	Roon the Ben	528	5
8	Goat Fell	427	4
9	Bruce's Castle	455	4
OUT		3,528	36
10	Dinna Fouter	452	4
11	Maidens	177	3
12	Monument	391	4
13	Tickly Tap	411	4
14	Risk-an-Hope	440	4
15	Ca Canny	209	3
16	Wee Burn	409	4
17	Lang Whang	500	5
18	Ailsa Hame	431	4
IN		3,420	35
TOTAL		6,948	71

several professional tournaments. By 1977, the R & A decided that the Ailsa was ready for an Open Championship, and it produced one of the greatest of all, an exceptional battle between Jack Nicklaus and Tom Watson. It was resolved only on the 72nd green with the two Americans paired. Watson followed a stunning last-throw birdie from Nicklaus with one of his own to score 65 against the 66 from Nicklaus. Watson won by that one stroke in perfect conditions, scoring 68-70-65-65 for 278, twelve strokes under par. Turnberry's second Open came in 1986, when Greg Norman's 280 total included a second round 63, a course record.

The Ailsa has a splendid variety of two-shot holes and two big par fives which run in completely opposite directions. The 7th at 528 yards has a demanding drive from a tee set high on the seaward ridge, across broken ground to carry another ridge and into a valley fairway. This then runs uphill to a rather small green. The 17th at 500 yards sees a drive down into a wide valley, then a pronounced and narrowing rise to another small green, this one protected by three bunkers. But perhaps the most famous and certainly the most photographed of Turnberry's delightful holes is the 9th, more specifically the 9th championship tee, perched out on a rocky promontory which was the site of King Robert the Bruce's castle in medieval times – or so, at least, Turnberry will claim. The drive from this tee demands a carry of almost 200 yards across an inlet to a hump-backed fairway on the clifftops, close by the century-old Turnberry lighthouse. The Ailsa course, its landscape, its seascape, is surely the most beautiful of all the Open Championship venues.

Ailsa Craig, the great granite boulder in the Firth of Clyde which dominates the Turnberry Hotel courses and gives its name to the Open Championship Course. It is seen here from the ninth hole of that Ailsa course. ➤

U

United States Golf Association (USGA)

Golf in the United States, as in so many other countries of the world, owes its origins to the wayward Scots – traders, travellers, emigrants. There is some evidence, fragmentary it is true, that golf was played in America in the 17th century, and there was certainly a golf club of sorts in Charleston, South Carolina in 1786 soon after the War of Independence. The first club formed and still surviving in North America is Royal Montreal, dating from 1873, but golf clubs were not truly established in the US until the 1880s, when the game was certainly being played at Oakhurst, West Virginia, in Vermont and Kentucky, in Foxburgh, Pennsylvania, and at the St Andrews Club in Yonkers, New York.

In the last two decades of the century the game spread rapidly and what is considered to be America's first 'public' course was opened in 1895 at Van Cortland Park in New York City. The growth of golf brought a situation in which the various clubs went their own ways and to some extent invented their own rules but in 1894, when the St Andrews Club of New York and the Newport Club in Rhode Island each held invitational tournaments and each declared that the winner was the 'Amateur Champion of the United States', it was time for something to be done. At the end of that year, on 22

December to be exact, at the Calumet Club in New York, delegates from five clubs met, no doubt to have a good dinner but also to establish an organisation which would administer the game, conduct recognised national championships and police the Rules of Golf. Thus the United States Golf Association was formed, and Theodore A Havemeyer, a national figure, 'The Sugar King', was appointed President.

The first choice of a name for this new association was in fact the 'Amateur Golf Association', discarded when they realised that they would be dealing also with professionals. Then the 'American Golf Association' was suggested, discarded when they had no authority in Canada. So the USGA it was. The Amateur and Open Championships were established for 1895 and Havemeyer gave a $1000 trophy for the Amateur.

The St Andrews Club, founded half a dozen years earlier by John Reid, an expatriate Scot from Dunfermline, had been a prime mover in all this. The other clubs represented at the Calumet Club meeting were Newport, The Country Club from Brookline near Boston, Shinnecock Hills from Long Island, and the Chicago Golf Club.

The first Amateur Championship was won by Charles Blair Macdonald, a powerful figure in the making of American golf, and the first Open Championship, over 36 holes or four times round the Newport club's course of nine holes in one day, and played the day following the Amateur, by Horace Rawlins, oddly an English and not a Scottish professional employed by the host club. Rawlins was a mere 21 and won his championship in a field of ten professionals and

one amateur because of a greater Newport attraction – the America's Cup yatch races. Mrs Charles S Brown won the the first Women's Amateur when 13 ladies played 18 holes at the Meadow Brook club at Hempstead, not far beyond the Brooklyn boundary on Long Island. She scored 132 on the round, but from the next year on, the women's test would be at match play.

Now the USGA conducts 13 different championships. The others are the Amateur Public Links, the Junior, the Girls Junior, Women's Open, Senior Amateur, Senior Women's Amateur, Women's Amateur Public Links, Senior Open, Mid-Amateur and Women's Mid-Amateur. In conjunction with the Royal & Ancient, it has conducted the Walker Cup matches between the United States and Great Britain & Ireland since 1922, and since 1932 has shared responsibility with the British Ladies' Golf Union for the presentation of the Curtis Cup matches. And on behalf of the World Amateur Golf Council, it has managed the World Amateur Team Championship for the Eisenhower Trophy since 1958, and the women's version of the same, for the Espirito Santo Trophy, since 1964.

The USGA is structured with an Executive Committee of 16 members, representing 7,500 member clubs and courses. There are 30 committees of a total of around 1,000 men and women volunteers. All provide their services and expenses freely. These committees cover various aspects of the governance of golf. The USGA is constantly refining the rules of golf and of Amateur Status. In May 1951 after some rules divergencies in the 1920s and 30s, a meeting of representatives from Great Britain, Australia, Canada

and the United States took place in London to unify a code. This is now recognised throughout the world. A rules conference is held, and the rules amended as deemed fit, only every four years.

Before the First World War, the Association developed a system of handicapping which could apply nationally. It is a system under constant review. In such a huge country, with such a variety of climates and weather, maintaining good playing conditions on all its courses has been a longtime concern of the governing body. A Green Section was formed in 1920 and in all, the USGA has spent more than $23 million on research, advisory visits to courses, films, videos, publications, grants, a bi-monthly magazine, grants to universities for research programmes and the employment of the USGA's staff agronomists.

At its headquarters at Far Hills, New Jersey, the USGA has a museum of golf artefacts and a library of more than 8,000 volumes, the largest golf library in existence.

US MASTERS

The youngest of the so-called Grand Slam championships, the US Masters, played on the course of the Augusta National Golf Club, enjoys a stature which has evolved in the simplest, but at the same time seemingly inevitable, way. The course and the club were the brainchild of Bobby Jones, who retired in 1930 having won the Open and Amateur Championships of both Britain and America in that single year. Jones, the Atlanta lawyer, wanted to build a course that would incorporate many of the architectural features he had noted on the great courses he had played, on both sides of

played in the warm Georgia spring, when flowering shrubs are in bloom, and when East Coast and Northern and Mid-West golfers were eager to escape from the snows and chills of winter.

And in Clifford Roberts, the Augusta National had a dictator who wanted the best of everything for the club and the event. The Masters was the first event to spread itself over four days. In time, Roberts roped off the fairways, allowing only players and caddies to walk them. He sold season tickets in advance to patrons. He provided free car-parking for them on club property. He arranged platoons of litter collectors so that the course

remained spotless even when thousands of people were using the grounds. He created a brilliant scoring system from central control to every scoreboard on the course, to show cumulative scores in red figures for under par, in green for over par, and a green zero for level par. After the event was first televised, for example, Roberts insisted that the television company lay permanent lines throughout the course, the cables remaining the property of the club. And every year, there seemed to be improvements made to the course, a spectator mound put in here, a bunker moved there.

Incidents in the tournament helped – there always seemed to be high drama at the Masters. When Horton Smith won the first one in 1934, he holed a 20 foot birdie putt on the 71st to do it. The next year Gene Sarazen holed his fairway

the ocean. Land was found in Augusta, Georgia, a small town 100 miles or so from Atlanta, and Jones and architect Dr Alister Mackenzie went to work with such effect that the course was ready for play in December 1932.

Jones wanted the club to be for men, with membership by invitation, and for winter golf, open from the end of October until the end of April. The club would have a nationwide membership from Jones' friends and acquaintances, and thus be called 'The Augusta National'. But its operation would be simple, modest and unostentatious. Jones asked Clifford Roberts, a Wall Street investment banker friend, to help structure and organise the club. Roberts, a gravel-voiced autocrat who had known Jones since they had both

used the existing Augusta Country Club's course for winter golf, did precisely that.

The Masters tournament was inaugurated in the spring of 1934 as the Augusta National Invitational, meant as an informal get-together of Jones' amateur and professional friends. Other players who received invitations were those who had been Open or Amateur champions and members of the current American Ryder Cup and Walker Cup teams. Jones wanted the event to remain as a relaxed reunion, but by 1938 he had to yield to the pressure to name it 'The Masters'. It had, after all, the best players of the day. It was played on a course that was quickly seen as quite challenging, and which developed into one of the most beautiful parkland courses in the world. It was

THE MASTERS TOURNAMENT

Winners US, except where stated

Year	Winner	Score	Year	Winner	Score
1934	Horton Smith	284	1966	Jack Nicklaus	288*
1935	Gene Sarazen	282*	1967	Gay Brewer	280
1936	Horton Smith	285	1968	Bob Goalby	277
1937	Byron Nelson	283	1969	George Archer	281
1938	Henry Picard	285	1970	Billy Casper	279*
1939	Ralph Guldahl	279	1971	Charles Coody	279
1940	Jimmy Demaret	280	1972	Jack Nicklaus	286
1941	Craig Wood	280	1973	Tommy Aaron	283
1942	Byron Nelson	280*	1974	Gary Player (SA)	278
1946	Herman Keiser	282	1975	Jack Nicklaus	276
1947	Jimmy Demaret	281	1976	Ray Floyd	271
1948	Claude Harmon	279	1977	Tom Watson	276
1949	Sam Snead	282	1978	Gary Player (SA)	277
1950	Jimmy Demaret	281	1979	Fuzzy Zoeller	280*
1951	Ben Hogan	274	1980	Seve Ballesteros (Sp)	280
1952	Sam Snead	286	1981	Tom Watson	280
1953	Ben Hogan	274	1982	Craig Stadler	284*
1954	Sam Snead	289*	1983	Seve Ballesteros (Sp)	280
1955	Cary Middlecoff	279	1984	Ben Crenshaw	277
1956	Jack Burke	289	1985	Bernhard Langer (Ger)	282
1957	Doug Ford	283	1986	Jack Nicklaus	279
1958	Arnold Palmer	284	1987	Larry Mize	285*
1959	Art Wall	284	1988	Sandy Lyle (GB)	281
1960	Arnold Palmer	282	1989	Nick Faldo (GB)	283*
1961	Gary Player (SA)	280	1990	Nick Faldo (GB)	278*
1962	Arnold Palmer	280*	1991	Ian Woosnam (GB)	277
1963	Jack Nicklaus	286	1992	Fred Couples	275
1964	Arnold Palmer	276	1993	Bernhard Langer (Ger)	277
1965	Jack Nicklaus	271	* *play-off*		

wood shot at the 15th for the famous 'double eagle' which allowed him to tie Craig Wood, then win the play-off. After the Second World War, the exploits of Sam Snead and Ben Hogan awoke America to the quality of the tournament, Snead winning in 1949, 1952 and 1954, Hogan in 1951 and 1953. Snead beat Hogan in a play-off in 1954. Great champions both, they took the Masters into the television age, the age of Palmer. The swashbuckling do-it-or-die style of Arnold Palmer was made for the television cameras and finally confirmed the Masters as a great, spectacular championship.

Yet the club makes no such claim. It is called simply 'The Masters Tournament'. Although there is a qualifying system for US players, entry is strictly by invitation and the field is restricted to less than 100 players, many of them amateurs. It is by no means an 'open' championship. But this great annual carnival in springtime Georgia, after 60 years has a secure place in the golfing year.

US OPEN

The United States National Open Championship was first played on 4 October 1885, less than a year after the five leading clubs of the day formed the United States Golf Association. It was played then, and has been played since, under the auspices of the USGA (Only

Lee Janzen, surprise winner of the US Open Championship at Baltusrol in 1993, enjoys one of the fruits of that success - an invitation to the Johnnie Walker World Championship.

in 1919 did the British Open Championship become the sole responsibility of the R & A at the request of the other British clubs.) The US Open was played over the course of the Newport, Rhode Island club as a 36-holes, one-day

competition. It had been scheduled for September, but was postponed because of a clash of dates with the America's Cup yacht races. The winner was Horace Rawlins, an English professional who had

crossed the ocean in January to be an assistant at the Newport club. He scored 91–82 for a 173 with the gutty ball and won $150, a $50 gold medal and the Open Championship cup for his club. Rawlins was 21 years

Year	Venue	Winner	Score
1895	Newport	Horace Rawlins	173
1896	Shinnecock Hills	James Foulis	152
1897	Chicago	Joe Lloyd	162
1898	Myopia Hunt	Fred Herd	328**
1899	Baltimore	Willie Smith	315
1900	Chcago	Harry Vardon (GB)	313
1901	Myopia Hunt	Willie Anderson	331*
1902	Garden City	Laurie Auchterlonie	307
1903	Baltusrol	Willie Anderson	307*
1904	Glen View	Willie Anderson	303
1905	Myopia Hunt	Willie Anderson	314
1906	Onwentsia	Alex Smith	295
1907	Philadelphia	Alex Ross	302
1908	Myopia Hunt	Fred McLeod	322*
1909	Englewood	George Sargent	290
1910	Philadelphia	Alex Smith	298*
1911	Chicago	John McDermott	307*
1912	Buffalo	John McDermott	294
1913	Brookline	Francis Ouimet†	304*
1914	Midlothian	Walter Hagen	290
1915	Baltusrol	Jerome Travers†	297
1916	Minikahda	Chick Evans†	286
1919	Brae Burn	Walter Hagen	301*
1920	Inverness	Ted Ray (GB)	295
1921	Columbia	Jim Barnes	289
1922	Skokie	Gene Sarazen	288
1923	Inwood	Bobby Jones†	296*
1924	Oakland Hills	Cyril Walker	297
1925	Worcester	Willie McFarlane	291*
1926	Scioto	Bobby Jones†	293
1927	Oakmont	Tommy Armour	301*
1928	Olympia Fields	Johnny Farrell	294*
1929	Winged Foot	Bobby Jones†	294*
1930	Interlachen	Bobby Jones†	287
1931	Inverness	Billy Burke	292*
1932	Fresh Meadow	Gene Sarazen	286
1933	North Shore	Johnny Goodman†	287
1934	Merion	Olin Dutra	293
1935	Oakmont	Sam Parks	299
1936	Baltusrol	Tony Manero	282
1937	Oakland Hills	Ralph Guldahl	281
1938	Cherry Hills	Ralph Guldahl	284
1939	Philadelphia	Byron Nelson	284*
1940	Canterbury	Lawson Little	287*
1941	Colonial	Craig Wood	284
1946	Canterbury	Lloyd Mangrum	284*
1947	St Louis	Lew Worsham	282*
1948	Riviera	Ben Hogan	276
1949	Medinah	Cary Middlecoff	286
1950	Merion	Ben Hogan	287*
1951	Oakland Hills	Ben Hogan	287
1952	Northwood	Julius Boros	281
1953	Oakmont	Ben Hogan	283
1954	Baltusrol	Ed Furgol	284
1955	Olympic	Jack Fleck	287*
1956	Oak Hill	Cary Middlecoff	281
1957	Inverness	Dick Mayer	282*
1958	Southern Hills	Tommy Bolt	283
1959	Winged Foot	Billy Casper	282
1960	Cherry Hills	Arnold Palmer	280
1961	Oakland Hills	Gene Littler	281
1962	Oakmont	Jack Nicklaus	283*
1963	Brookline	Julius Boros	293*
1964	Congressional	Ken Venturi	278
1965	Bellerive	Gary Player (SA)	282*
1966	Olympic	Billy Casper	278*
1967	Baltusrol	Jack Nicklaus	275
1968	Oak Hill	Lee Trevino	275
1969	Champions	Orville Moody	281
1970	Hazeltine	Tony Jacklin (GB)	281
1971	Merion	Lee Trevino	280*
1972	Pebble Beach	Jack Nicklaus	290
1973	Oakmont	Johnny Miller	279
1974	Winged Foot	Hale Irwin	287
1975	Medinah	Lou Graham	287*
1976	Atlanta	Jerry Pate	277
1977	Southern Hills	Hubert Green	278
1978	Cherry Hills	Andy North	285
1979	Inverness	Hale Irwin	284
1980	Baltusrol	Jack Nicklaus	272
1981	Merion	David Graham (Aus)	273
1982	Pebble Beach	Tom Watson	282
1983	Oakmont	Larry Nelson	280
1984	Winged Foot	Fuzzy Zoeller	276*
1985	Oakland Hills	Andy North	279
1986	Shinnecock Hills	Ray Floyd	279
1987	Olympic	Scott Simpson	277
1988	Brookline	Curtis Strange	278*
1989	Oak Hill	Curtis Strange	278
1990	Medinah	Hale Irwin	280*
1991	Hazeltine, Minn.	Payne Stewart	282
1992	Pebble Beach	Tom Kite	285
1993	Baltusrol	Lee Janzen	272

*play-off **Competition extended over 72 holes † amateur*

old. Ten professionals and one amateur had taken part. The first US Amateur Championship took place in the same week over the same course, with 32 competitors.

The early US Opens were considered side-shows to the US Amateur. In the early years they were dominated by Scottish and English professionals who had emigrated to the New World in search of fortune if not of fame. The second championship, played at another founder club, Shinnecock Hills at Southampton on Long Island, attracted 35 entrants. Over a course measuring 4,423 yards Jim Foulis, a Scot from the Chicago Golf Club, won with 78-74 for a 152. The 74 was a record that lasted for seven years when the rubber-cored ball was coming into favour.

In 1898, the USGA decided to extend their Open to 72 holes (the British had done this seven years earlier). Also in 1898, the Americans played their Open in June, separating it from the Amateur in September. In 1900 the Open title went abroad for the first time when Harry Vardon of England won at the Chicago Golf Club by two strokes from his fellow tourist, JH Taylor. Vardon's win included a complete miss on the last green, when he stabbed unsuccessfully at a tap-in putt. In 1901 Willie Anderson, a dour Scot, won the first of his four Opens, three of them (1903 – 5) coming in successive years. He is one of only four players to have done this, the others being Bobby Jones, Ben Hogan and Jack Nicklaus. The 'immigrants' remained in control until 1911 when Johnny McDermott, a cocky young Philadelphian aged only 19, won in a play-off. When he retained his title the following year, the native-born Americans were firmly in control of their title.

They have yielded it seldom, only to Ted Ray of England in 1920, Gary Player of South Africa in 1965, Tony Jacklin of England in 1970, and David Graham of Australia in 1981. The stunning victory of Francis Ouimet over Vardon and Ray in 1913 gave the amateurs a taste for the Open. Jerome

Travers, a winner of four Amateur titles, won at Baltusrol in 1915 and then Chick Evans won at Minikahada, Minneapolis, breaking par in all four rounds and making it three amateur wins in four years. His 70–69–74–73 for 286 was two under par and stood unbettered for 20 years. After the First World War, the prize fund stood at $1,745 with the first professional prize $500. In 1922 the entry was a record 323 and spectator admission was charged for the first time. In 1924, the use of steel-shafted putters was permitted. In 1925, three elimination rounds were needed at New York, Chicago and San Francisco for an entry of 445. It rose above 1000 for the first time in 1928. The following year the total purse was up to $5000 with a first professional prize of $1000. Entries, and prize money, rose inexorably, stimulated by the achievements of great champions – the twenties was the decade of Bobby Jones, the fifties belonged to Ben Hogan, the sixties and early seventies to Jack Nicklaus. In 1947, first prize became $2000; by 1953 that was $5000. By 1960, total prize money topped $50,000, in 1965 $100,000. By 1990, it had passed $1 million, with an entry of more than 5000 golfers playing through sophisticated pre-qualifying systems for places in the Open proper.

In the main, the USGA has prepared very difficult parkland courses for its championship. Recent hugely successful exceptions have been Pebble Beach in California, that marvellous clifftop course, and Shinnecock Hills on Long Island, one of the original links-type designs, where Raymond Floyd in 1986 became the oldest winner to that time, at the age of 43 years and nine months.

US PGA CHAMPIONSHIP

The US Professional Golfers' Association was formed in 1916, fifteen years after the original British PGA, and was able to stage its first championship that same year. It was played at the Siwanoy Club in New York and won by Jim Barnes, the Cornishman, who beat Jock Hutchison by one hole. Match play golf was the fashion of the times to a great extent. Just as immigrant Scottish and English players had dominated American golf up to the outbreak of the First World War, so they continued briefly in the post-war period. Barnes won again when the championship resumed in 1919, this time by 6 & 5 over Freddie McLeod, and in 1920 Jock Hutchison prevailed over Englishman Douglas Edgar by one hole. But when Barnes went down in the final the following year to Walter Hagen, the PGA Championship became 'native-born' and entered the

A dream comes true. For Paul Azinger, the long quest for his first major championship ended with victory in the US PGA Championship of 1993.

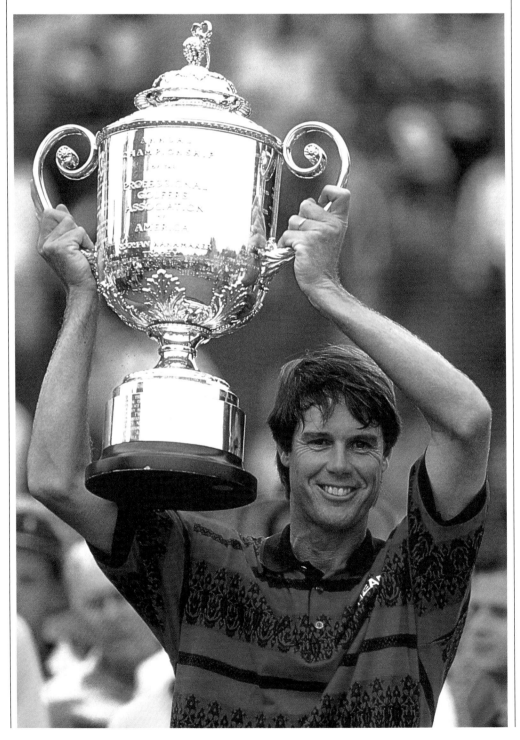

THE US PGA CHAMPIONSHIP

Winners US, except where stated

Year	Venue	Winner	Margin/Score	Year	Venue	Winner	Margin/Score
1916	Siwanoy	Jim Barnes	1 up	1957	Miami Valley	Lionel Hebert	2 & 1
1919	Engineers	Jim Barnes	6 & 5	1958	Llanerch	Dow Finsterwald	276
1920	Flossmoor	Jock Hitchinson	1 up	1959	Minneapolis	Bob Rosburg	277
1921	Inwood	Walter Hagen	3 & 2	1960	Firestone	Jay Hebert	281
1922	Oakmont	Gene Sarazen	4 & 3	1961	Olympia Fields	Jerry Barber	277*
1923	Pelham	Gene Sarazen	4 & 3	1962	Aronimink	Gary Player (SA)	278
1924	French Lick	Walter Hagen	2 up	1963	Dallas	Jack Nicklaus	279
1925	Olympia Fields	Walter Hagen	6 & 5	1964	Columbus	Bobby Nichols	271
1926	Salisbury	Walter Hagen	5 % 3	1965	Laurel Valley	Dave Marr	280
1927	Cedar Crest	Walter Hagen	1 up	1966	Firestone	Al Geiberger	280
1928	Five Farms	Leo Diegel	6 & 5	1967	Columbine	Don January	281*
1929	Hillcrest	Leo Diegel	6 & 4	1968	Pecan Valley	Julius Boros	281
1930	Fresh Meadow	Tommy Armour	1 up	1969	NCR (Dayton)	Ray Floyd	276
1931	Wannamoisett	Tom Creavy	2 & 1	1970	Southern Hills	Dave Stockton	279
1932	Keller	Olin Durra	4 & 3	1971	PGA National (Palm Beach)	Jack Nicklaus	281
1933	Blue Mound	Gene Sarazen	5 & 4	1972	Oakland Hills	Gary Player (SA)	281
1934	Park	Paul Runyan	at 38th	1973	Canterbury	Jack Nicklaus	277
1935	Twin Hills	Johnny Revolta	5 & 4	1974	Tanglewood	Lee Trevino	276
1936	Pinehurst	Densmore Shute	3 & 2	1975	Firestone	Jack Nicklaus	277
1937	Pittsburgh	Densmore Shute	at 37th	1976	Congressional	Dave Stockton	281
1938	Shawnee	Paul Runyan	8 & 7	1977	Pebble Beach	Lanny Wadkins	282*
1939	Pomonok	Henry Picard	at 37th	1978	Oakmont	John Mahaffey	276*
1940	Hershey	Byron Nelson	1 up	1979	Oakland Hills	David Graham (Aus)	272*
1941	Cherry Hills	Vic Ghezzi	at 38th	1980	Oak Hill	Jack Nicklaus	274
1942	Seaview	Sam Snead	2 & 1	1981	Atlanta	Larry Nelson	273
1944	Manito	Bob Hamilton	1 up	1982	Southern Hills	Ray Floyd	272
1945	Morraine	Byron Nelson	4 & 3	1983	Riviera	Hal Sutton	274
1946	Portland	Ben Hogan	6 & 4	1984	Shoal Creek	Lee Trevino	273
1947	Plum Hollow	Jim Ferrier	2 & 1	1985	Cherry Hills	Hubert Green	278
1948	Norwood Hills	Ben Hogan	7 & 6	1986	Inverness	Bob Tway	276
1949	Hermitage	Sam Snead	3 & 2	1987	PGA National (Palm Beach)	Larry Nelson	287*
1950	Scioto	Chandler Harper	4 & 3	1988	Oak Tree	Jeff Sluman	272
1951	Oakmont	Sam Snead	7 & 6	1989	Kemper Lakes	Payne Stewart	276
1952	Big Spring	Jim Turnesa	1 up	1990	Shoal Creek	Wayne Grady (Aus)	282
1953	Birmingham	Walter Burkemo	2 & 1	1991	Crooked Stick	John Daly	276
1954	Keller	Chick Harbert	4 & 3	1992	Bellerive	Nick Price (Zim)	278
1955	Meadowbrook	Doug Ford	4 & 3	1993	Inverness	Paul Azinger	272
1956	Blue Hill	Jack Burke	3 & 2				

play-off

age of Hagen and Gene Sarazen.

One of the epic achievements in the history of golf was to follow. Hagen, the ebullient, larger-than-life superstar, won in 1921; lost an animated final at the 38th hole in 1923 to Gene Sarazen; then won, at match play, the next four championships! So in six years, Hagen won five times, was a finalist six times, and won four successive championships. There is virtually nothing to compare with this in the game. Sarazen's first win in 1922 gave him a unique double, since he had also won the US Open that year, and he came closest to Hagen's successes, winning again in 1933 for a tally of three PGA wins in a

decade of growth and expansion famously dubbed 'The Roaring Twenties'. In the forties and fifties, Sam Snead won three and Byron Nelson and Ben Hogan, perhaps surprisingly, only two each, although Nelson was three times a losing finalist.

With the expansion of the golf tour in the fifties, the professionals became increasingly edgy about match play, pointing out that in one match, a player scoring 69 might lose, while in another match, a player scoring 73 might win. This of course is the essence of match play, but as the competition reduces down to four players in the semi-finals, and only two in the final, there was that much

less for the spectators to see.

Even more important, it left diminishing scope for television coverage. The USGA had started national television coverage at their Open in 1954 and three years later, the PGA decided that the change had to be made. Fittingly enough, Dow Finsterwald bridged the gap, losing at match play in the 1957 final and winning at stroke play in 1958 with total of 276. To come was the Age of Nicklaus, who won first in 1963 then dominated the seventies with four more wins to equal Hagen's record total of five.

The championship has remained rather a poor relation of the other three in golf's 'Grand Slam' quartet. Criticisms aimed at it

included the poor quality of the courses selected to stage it, at least until perhaps 15 years ago, and the policy adopted for qualifying. To counter the first of these, in recent years the PGA has gone to such fine courses as Pebble Beach, Oakmont, Oak Hill, Oakland Hills, Shoal Creek and Bellerive. But the nature of the championship has meant that foreign players have had great difficulty in finding places in the field, so much so that Gary Player of South Africa in 1962 and 1972, David Graham of Australia in 1979, and Nick Price of Zimbabwe in 1992, are the only foreign players to have won it since the early 1920s.

VARDON, Harry

Born 1870

Nationality British

Turned Pro 1887

Majors Open Championship 1896, 1898, 1899, 1903, 1911, 1914; US Open 1900

In many ways the single most important figure in the game's history, Harry Vardon is always considered first among equals with Bobby Jones, Ben Hogan and Jack Nicklaus. He had a profound effect on how the golf club should be held and swung, but one element of his uniqueness is clear. He won the Open Championship six times. James Braid, JH Taylor, Peter Thomson and Tom Watson have each won five championships, but only Vardon has six, a total unlikely ever to be equalled. His immortality does not rest on his playing achievements alone. He was the first truly international champion. He was the first 'modern' professional in the sense that more than 50 years after his death, almost 65 years since his last major competition, we can still relate to how he swung the golf club, and to the modern swing which he developed.

Harry Vardon was the fourth of six sons in a family of eight, and was born in 1870 in the village of Grouville in Jersey, Channel Islands. His father was a gardener. When he was seven years old, some English vacationers laid out a few golf holes on a piece of common land near the Vardon home – and incidentally planted the seed that was to grow into the Royal Jersey Golf Club. Vardon was one of a bunch of local boys who, as they grew up, became caddies and learned to play with cut-down clubs and cast-off balls. Harry left school at the age of 12 to work on a dairy farm, then in the service of a local doctor. He was taken on the staff of a local squire, one Major Spofford of Beauview, who encouraged his golf. A younger brother Tom, a better player, left to become an assistant professional at St Annes in Lancashire, and soon summoned Harry. He helped him find work at Studley Royal, then at Bury, and finally at Ganton in Yorkshire as greenkeeper-professional.

In 1893, Harry played in his first Open. The following year he finished fifth behind JH Taylor at Sandwich and in 1895 he finished ninth, again behind Taylor. In 1896, JH, the top man of the day, was going for a third successive Open. He already knew all about Harry Vardon. Earlier in the year, he had been spanked 8 & 6 by the Jerseyman in a match played at Ganton; JH did not enjoy it.

Sure enough, the 1886 Open at Muirfield came down to a battle between the two. Taylor had posted his final score, and Vardon came to the last hole, a stiff par four then as now, with a four needed to win his first Open. He was faced with a second shot of 200 yards, which would have to carry cross-bunkers at the front of the green. Vardon played short, pitched on, scored five to tie, and won the play-off handily 157 to 161. It was a neat illustration of tactical golf by Vardon.

He won again in 1898 and 1899, and in 1900 made the first of three extensive tours to the US, where golf was expanding. He played exhibitions and challenge matches, held store exhibitions the entire length of the country and won the US Open at the Chicago Golf Club in October. Huge crowds followed him and marvelled at his skill and artistry. Early in the new century, he fell ill with tuberculosis. It was to plague him for the rest of his life (he died in 1937) and many of his friends claimed that the rigours of his American sojourn were responsible. Vardon played in three US Opens. His record? A win in 1900, joint second with Ted Ray in 1913 after a play-off with Francis Ouimet, and joint second again in 1920 behind Ted Ray. Vardon's visits contributed enormously to publicising and popularising the game in the US.

In his contributions to the evolution of the golf grip and swing, he is remembered above all for the 'Vardon Grip', in which the little finger of the right hand rides over the index finger of the left. It had been used by Johnny Laidlay, an Edinburgh golfer who had been Amateur Champion in 1889 and 1891, but Vardon had spent a year experimenting with grips before deciding that this was the optimum for him, and he revolutionised the swinging of the club. The prevalent St Andrews swing, evolved through the years from the feathery ball to the gutty, featured a solid two-fisted grip, an open and wide stance, a huge backswing and much lurching and swaying. Another swing, an extreme, had been developed principally by JH Taylor, who called it 'flat-footed golf, sir'. Taylor was a short, stocky man and his swing was short and compact, with a rather fierce smash at the ball. Vardon brought grace and rhythm and style to the swing. He took the club back slowly, gripping the club quite lightly, and letting the clubhead swing. He went through to a high, controlled finish, with his weight moving smoothly to his left foot.

This was a thoroughly modern swing, which clipped the ball away smoothly without taking much in the way of a divot. Of Vardon's six Open titles, three were won with the gutty ball, three with the rubber-wound ball. No man has influenced the game more, no man has played it better, than Harry Vardon, of Grouville, Jersey.

Harry Vardon, in many ways the single most important figure in the game of golf.

VICENZO, Roberto de

Born 1923

Nationality Argentinian

Turned Pro 1940

Majors Open Championship 1967

The greatest of the South American golfers, Roberto de Vicenzo was also one of the most successful of all international players. He was born in Buenos Aires in 1923, won the Argentine Open at the age of 21, and is reckoned to have won more than 230 events of all kinds, including more than 100 major tournaments and 39 national championships. In his career he won the National Opens of Brazil, France, Germany, Holland, Mexico and Spain. His British Open win at Hoylake in 1967 was the last played at the

famous course of the Royal Liverpool club, because the championship had outgrown the off-course facilities. Roberto was the oldest winner of the Open to that date, at 44 years 93 days.

Powerfully built and 6' 1" tall, he was immensely long but with a controlled, powerful swing. In the US Masters of 1968, he lost the possibility of a play-off with Bob Goalby by signing an incorrect scorecard, which showed a four on a hole on which he had scored three. He represented Argentina 17 times in World (Canada) Cup play, winning the inaugural event with Antonio Cerda at Montreal in 1953, and won the Individual Trophy twice, in 1969 and 1972. Later in his career he played successfully on the US Senior Tour, winning the US Senior Open in 1980 with a score of 285 at Winged Foot. He became an honorary member of the Royal & Ancient Club in 1976.

VOCABULARY of Golf, The

Ace American slang for a hole in one.

Albatross Term used in Britain for a score of three under the par of the hole. In America this is known as a double eagle.

Address The position the golfer takes up in order to strike at the ball.

Approach Shot played to the green.

Away The player whose ball is furthest from the hole is said to be 'Away' (Americanism).

Back nine The second half of an 18 hole course, i.e. holes 10–18

Baffy A lofted wooden club used in the days of the feathery and gutty balls – now obsolete, its modern equivalent would be the 3 or 4 wood.

Bent grass A species of grass of fine texture ideally suited to golf greens. Difficult to maintain in hot climates.

Bermuda grass A species of coarsely textured grass in which the strands matt and intertwine. Used for both fairways and greens in hot climates.

Birdie A hole scored in one stroke under par.

Bisque A handicap stroke allotted to an opponent who can use it at his discretion, but only if he announces his desire to do so before the next hole is played.

Bogey In British golf, originally the score that a first-class player would be expected to make on a hole. Its American meaning of one stroke over the par of the hole is now common.

Blind A hole is said to be blind when the approaching player cannot see the green.

Borrow British term for the amount a putt will deviate from a direct line to the hole because of the slope on the green. The American useage is 'break'.

Brassie A wooden club used from the fairway for long shots, the modern equivalent being a 2-wood.

Caddie A person who carries the golfer's clubs.

Carry The distance the ball flies through the air from the point of being hit to the point where it first strikes the ground.

Chip A running shot usually played from just off the green.

Cleek A word of Scottish origin describing an iron-headed club, usually used from long distances.

Cuppy lie A lie in which the ball rests in a small depression in the ground.

Cut To 'Miss the Cut' is an Americanism meaning failure to qualify for the final 36 holes in a 72 holes medal tournament or championship.

Cut shot A shot that makes the ball spin in a clockwise manner resulting in a left to right flight.

Dead Description of a putt that is so close to the hole that the holing of the ball is certain.

Divot The piece of turf displaced when a shot is played.

Dog-leg A hole that turns sharply to one side or the other.

Dormie In match play, the player who is as many holes ahead of his opponent as there are holes left to play is said to be 'Dormie'. He thus cannot be beaten.

Draw A slight turn from right to left in the flight of a ball.

Double-eagle An American term for scoring three under par on a hole. The British term is 'albatross'.

Driver The number one

Corey Pavin of the US and Peter Baker representing Europe in the 1993 Ryder Cup – perhaps the ultimate match play competition.

wood club for long play, with a very slight loft in the face.

Eagle A hole played in two strokes less than par.

Fairway The stretch of ground extending from tee to green, specially prepared for play.

Feathery An early golf ball made of leather stuffed with boiled feathers and stitched into shape. It was superseded by the 'gutty' from 1848.

Flat Either a very obtuse angle between the shaft and the sole of the club, or the swing (flat swing) of a player whose swing seems more horizontal than upright.

Fescue A particular species of grass; fine-leaved and deep, straight-rooted, common in the British Isles and highly suitable for links or heathland greens.

Fourball A match involving four players in teams of two, each player playing his own ball.

Foursome A match involving four players in teams of two, each team playing one ball with alternate strokes.

Follow through The continuation of the swing after the ball has been struck.

Free Drop A ball dropped away from an immoveable obstruction, or in any circumstances in accordance with the Rules of Golf.

Front Nine The first half of an 18 holes golf course, i.e. holes 1–9 inclusive. The second half is known as the 'back-nine'.

Gobble Slang expression for a firmly hit putt that surprisingly goes into the hole.

Green In early times, this meant the entire course. Now it is understood to be that piece of the course which is prepared for putting and in which the hole is cut.

Grip The part of the club shaft that is held in the hands *or* the material that covers it *or* the actual conformation of the hands on the club.

Guttie A ball introduced in 1848 and made from gutta percha, a rubber-like substance produced by trees in Malaysia.

Handicap A system that provides the golfer with a classification, established by his abilities, of strokes that he may deduct from his actual score, thus enabling players of varying abilities to play against each other on theoretically equal terms.

Half shot. A shot played with rather less than a full swing.

Hole The area between tee and green *or* the hole cut in the putting green.

Hole out The final stroke in playing the ball into the hole on the putting green.

Honour The privilege of playing first from the tee. Such a player 'has the honour'.

Haskell ball The name of the first rubber-cored, wound golf ball, named after Coburn Haskell, an American who invented it in 1898.

Hook The result of a counter-clockwise spin imparted to the ball – a flight that bends to the left.

Hosel The socket on an iron-head club into which the shaft is fitted. Modern technology is increasingly dispensing with it.

Iron A club with a metal head, although modern golf is now accustomed to 'metal woods' i.e. the former driver, 3–wood etc, now being made with metal heads.

Lie The state of the ball's position on the ground *or* the 'lie of the club', the angle formed by the clubhead and the shaft.

Like as we lie Outdated expression meaning that both sides have played the same number of strokes.

Line The line from the ball to the target.

Loft The angle of the slope of the face of the club, related to the vertical. The higher the loft on the face of the club, the higher the trajectory of the ball.

Links The sandy soil left between the beach and the beginning of agricultural land, left by receding tides. On such ground the original golf courses were laid, and it has come to mean seaside golf courses.

Long game The shots played from a distance in the golfing sense.

Long Iron An iron club designed for long and accurate shots from the fairway, with a minimum amount of loft – modern 1, 2 and 3–irons.

Loose Impediments Any object in the vicinity of the ball not attached to the earth.

Marker A scorer in stroke play appointed by the committee to record a competitor's score. He may be a fellow-competitor, but is not a referee or a forecaddie.

Match play A competition conducted by holes won and lost, and not by strokes taken, to decide the outcome. The alternative is stroke or medal play.

Mixed foursomes Foursomes in which each team includes one male and one female player.

Nassau A system which offers three matches in one – a competition over the first nine holes, over the second nine holes, and over the entire 18.

Neck The junction between the head and shaft of a club.

Niblick An early lofted iron.

Observer One appointed by the committee to decide questions of fact and to report any breach of the Rules.

Odd, the A stroke more than an opponent has played.

Par The standard score for a hole, based on the length of the hole and the number of strokes a first-class player would expect to score in normal conditions.

Pitch A lofted shot to the green.

Pitch and run A lofted shot to the green, which runs forward rather than stopping quickly.

Pot bunker A small, round, deep bunker, found particularly on the Old Course at St Andrews.

Press To swing so hard that the ball cannot be hit properly. Also to double the bet in a Nassau when two down.

Pull A shot dragged off to the left.

Push A shot pushed straight to the right.

Putt, putter A short shot on the green, and the club used for it.

Pro-Am The game in which a professional forms a team with an amateur or amateurs.

R & A The Royal and Ancient Golf Club of St Andrews

Rough Part of the course that is not tee, fairway, green or hazards. Usually unkempt to punish the wayward shot.

Rub-of-the-green A chance deflection of the ball while in play.

Sand iron, sand wedge Lofted club, with heavy flange designed for play from bunkers. The flange 'bounces' the clubhead through the sand.

Sclaff Outdated expression meaning to strike the ground before striking the ball on the downswing.

Scoop A piece of equipment, horse-drawn, designed to strip earth in the early days of course construction.

Scratch Zero handicap – a scratch player is one who needs no handicap.

Shank The part of the hosel nearest the club's face. Also the act of striking the ball on the shank.

Short game Pitching, chipping and putting.

Side The player or players forming one part of a match.

Single A match between two players.

Slice Shot with clockwise spin which makes the ball swerve to the right – opposite to a hook.

Spoon Early name for a fairway wood club, equivalent to the present day 3-wood.

Stroke play A form of competition in which the number of strokes a player takes is compared with all those of all other competitors to determine a winner.

Stymie Situation in which one player's ball lay between another player's ball and the hole. It was abolished in 1951 by the Joint Committee on the Rules established by the R & A and USGA

Sweet Spot The point on the face of a club which will deliver the maximum possible mass behind the ball at impact. This will produce the longest possible shot with that club by that player.

Stroke The forward movement of the club with intent to strike the ball.

Swing The physical movement in the operation of striking the ball.

Tee The prescribed teeing ground. The wooden peg on which the ball is usually placed for the drive.

Three ball A match in which three players compete, each playing his own ball.

Threesome A match in which one player competes against two others forming a side, these two playing alternate strokes with the same ball.

Through the green The entire course, with the exception of the tee and green at the hole being played, and all the hazards on the course.

Yips Nervous trauma that inhibits or destroys the ability to putt, making it impossible to move the putter head, or makes the stroke a convulsive twitch. It has affected the very greatest players from time to time.

WALKER CUP

The Walker Cup is the trophy played for in matches between the gentlemen amateur golfers of the United States on the one hand, and a Great Britain & Ireland team on the other. It is played for every two years, alternately in the US and the British Isles. The country winning the Cup takes custody of it for the following two years. In the case of a tie, each country holds the Cup for one year.

The match grew in part out of international matches held between the US and Canada in 1919 and 1920. The Royal Canadian Golf Association had invited the US Golf Association to a match, and a US team beat the Canadians 12-3 at the Hamilton, Ontario Club in July 1919 and 10-4 in the return match in September of the following year. After the First World War, players on both sides of the Atlantic began to challenge for each other's championships. Cyril Tolley, Roger Wethered, Tommy Armour and others tilted at the US Amateur Championship while the American Bob Gardner reached the final of the 1920 Amateur Championship at Muirfield, losing to Tolley only at the 37th hole.

In the meantime, the Royal and Ancient had invited the executive committee of the USGA to travel to St Andrews to discuss changes that might be needed to the Rules of Golf. George Herbert Walker of the National Golf Links of America, president of the USGA in 1920, led the delegation. On their return home, the Americans discussed the possibility of getting international matches started. Walker, a low handicap player in his day, put up a plan for international golf and offered to donate an 'International Challenge Trophy'. When the Press heard of this, they immediately dubbed it the 'Walker Cup', much to Walker's chagrin, and so it has remained. George Walker was the grandfather of George Bush, President of the US 1988 – 1992. Walker died in 1953.

Early in 1921, the USGA invited all interested countries to send teams to compete for the trophy. None was able to accept that year. But William C Fownes, the 1910 US Amateur Champion, and son of the founder of the famous Oakmont Club in Pittsburgh, had organised the teams which played against Canada, and he rounded up another team in 1921 and took it to Hoylake where, in an informal match on the day before the Amateur Championship, it beat a British team 9-3.

In 1922, the R & A sent a team to America and the first official match was played at the National Links on Long Island, the Americans winning 8-4. The original concept had been that the competition would be a worldwide affair, and more than 35 years were to pass before that became a fact with the World Amateur Team Championship for the

The GB & I team rejoice at their victory in the 1989 Walker Cup match, as Jim Milligan clinches a stunning win in his final match with a half against Jay Sigel at the Peachtree club in Atlanta.

THE WALKER CUP

Year	Venue	Winner	Margin
1922	National Golf Links	William Fownes (US)	8 - 4
1923	St Andrews	Robert A Gardner (US)	6½ - 5½
1924	Garden City	Robert A Gardner (US)	9 - 3
1926	St Andrews	Robert A Gardner (US)	6½ - 5½
1928	Chicago	Bobby Jones (US)	11 - 1
1930	Royal St George's (Sandwich)	Bobby Jones (US)	10 - 2
1932	Brookline	Francis Ouimet (US)	9½ - 2½
1934	St Andrews	Francis Ouimet (US)	9½ - 2½
1936	Pine Valley	Francis Ouimet (US)*	10½ - 1½
1938	St Andrews	John Beck (GB)*	7½ - 4½
1947	St Andrews	Francis Ouimet (US)*	8 - 4
1949	Winged Foot	Francis Ouimet (US)*	10 - 2
1951	Royal Birkdale	William Turnesa (US)	7½ - 4½
1953	Kittansett	Charlie Yates (US)*	9 - 3
1955	St Andrews	William C. Campbell (US)*	10 - 2
1957	Minikahda	Charles Coe (US)*	8½ - 3½
1959	Muirfield (Scotland)	Charles Coe (US)	9 - 3
1961	Seattle	Jack Westland (US)*	11 - 1
1963	Turnberry	Richard Tufts (US)*	14 - 10
1965	Baltimore	John Fischer (US)*	12 - 12
		tied Joe Carr (GB)*	
1967	Royal St George's (Sandwich)	Jess Sweetser (US)*	15 - 9
1969	Milwaukee	Billy Joe Patton (US)*	13 - 11
1971	St Andrews	Michael Bonallack (GB)	13 - 11
1973	Brookline	Jess Sweetser (US)*	14 - 10
1975	St Andrews	Ed Updegraff (US)*	15½ - 8½
1977	Shinnecock Hills	Lou Oehmig (US)*	16 - 8
1979	Muirfield (Scotland)	Dick Siderowf (US)*	15½ - 8½
1981	Cypress Point	Jim Gabrielsen (US)*	15 - 9
1983	Royal Liverpool (Hoylake)	Jay Sigel (US)	13½ - 10½
1985	Pine Valley	Jay Sigel (US)	13 - 11
1987	Sunningdale	Fred Riley (US)*	16½ - 7½
1989	Peachtree	Geoffrey Marks (GB & Ire)	12½ - 11½
1991	Portmarnock	Jim Gabrielson	14 - 10
1993	Interlachen	Vinney Giles	19 - 5

non-playing captain

Eisenhower Trophy. But only the British accepted the initial invitation to compete and that first result was the start of a long American dominance in the competition – not until 1938 were they defeated, by 7-4 with one match halved at St Andrews. The Walker Cup match was played annually until 1924, when it was felt that the financial strain of annual matches, plus a decline of interest if they were played too frequently, indicated that a match every two years would be more sensible.

The US dominance, reflecting the strength of amateur golf in that country, continued after the Second World War. In 1965 at Baltimore the match was halved for the first time, a critical long and late putt by Clive Clark sealing the result, and in 1971, captained by Michael Bonallack, the Great Britain & Ireland team won for a second time, also at St Andrews. Their first win in the United States came in 1989 at the Peachtree club in Atlanta, by 12½ – 11½ in one of the closest and most thrilling of all Walker Cup matches. The visitors shot ahead from the start and led by 7½ – 4½ points at the end of the first day. They extended that lead to 11-5 by winning three of the four foursomes the following morning. The Americans thus needed to win seven of the eight singles in the afternoon, and as so often in the past, rallied brilliantly and almost did it, winning five singles outright.

In the first of the three halved matches, Andrew of Great Britain and Ireland was two down with two to play against Doug Martin, and won both holes. Eoghan O'Connell won the 17th hole when Phil Mickleson three-putted and thus ensured a tie in the match for the visitors, and in the last match, the Walker Cup was won and lost. The experienced Jay Sigel of the US was two up with three to play against Jim Milligan. The Scot birdied the 16th and chipped in from behind the 17th green to square his match, and a half at the 18th gave Great Britain & Ireland the Walker Cup.

But regardless of the results, the matches without exception since 1922 have been played in true Corinthian spirit and selection for the team remains a pinnacle in the careers of all amateur players on both sides of the ocean.

WATSON, Tom

Born 1949

Nationality United States

Turned Pro 1971

Majors Open Championship 1975, 1977, 1980, 1982, 1983; US Open 1982; US Masters 1977, 1981

For Tom Watson, one of the greatest honours in a career of exceptional success was to be captain of the US team in the Ryder Cup match against Europe at The Belfry in September 1993. Watson, five times an Open Champion, is a traditionalist for whom the spirit of the game, the behaviour of its champions and a keen awareness of its history are everything.

He was born in Kansas City, Missouri, in the very heartland of America on 4 September 1949, yet came to have a remarkable affinity with the linksland golf of Great Britain and Ireland. Apart from the great Open Championship courses he played, he made pilgrimages to Royal Dornoch in the far north of Scotland, and to those marvellous courses on the Atlantic coasts of Ireland, Ballybunion and Lahinch, simply to play friendly golf and savour their designs and challenges. Tom Watson is an internationalist but nothing thrills him more than playing for the United States, which he did four times in Ryder Cup matches.

Tom's father was an insurance broker. His grandfather had been a judge. He grew up in an atmosphere of affluence, living at the better end of Kansas City, and learned his golf not in backyards or driving ranges, but at the Prairie Dunes club. Tom was state amateur champion more than once, but had no amateur career to speak of at national level. He played on the golf team at Stanford University, the 'Harvard of the West', near San Francisco, where he graduated in psychology, then promptly turned professional. Within three years he had broken through, winning the 1974 Western Open. That same year, he led the field of the US Open into the final round, one ahead of Hale Irwin, but blew up with a 79. The following year at Carnoustie he won the Open Championship at his very first attempt. Down to the 70th hole it was a helter-skelter finish and at the end, two strokes covered half a dozen players including Jack Nicklaus, Johnny Miller, Bobby Cole and Graham Marsh. Watson and Jack Newton tied, and Watson won on the 18th hole of the play-off, 71 to 72.

If this was the end of Carnoustie as a major venue, it was the beginning of a golden decade for Watson. Less than a month earlier, in

Still one of the major figures in the game, Tom Watson has achieved as much as any man could wish for in golf – five times Open Champion, twice a US Masters winner and once the winner of the US Open, and perhaps above all, captain of the winning US Ryder Cup team in the 1993 match at The Belfry.

At 5' 9", Tom Sturges Watson was no giant, but he was strongly built where it mattered, in the legs and in the hands and arms. He drove the ball very long, if not relentlessly into the fairway, but in his golden decade, it was always his finishing – pitch, chip, putt – that left the others trailing. He would often putt as though he didn't know how difficult it was. In fact, nothing was more reminiscent of Arnold Palmer at his peak than Watson's holing out. Tom was brisk. If he was not quite as jaunty as was, at times, Peter Thomson, there was the same self-possessed, confident air, the business-like approach to the task in hand, to the whole game. On the tee, as on the green, he wasted no time. Once he was set over the ball, away it would go at flashing speed. The swing was quick – if his game went wrong it was almost always down to tempo, too much speed in the backswing. This then was the man who came to the Ailsa Course in July 1977, reigning Masters champion, and a golfer more than set on putting his 1976 Open – he missed the cut defending his title – behind him. Unusually the championship saw a week of freak summer weather in Scotland – brilliant sunshine, no wind and temperatures which had the Scots talking of

the US Open at Medinah, Chicago, he had again led the field, this time by seven shots at the halfway mark having scored 67, 68. He then scored 78, 77, and tied for ninth place. The American critics declared him to be a 'never winner'. His success at Carnoustie was not considered by them. The year 1977 was to change all that. Watson came to the Open at the Ailsa Course of the Turnberry Hotel as the US Masters champion, a championship he had won with a birdie on the 72nd hole to beat the man who mattered most – Jack Nicklaus. An hour spent with Byron Nelson, his friend and mentor, before the event had put his swing into place.

heatwaves. In the opening rounds, he and Jack Nicklaus scored 68, then 70. Paired together in the third round, they each scored a dazzling 65. Paired together in the final round, Nicklaus scored 66, Watson an even more dazzling second 65. 'Duel in the Sun' the writers called it. Early in the round, Nicklaus in fact had gone three strokes ahead. Watson clawed them back, levelling the scores at the short 15th by holing out with his putter from the left fringe of the green a good 60 feet away. And when Watson birdied the long 17th, and Nicklaus didn't, Watson said to his caddie, Alfie Fyles, 'I think we've got him.' They both made dramatic birdies at the last hole, but Watson had got him, by a stroke. The man in third place, Hubert Green, was 11 strokes behind Watson.

And five years later, at the US Open Championship at Pebble Beach, Tom Watson 'got' Jack Nicklaus again, holing again from off the green at a par 3, this time the 71st hole for a birdie and a victory by two strokes. His own National Open had fallen to him at last. Indeed he was Open Champion of both countries that same year of 1982.

Tom Watson was always the man for the low round. Perhaps the most dominating of his five Open victories was that of 1980, when his third round 64 shattered the field at Muirfield.

WEISKOPF, Tom

Born 1942

Nationality United States

Turned Pro 1964

Majors Open Championship 1973

One of the greatest mysteries in an often mysterious game is why Tom Weiskopf won only one major championship. At the height of his career he was close to being the best golfer in the world, and that at a time when his main opposition was of the calibre of Jack Nicklaus, Johnny Miller, Lee Trevino and Gary Player.

Tom, at 6' 3" a majestic figure, was a wonderful golfer, a magnificent driver of the ball with a swing that seemed made in heaven. When he won the Open Championship at Troon, he led from beginning to end, the first time this had been done since Henry Cotton's win at Royal St George's in 1934. In a golden spell in that year of 1973, Weiskopf won five events in eight weeks including the Open and Canadian Open. He tied for second in the US Open of 1976, won by Jerry Pate, and was four times runner-up in the Masters. He played on two Ryder Cup teams, and in two decades on the US Tour, won 15 events. Often Tom gave the impression that he preferred hunting mountain sheep and elk in the Rockies and once declined a place on a Ryder Cup team in favour of a hunting trip. His temper was often suspect, so much so that he was dubbed the 'Towering Inferno', after a disaster movie of the time.

Following surgery on a shoulder in 1986, he cut down his tournament play in favour of some television commentating and golf course designing, in partnership with Jay Morrish. Their Loch Lomond course, at Luss on the 'bonnie banks', has been described by many Scottish critics as one of the best in the world.

Tom Weiskopf, Open Champion at Troon in 1973.

WENTWORTH

The best known golfing venue in the British Isles, St Andrews not excluded, is Wentworth in Surrey. And the best known event in the British Isles, the Open Championship not excluded, may well be the World Match Play Championship, played traditionally over the Wentworth Club's West Course in autumn. Since it started in 1964, it has provided marvellous entertainment for huge television audiences and made Wentworth a household name, and one famous far beyond Britain. The quality of the West course – there is also an 'East', an 'Edinburgh' and a 9-holes 'Executive' – and the events it has staged, have given it a secure place in golfing lore.

The first Curtis Cup match was staged on Wentworth's East course in 1932, when the amateur ladies of the US beat their British Isles counterparts by 5½–3½. In 1953, a desperately close Ryder Cup match was played

WENTWORTH CLUB

HOLE	YARDS	PAR
1	471	4
2	155	3
3	452	4
4	501	5
5	191	3
6	344	4
7	399	4
8	398	4
9	450	4
OUT	3,361	35
10	186	3
11	376	4
12	483	5
13	441	4
14	179	3
15	466	4
16	380	4
17	571	5
18	502	5
IN	3,584	37
TOTAL	6,945	72

The 8th hole on the West Course at Wentworth, with the water providing an ample distraction.

over the West course, the US winning by 6½–5½. And in 1956, the Canada Cup, subsequently the World Cup, was played over the West and won by Ben Hogan and Sam Snead for the US. Wentworth's international credentials are thus assured. Although the club is comparatively young, dating from the 1920s, the Wentworth Estate has a much longer history. A small 19th century estate centred on

'Wentworths', the family home of a brother-in-law of the Duke of Wellington and in 1850, the property was acquired by Ramon Cabrera, a Spanish count. On his death, his wife, the Countess de Morella, bought up adjoining lands to make an estate which ran to 1750 acres.

In 1923 development rights were established by WG Tarrant, builders who built up-market estates at Woking and St George's Hill, Weybridge. Two 18-holes and one 9-hole golf courses, swimming pool, tennis and squash made Wentworth one of the first American-style 'country club' developments

in Britain. The sale of spacious properties adjoining the fairways was the key to the viability of the whole project. Henry Colt, an architect with an outstanding reputation, designed the courses, the East opening first, then the West, dating from 1927. Colt had a splendid piece of ground on which to work, and now these courses thread through heather and pine, oak and silver birch, over sandy sub-soil with massive banks of rhododendron. One of the singular delights of the West course is that almost every fairway is secluded from its neighbours.

The West course, which is

WETHERED, Joyce (Lady Heathcoat-Amory)

Born 1901

Nationality British

At the age of 18, Joyce Wethered entered the 1920 English Ladies Championship and rather to her surprise, won it, beating Cecil Leitch, the dominant woman player of the age, by 2 and 1 at Sheringham in Norfolk. She was to compete in four more of these national championships, winning all of them. In the more demanding, more international British Ladies Championship, Miss Leitch had some kind of revenge the following year, with a 4 and 3 win in the final at Turnberry. Joyce played in three more British finals – 1924, 1925, 1929 – and won all three.

Her brother Roger, who was to become Amateur Champion and play off for the Open Championship, persuaded her into competitive golf after the First World War, when he was captain of golf at Oxford University. She quickly acquired a taste for it. From 1920 to 1925 when she 'retired', she was nine times a finalist. In 1922 and again in 1924, she won both English and British titles.

The Wethereds, a family of means if not quite wealth, learned their golf to a great extent at Dornoch in the far north of Scotland. Their father would take a house there for the entire summer,

A rather sombre Joyce Wethered with the Ladies Championship trophy at St Andrews in 1929, after her classic final against America's Glenna Collett. She won 3 and 1.

always the one in mind when one speaks of Wentworth, plays a shade under 7000 yards at championship length, and the two closing holes take up 1000 of these yards. They are two hulking par fives and the drive on the 17th hole is one of the classic challenges in golf. An out of bounds woodland runs tight along the left side. The fairway slopes down from it, from left to right. A ball finishing too far to the right will almost certainly find rough, and most certainly face a blind shot over a rise. It is a hole where 'who dares the tight left line, wins'.

The course's nickname of 'Burma Road' is little spoken

of, as the Second World War fades further into history. The original Burma Road was one on which the Japanese used British and other prisoners of war as labour which was dreadfully maltreated. During that war, when Wentworth was adapted as an alternative headquarters for the Army General Staff if that became necessary, extensive tunnels and underground apartments were dug out, and the course was abandoned. After the war, when a group of German prisoners of war were brought in to clear and restore it, 'Rawly' Rawlinson, the then club secretary, said it was 'just like another Burma Road'.

and there were lots of competitions. Joyce was a tall, slender, reserved girl, close on six foot, and she developed a fluid, rhythmic swing with an arc that was particularly wide with her wood clubs and let her knock drives consistently more than 225 yards down the fairway. With her irons, her hands seldom went higher than her shoulder level on either the backswing or follow through.

At a time of hickory shafts, when most lady golfers had a hard time in getting under 80, she would be scoring in the mid or low seventies. When she beat the brilliant American Glenna Collett in the third round of the British Ladies at Troon in 1925, when the match ended 4 and 3 to Joyce, she played ten holes in six under par. She retired after that championship but reappeared in 1929, a year in which there was a large overseas entry, to beat the same Glenna Collett in the final at St Andrews by 3 and 1, in what has been described as the finest match in the history of women's golf.

Graceful, and with a perfect temperament, she made the game seem effortless. In spite of appearing cool and saying little to opponents, like Bobby Jones she found the stress of championship play crushing. She believed that the first yard of the backswing was critical to the tempo of the swing, and 'always wanted to be conscious of the clubhead'. Just before an Amateur Championship at St Andrews, Joyce Wethered played a friendly round over the Old Course with Jones, her brother Roger and Dale Bourne, then English champion. She went round the course in 75 – these were still the days of hickory shafts – never missed a shot, and

An outstanding amateur in the 1920s, Roger Wethered twice won the Amateur Championship, and tied for the Open of 1921 at St Andrews. He was Captain of the Royal and Ancient in 1946.

never 'half-missed' a shot. Jones later wrote that 'I had never played golf with anyone, man or woman, amateur or professional, who made me feel so utterly outclassed…I have no hesitancy in saying that, accounting for the unavoidable handicap of a woman's lesser physical strength, she is the finest golfer I have ever seen.'

The family fortunes were dented by the Wall Street crash and subsequent depression, and Joyce forfeited her amateur status by taking a job in the golf department of Fortnum and Mason, the famous London store. After more than four years there, she made a four month tour of the United States in 1935, which, it was said, paid £4000. She was reinstated as an amateur after the Second World War.

WETHERED, Roger

In the Open Championship of 1921 at St Andrews, Roger Wethered asked for an early start time on the final round, since he wanted to take an overnight train that would get him to London in time for a cricket match to which he was committed, the

following day. Then, the final 36 holes were played on a Friday, and at the halfway mark, Wethered was six strokes behind. In walking backwards from lining up a putt in the third round, he inadvertently trod on his ball, suffering a penalty stroke that was to prove immensely expensive. Nevertheless, a magnificent fourth round of 71 meant that Jock Hutchison would have to score 70 to tie the young English amateur. He did just that. It was a remarkable championship in that Hutchinson, in the first round, played two holes in only three strokes – a hole in one at the short 8th, and a two from a matter of a few inches at the reachable 9th.

In the play-off over 36 holes, the professional prevailed, 150 to 159, and Hutchison, a native-born Scot, became the first man to take the championship trophy across the Atlantic. He was to be the first of many.

Wethered, with Cyril Tolley, dominated amateur golf in Britain in the 1920s, and the 1921 Open merely underlined what Wethered firmly believed – that they were just as good as the leading professionals. To support his conviction, he pointed to his experience at St Andrews; to the fact that Cyril Tolley twice won the French Open against the best of the professionals; and of course, to the achievements of Bobby Jones against the US professionals. Wethered won the Amateur Championship in 1923 and was a finalist in 1928 and 1930, and played in all the early Walker Cup matches.

Tall and leggy, Wethered could be a rather unbridled driver, but was a brilliant iron player from all distances and, so it often seemed, from all lies. A successful London stockbroker, he was Captain of the R & A in 1946. He died in 1983, aged 84.

WHITWORTH, Kathy

The most 'decorated' player in America's LPGA history, Kathy Whitworth is the Sam Snead of women's golf. She has won no fewer than 88

Kathy Whitworth, the 'Sam Snead' of women's golf in America, with 88 professional victories.

events, but like Snead, has won everything except her National Open championship. Born in Texas, she started playing golf at 15 and turned professional at 19. Three years later, she won two tournaments and started on an unprecedented winning career that spanned 30 years. In 1968, she won no fewer than ten tournaments.

WOMEN'S GOLF

Mary Queen of Scots may have some claim to being the first lady golfer, having been recorded as playing at various places in Fife and the Lothians in the middle of the 16th century. No doubt women played the game from then on, often on sufferance from the men, but not until the end of the 19th century did they begin to make a direct impact on the game. In 1891, the Lundin Ladies Golf Club was formed in Fife and claims to be the oldest such club extant, with its own course and clubhouse, for women only!

The Ladies Golf Union was founded in 1893. It upholds the Rules of Golf and of Amateur Status, as laid down by the Royal & Ancient, but in every other respect is a separate independent entity

THE US WOMEN'S OPEN CHAMPIONSHIP

Winners US, except where stated

Year	Venue	Winner	Margin/Score
1946	Spokane	Patty Berg	5 & 4
1947	Greensboro	Betty Jameson	295
1948	Atlantic City	Babe Zaharias	291
1949	Landover	Louise Suggs	291
1950	Wichita	Babe Zaharias	291
1951	Atlanta	Betsy Rawls	293
1952	Bala	Louise Suggs	284
1953	Rochester	Betsy Rawls	302*
1954	Salem	Babe Zaharias	291
1955	Wichita	Fay Crocker	299
1956	Duluth	Kathy Cornelius	302*
1957	Winged Foot	Betsy Rawls	299
1958	Bloomfield Hills	Mickey Wright	290
1959	Pittsburgh	Mickey Wright	287
1960	Worcester	Betsy Rawls	292
1961	Baltusrol	Mickey Wright	293
1962	Myrtle Beach	Murle Lindstrom	301
1963	Kenwood	Mary Mills	289
1964	San Diego	Mickey Wright	290*
1965	Atlantic City	Carol Mann	290
1966	Hazeltine National	Sandra Spuzich	297
1967	Hot Springs	Catherine Lacoste (Fr)†	294
1968	Moselem Springs	Susie Berning	289
1969	Scenic Hills	Donna Caponi	294
1970	Muskogee	Donna Caponi	287
1971	Erie	JoAnne Gunderson Carner	288
1972	Winged Foot	Susie Berning	299
1973	Rochester	Susie Berning	290
1974	La Grange	Sandra Haynie	295
1975	Atlantic City	Sandra Palmer	295
1976	Springfield	JoAnne Gunderson Carner	292*
1977	Hazeltine National	Hollis Stacy	292
1978	Indianapolis	Hollis Stacy	289
1979	Brooklawn	Jerilyn Britz	284
1980	Richland	Amy Alcott	280
1981	La Grange	Pat Bradley	279
1982	Del Paso	Janet Alex	283
1983	Cedar Ridge	Jan Stephenson (Aus)	290
1984	Salem	Hollis Stacy	290
1985	Baltusrol	Kathy Baker	280
1986	NCR (Dayton)	Jane Geddes	287*
1987	Plainfield	Laura Davies (GB)	285*
1988	Baltimore	Liselotte Neumann (Swe)	277
1989	Indianwood	Betsy King	278
1990	Duluth	Betsy King	284
1991	Colonial	Meg Mallon	283
1992	Oakmont	Patty Sheehan	280
1993	Crooked Stick	Lauri Merten	280

* play-off † amateur

THE WOMEN'S BRITISH OPEN CHAMPIONSHIP

Winners British, except where stated

Year	Venue	Winner	Score
1976	Fulford	Jennifer Lee Smith †	299
1977	Lindrick	Vivien Saunders	306
1978	Foxhills	Janet Melville †	310
1979	Southport & Ainsdale	Alison Shead (SA)	301
1980	Wentworth	Debbie Massey (US)	294
1981	Northumberland	Debbie Massey (US)	295
1982	Royal Birkdale	Marta Figueras-Dotti (Sp) †	296
1984	Woburn	Ayako Okamoto (Jap)	289
1985	Moor Park	Betsy King (US)	300
1986	Royal Birkdale	Laura Davies	283
1987	St Mellion	Alison Nicholas	296
1988	Lindrick	Corinne Dibnah (Aus)	295*
1989	Ferndown	Jane Geddes (US)	274
1990	Woburn	Helen Alfredsson (Swe)	288*
1991	Woburn	Penny Grice-Whittaker	284
1992	Woburn	Patty Sheehan	207
1993	Woburn	Karen Lunn	275

play-off † amateur

THE US WOMEN'S AMATEUR CHAMPIONSHIP

Winners US, unless otherwise stated

Year	Venue	Winner	Score/Margin
1895	Meadowbrook	Mrs Charles Brown	132
1896	Morris County	Beatrix Hoyt	2 & 1
1897	Essex	Beatrix Hoyt	5 & 4
1898	Ardsley	Beatrix Hoyt	5 & 3
1899	Philadelphia	Ruth Underhill	2 & 1
1900	Shinnecock Hills	Frances Griscom	6 & 5
1901	Baltusrol	Genevieve Hecker	5 & 3
1902	Brookline	Genevieve Hecker	4 & 3
1903	Chicago	Bessie Anthony	7 & 6
1904	Merion	Georgianna Bishop	5 & 3
1905	Morris County	Pauline Mackay	1 up
1906	Brae Burn	Harriot Curtis	2 & 1
1907	Midlothian	Margaret Curtis	7 & 6
1908	Chevy Chase	Katherine Harley	6 & 5
1909	Merion	Dorothy Campbell (GB)	3 & 2
1910	Homewood	Dorothy Campbell (GB)	2 & 1
1911	Baltusrol	Margaret Curtis	5 & 3
1912	Essex	Margaret Curtis	3 & 2
1913	Wilmington	Gladys Ravenscroft (GB)	2 up
1914	Glen Cove	Mrs Arnold Jackson	1 up
1915	Onwentsia	Mrs CH Vanderbeck	3 & 2
1916	Belmont Springs	Alexa Stirling	2 & 1
1919	Shawnee	Alexa Stirling	6 & 5
1920	Mayfield	Alexa Stirling	5 & 4
1921	Hollywood	Marian Hollins	5 & 4
1922	Greenbrier	Glenna Collett	5 & 4
1923	Westchester-Biltmore	Edith Cummings	3 & 2
1924	Rhode Island	Dorothy Campbell (GB)	7 & 6
1925	St Louis	Glenna Collett	9 & 8
1926	Merion	Helen Stetson	3 & 1
1927	Cherry Valley	Miriam Burns Horn	5 & 4
1928	Hot Springs	Glenna Collett	13 & 1
1929	Oakland Hills	Glenna Collett	4 & 3
1930	Los Angeles	Glenna Collett	6 & 5
1931	Buffalo	Helen Hicks	2 & 1
1932	Salem	Virginia Van Wie	10 & 8
1933	Exmore	Virginia Van Wie	4 & 3
1934	Whitemarsh Valley	Virginia Van Wie	2 & 1
1935	Interlachen	Glenna Collett Vare	3 & 2
1936	Canoe Brook	Pam Barton (GB)	4 & 3
1937	Memphis	Mrs Julius Page	7 & 6
1938	Westmoreland	Patty Berg	6 & 5

1939	Wee Burn	Betty Jameson	3 & 2
1940	Del Monte	Betty Jameson	6 & 5
1941	Brookline	Betty Hicks Newell	5 & 3
1946	Southern Hills	Babe Zaharias	11 & 9
1947	Franklin Hills	Loiuse Suggs	2 up
1948	Del Monte	Grace Lenczyk	4 & 3
1949	Merion	Dorothy Porter	3 & 2
1950	Atlanta	Beverly Hanson	6 & 4
1951	St Paul	Dorothy Kirby	2 & 1
1952	Waverley	Jacqueline Pung	2 & 1
1953	Rhode Island	Mary Lena Faulk	3 & 2
1954	Allegheny	Barbara Romack	4 & 2
1955	Myers Park	Patricia Lesser	7 & 6
1956	Meridian Hills	Marlene Stewart (Can)	2 & 1
1957	Del Paso	JoAnne Gunderson	8 & 6
1958	Wee Burn	Anne Quast	3 & 2
1959	Congressional	Barbara McIntire	4 & 3
1960	Tulsa	JoAnne Gunderson	6 & 5
1961	Tacoma	Anne Decker	14 & 13
1962	Rochester	JoAnne Gunderson	9 & 8
1963	Taconic	Anne Welts	2 & 1
1964	Prairie Dunes	Barbara McIntire	3 & 2
1965	Lakewood	Jean Ashley	5 & 4
1966	Sewickley Heights	JoAnne Gunderson Carner	at 41st
1967	Annandale	Mary Lou Dill	5 & 4
1968	Birmingham	JoAnne Gunderson Carner	5 & 4
1969	Las Colinas	Catherine Lacoste (Fr)	3 & 2
1970	Wee Burn	Martha Wilkinson	3 & 2
1971	Atlanta	Laura Baugh	1 up
1972	St Louis	Mary Anne Budke	5 & 4
1973	Rochester	Carol Semple	1 up
1974	Broadmoor (Seattle)	Cynthia Hill	5 & 4
1975	Brae Burn	Beth Daniel	3 & 2
1976	Del Paso	Donna Horton	2 & 1
1977	Cincinnati	Beth Daniel	3 & 1
1978	Sunnybrook	Cathy Sherk (Can)	4 & 3
1979	Memphis	Carolyn Hill	7 & 6
1980	Prairie Dunes	Juli Inkster	2 up
1981	Waverley	Juli Inkster	1 up
1982	Broadmoor (Colorado Springs)	Juli Inkster	4 & 3
1983	Canoe Brook	Joanne Pacillo	2 & 1
1984	Broadmoor (Seattle)	Deb Richard	1 up
1985	Fox Chapel	Michiko Hattori (Jap)	5 & 4
1986	Pasatiempo	Kay Cockerill	9 & 7
1987	Barrington	Kay Cockerill	3 & 2
1988	Minikahda	Pearl Sinn	6 & 5
1989	Pinehurst	Vicki Goetze	4 & 3
1990	Canoe Brook	Pat Hurst	at 37th
1991	Prairie Dunes	A Fruwirth	5 & 4
1992	Kemper Lakes	Vicki Goetze	1 hole
1993	San Diego C.C.	Jill McGill	1 hole

which governs the women's game. In the United States by contrast, and perhaps surprisingly, there is no separate organisation for women. They form simply a division of the United States Golf Association (1894).

The LGU establishes a uniform system of handicapping and administers the Ladies Championship (which dates back from 1893), the home international matches, the Curtis Cup, European and Commonwealth matches. Outstanding lady champions have been Lady Margaret Scott, Cecil Leitch, Joyce Wethered, Pam Barton, Marley Spearman and the French girls Viscomtesse de Saint-Sauveur, Brigitte Varangot and Catherine Lacoste. In America, Dorothy Campbell, the Curtis sisters, Alexa Stirling, Glenna Collett, Patty Berg, Babe Didrikson, Joanne Carner and Nancy Lopez have famous names.

Just before the Second

Winners British, unless otherwise stated

Year	Venue	Winner	Margin
1893	Royal Lytham & St Annes	Lady Margaret Scott	7 & 5
1894	Littlestone	Lady Margaret Scott	3 & 2
1895	Royal Portrush	Lady Margaret Scott	3 & 2
1896	Royal Liverpool (Hoylake)	Amy Pascoe	3 & 2
1897	Gullane	Edith Orr	4 & 2
1898	Yarmouth	Lena Thomson	7 & 5
1899	County Down (Newcastle)	May Hezlet (Ire)	2 & 1
1900	Royal North Devon (Westward Ho!)	Rhona Adair	6 & 5
1901	Aberdovey	Miss Graham	3 & 1
1902	Cinque Ports (Deal)	May Hezlet (Ire)	2 & 1
1903	Royal Portrush	Rhona Adair	4 & 3
1904	Troon	Lottie Dod	1 hole
1905	Cromer	Bertha Thompson	3 & 2
1906	Burnham	Mrs Kennion	4 & 3
1907	County Down (Newcastle)	May Hezlet (Ire)	2 & 1
1908	St Andrews	Maud Titterton	at 19th
1909	Birkdale	Dorothy Campbell	4 & 3
1910	Royal North Devon (Westward Ho!)	Grant Suttie	6 & 4
1911	Royal Portrush	Dorothy Campbell	3 & 2
1912	Turnberry	Gladys Ravenscroft	3 & 2
1913	Royal Lytham & St Annes	Muriel Dodd	8 & 6
1914	Hunstanton	Cecil Leitch	2 & 1
1920	Royal County Down (Westward Ho!)	Cecil Leitch	7 & 6
1921	Turnberry	Cecil Leitch	4 & 3
1922	Prince's (Sandwich)	Joyce Wethered	9 & 7
1923	Burnham	Doris Chambers	2 holes
1924	Royal Portrush	Joyce Wethered	7 & 6
1925	Troon	Joyce Wethered	at 37th
1926	Royal St David's (Harlech)	Cecil Leitch	8 & 7
1927	Royal County Down (Newcastle)	Simone Thion de la Chaume (Fr)	5 & 4
1928	Hunstanton	Nanette Le Blan (Fr)	3 & 2
1929	St Andrews	Joyce Wethered	3 & 1
1930	Formby	Diana Fishwick	4 & 3
1931	Portmarnock	Enid Wilson	7 & 6
1932	Saunton	Enid Wilson	7 & 6
1933	Gleneagles	Enid Wilson	5 & 4
1934	Royal Porthcawl	Helen Holm	6 & 5
1935	Royal County Down (Newcastle)	Wanda Morgan	3 & 2
1936	Southport & Ainsdale	Pam Barton	5 & 3
1937	Turnberry	Jessie Anderson	6 & 4
1938	Burnham	Helen Holm	4 & 3
1939	Royal Portrush	Pam Barton	2 & 1
1946	Hunstanton	Jean Hetherington	1 hole
1947	Gullane	Babe Zaharias (US)	5 & 4
1948	Royal Lytham & St Annes	Louise Suggs (US)	1 hole
1949	Royal St David's (Harlech)	Frances Stephens	5 & 4
1950	Royal County Down (Newcastle)	Viscomtesse de Saint Sauveur (Fr)	3 & 2
1951	Broadstone	Kitty MacCann (Ire)	4 & 3
1952	Troon	Moira Paterson	at 39th
1953	Royal Porthcawl	Marlene Stewart (Can)	7 & 6
1954	Ganton	Frances Stephens	4 & 3
1955	Royal Portrush	Jessie Valentine	7 & 6
1956	Sunningdale	Margaret Smith	8 & 7
1957	Gleneagles	Philomena Garvey (Ire)	4 & 3
1958	Hunstanton	Jessie Valentine	1 hole
1959	Ascot	Elizabeth Price	at 37th
1960	Royal St David's (Harlech)	Barbara McIntire (US)	4 & 2
1961	Carnoustie	Marley Spearman	7 & 6
1962	Royal Birkdale	Marley Spearman	1 hole
1963	Royal County Down (Newcastle)	Brigitte Varangot (Fr)	3 & 1
1964	Prince's (Sandwich)	Carol Sorenson	at 37th
1965	St Andrews	Brigitte Varandot (Fr)	4 & 3
1966	Ganton	Elizabeth Chadwick	3 & 2
1967	Royal St David's (Harlech)	Elizabeth Chadwick	1 hole
1968	Walton Heath	Brigitte Varandot (Fr)	at 20th
1969	Royal Portrush	Catherine Lacoste (Fr)	1 hole
1970	Gullane	Dinah Oxley	1 hole
1971	Alwoodley	Michelle Walker	3 & 1
1972	Hunstanton	Michelle Walker	2 holes
1973	Carnoustie	Ann Irvin	3 & 2
1974	Royal Porthcawl	Carol Semple (US)	2 & 1
1975	St Andrews	Nancy Syms (US)	3 & 2
1976	Silloth	Cathy Panton	1 hole
1977	Hillside	Angela Uzielli	6 & 5
1978	Notts	Edwina Kennedy (Aus)	1 hole
1979	Nairn	Maureen Madill (Ire)	2 & 1
1980	Wodhall Spa	Anne Sander (US)	3 & 1
1981	Caernarvonshire	Belle Robertson	at 20th
1982	Walton Heath	Katrina Douglas	4 & 2
1983	Silloth	Jill Thornhill	4 & 2
1984	Royal Troon	Jody Rosenthal (US)	4 & 3
1985	Ganton	Lilian Behan (Ire)	1 hole
1986	West Sussex	Marnie McGuire (NZ)	2 & 1
1987	Royal St David's (Harlech)	Janet Collingham	at 19th
1988	Royal Cinque Ports (Deal)	Joanne Furby	4 & 3
1989	Royal Liverpool (Hoylake)	Helen Dobson	6 & 5
1990	Dunbar	Julie Hall	3 & 2
1991	Pannal	Valerie Michaud (Fr)	3 & 2
1992	Saunton	Pernille Pedersen (Den)	1 hole
1993	Royal Lytham	Katrina Lambert	3 & 2

World War, there were enough players and enough potential to form a professional 'tour' in America. The US Ladies PGA Tour has developed enormously and now has its own complete organisation. Over the past decade, its equivalent in Europe has been progressing, rather more slowly.

WOOSNAM, Ian

Born 1958

Nationality British

Turned Pro 1976

Majors US Masters 1991

A small, pugnacious Welshman won the Masters at Augusta in 1991 and punched the air with such ferocity that even years later the intensity leaps out of the photographs. The image sums up the man. Ian Woosnam, perhaps because of his size (5' 4½" at full stretch), has always reacted aggressively to the world and his attitude could be summed up in the phrase he used when a few fans heckled at him at Augusta: 'I'll show you what I'm made of, pal.' He did, too, becoming the first Welshman to win a major championship.

Woosnam, in fact, comes of sturdy, yeoman farming stock from near Oswestry, in the border country of England and Wales. He learned his golf at a course called Llanymynech, which has 15 holes in Wales and three in England, and spent his youth being overshadowed by a lad called Sandy Lyle. They both played for Shropshire and one year, having lost the junior championship to Lyle, Woosnam's gracious loser's speech consisted of, 'I'll beat you one day.'

Lyle was the child star but Woosnam, so ferocious in the tackle at football that his father feared for his son's safety and his opponents feared for theirs, and such a flailing windmill of assault in the boxing ring that his opponents, their mothers and his own mother wept,

Ian Woosnam proving the old adage that if you're good enough, you're big enough. One of the shorter golfers in the professional game today, 'Woosie' relies upon timing and technique for his enormous drives.

baked beans straight out of the tin and sleeping in his waterproofs on really cold nights. Money, which he now has in such abundance that he runs a private plane and has upped sticks from Oswestry to Jersey, was notable by its absence.

The little man who could hit the ball a country mile made little progress until he was persuaded to accept that a less than perfect shot was not necessarily a bad shot. He finished third on the Safari tour to be exempt from qualifying and his career, if not flying high, was at least off and running.

In 1982 he won the Cacharel Under-25 championship and later that year the first big success came: victory in the Swiss Open. The ambitious Woosnam was on his way and over the next decade he won more than a score of tournaments and over £3 million in prize money in Europe alone.

His simple style earned the plaudits of the experts. 'Marvellously fluent,' was how Tony Jacklin described it. 'It shows that timing, balance and technique are just as important as stature when it comes to hitting a golf ball a long way.' He made it all look so easy and although people marvelled at how so small a body could propel the ball so far, he was immensely strong, thanks in part to years of helping out on his father's farm.

Reeling in the tournaments and the money became the Woosnam forte and in 1987

had few doubts. 'Golf was always my first love,' he said. 'I always knew deep down that I could make the grade'.

That conviction was tested to its limits. His amateur record was not one of great distinction and when he turned professional in 1976 at the age of 18, it was a struggle. He had to attend that chamber of horrors, the tour qualifying school, three times and his early years as a travelling professional have become the stuff of legend – touring round in a battered caravanette, eating cold

he won seven times worldwide, including five in Europe, one of which was the World Matchplay championship, in which he beat Lyle in the final to become the first British winner. He was a crucial member of the Ryder Cup team that won at Muirfield Village, topped the European Order of Merit and confirmed himself as one of the world's leading players. In fact, he and David Llewellyn won the World Cup for Wales in Hawaii (beating Lyle and Sam Torrance of Scotland in a play-off) and Woosnam won the individual title. He was No. 1 on the European money list again in 1990, winning five times and amassing huge earnings of nearly £740,000. He had a round of 60, the lowest of his career, in Monte Carlo but the major championship that would confirm his standing still eluded him.

It was a friendly – but competitive – Christmas round at homely Oswestry that spurred his tilt at greatness. He shot 57, 13 under par, and said, 'I realised then it was time I believed in myself.' In 1991, he proceeded to prove that few people could live with his self-belief.

His goals for the year were to win in America, win a major and head the Sony world rankings. He achieved all three in his first five outings. He won the Mediterranean Open (surplus to requirements), then won in New Orleans and arrived in Augusta as No. 1 in the world, according to the rankings and his own estimation. He won the Masters.

Playing the 18th, Jose Maria Olazabal and Tom Watson were tied with

Mickey Wright (back) drapes Betsy Rawls with a winner's blazer

Woosnam at 11 under par. The Spaniard took five, the American six and the Welshman took four. In keeping with his philosophy – 'I just stand there and hit it' – he smashed a drive miles left, carrying the bunker 260 yards away, hit an eight iron to the front of the green and two putted, holing triumphantly from six feet for the title he craved.

'You dream all your life about making a putt to win the Masters,' said the mighty atom who had made it reality.

WRIGHT, Mickey

A near-contemporary of Kathy Whitworth, Mickey Wright from San Diego is considered by many to be the doyenne of America's women golfers. She won 82 events in her career as against Whitworth's 88, but has four US Opens and four LPGA Championships to her credit. In 1963, she won 13 of a total of 32 events, a record that may never be equalled, and in 1962 and again in 1963 she won four consecutive tournaments. She had started at the age of 12 and won the US Junior championship. Mickey was leading amateur in the US Open of 1954, won by Babe Zaharias, when she was joint fourth; she turned professional that same year, aged 19. Injuries reduced her play to a large extent after 1969.

Z

ZAHARIAS, Babe

Born 1915

Nationality United States

Turned Pro 1947

The sixth of seven children of Norwegian immigrant parents, Mildred Lee Didrikson grew up in Port Arthur, then Beaumont, near the Texas gulf coast. She grew into a lean, boyish, extrovert teenager who, with her three brothers, tackled any sport that came along and earned the nickname 'Babe' after the baseball hero Babe Ruth when she hit five home runs in one game. And beyond any reasonable doubt, she grew into the greatest female athlete of the 20th century.

When she was still in high school, her exceptional talents were noted. Before the Olympic Games of 1932 in Los Angeles, she took part in the US championships, the final selection ground for the US team. Babe promptly won the javelin, shot putt, long jump, baseball throw and 80 metres hurdles and tied in the high jump. In her seventh event, she finished fourth in the discus. At the time, the US athletics authorities limited any athlete's participation to a maximum of three events. Babe in the Olympics set a new record in winning the javelin, a new record in winning the 80 metres hurdles and tied with Jean Shiley in the high jump. The authorities settled that issue by disqualifying Babe for clearing the bar head first,

a technique that was merely postponed. Miss Didrikson was 19 years old.

She was also an outstanding basketball player, nominated for the All-America team. She was a talented swimmer and diver and an exceptional softball pitcher. She turned professional shortly after the 1932 Olympics had made her a household name. She was also an excellent tapdancer and harmonica player and she embarked on a highly paid tour of the nation's theatres, singing, dancing and playing. She also took

part in baseball exhibition games with the men, then in 1934 began to concentrate on golf with such success that in 1935 she was able to tour the country with Gene Sarazen, belting out 250 yard drives to the astonishment of the crowds. She took lessons from Tommy Armour and worked seriously at the game.

In 1938, she married George Zaharias, a professional wrestler who became a wrestling promoter, and who was a constant companion for Babe in her later years. She was

reinstated as an amateur by the USGA in 1944, and promptly won the US Women's Amateur in 1946 and the British Ladies at Gullane in 1947, taking the trophy across the Atlantic for the first time after proving herself immensely popular with the Scottish galleries. In 1946 and 1947, Babe won 17 consecutive amateur events.

The development of

'The Babe', the greatest female athlete of the 20th century!

professional tournament golf for women in the US, and the eventual formation of the LPGA of which Babe was a founder member, saw her turn professional yet again only two months after her Gullane triumph, and almost inevitably she underlined her immense power in the women's game by winning the US Open in 1948 and repeating in 1950 and 1954. From 1948 to 1955, Babe won 31 professional tournaments.

Her greatest single achievement may well have been her third US Open win in 1954 at Salem, near Boston, a few months after she had undergone surgery for cancer. Her score of 291 put her an astonishing 12 strokes ahead of the field. She had further surgery in 1956, before she died in September of that year at the age of 45. A Babe Didrikson Zaharias Memorial Center, a museum, has been established in Beaumont and a Babe Zaharias Foundation raises funds for cancer research.

The Babe was one of the greatest personalities of her time, chattering with galleries and swapping wisecracks with them. When asked how she was able to hit the ball such vast distances, her stock answer was, 'Why, I just loosen my girdle and let fly.'

ZOELLER, Fuzzy

Born 1951

Nationality United States

Turned Pro 1973

Majors US Masters 1979; US Open 1984

Life, courtesy of his parents, gave Frank Urban Zoeller the initials FUZ and inevitably he was once and forever known as Fuzzy. The name seldom typified his golf. His principal distinctions in the game are that he won both of his major championships in play-offs, and in the first of them, he took the Masters on his very first appearance at the Augusta National course, in 1979.

Zoeller, born in New Albany, Indiana on Armistice Day, 1951, rivalled Lee Trevino as an outgoing, chattering golfer, even on rather solemn occasions. Powerfully built, he drove the ball long distances with a distinctive swing which had the hands rather low at the address, an early break of the wrists, and a rather long, low action. He had a very exaggerated putting stance, open towards the hole. He was plagued with back strain which required surgery in the mid-1980s. Zoeller went into the 1979 Masters third on the money list at the time, although he was seldom seen as a winner. But he tied with Ed Sneed and Tom Watson, and won with a birdie on the second extra hole.

Five years later, in the US Open at Winged Foot, he watched from the middle of the fairway as Greg Norman, up ahead on the last green, holed a huge putt for what Zoeller thought was a winning birdie. He waved a white towel in mock surrender, but Norman's putt was in fact for a par; they tied and Zoeller won the 18 holes play-off, 67 to 75. He played three times on Ryder Cup teams, but as he moved into his forties, Fuzzy Zoeller cut down on his tournament play in favour of course design and development consultancy.

Fuzzy Zoeller, swinging high from a deep Augusta bunker.

Index

(Where individual place names are used in the index, this refers to the golf club of the same name)